Development Policy II—The Pakistan Experience

Studies based on the work of the Development Advisory Service, and written under the auspices of the Center for International Affairs, Harvard University

Development Policy II—

The Pakistan Experience

Edited by Walter P. Falcon

and Gustav F. Papanek

Harvard University Press, Cambridge, Massachusetts, 1971

Library of Congress Catalog Card Number 70-160113
SBN 674-20270-8
Printed in the United States of America

To Richard V. Gilbert
Teacher, Activist and Humanist

As head of the Development Advisory Service project in Pakistan during 1960–66 and 1969–70 he made a lasting impression on the country's development policy, its growing pool of skilled government economists and several generations of DAS advisors. Always the incisive and persuasive advocate, he demonstrated the power of an artful combination of sound theory, respect for the facts, political sensitivity, and a strong sense of priorities.

Though Richard Gilbert is most widely known for the many economic policies and programs he conceived and influenced over more than thirty years of active involvement in the U.S. Government and abroad, his most lasting contribution may well be as a teacher. Although the essays which follow should not be blamed on him, they reflect in a myriad of ways his questions, his arguments, and his beliefs.

Those who know Richard Gilbert value him for more than his considerable skills as an economist and teacher, however. They know him as, above all, a man concerned with the impact of economic policy on people. It is to his unflagging interest in humanity and his vision of economics as its servant that this volume is dedicated.

Preface

The eleven essays in the first volume of *Development Policy,* subtitled *Theory and Practice,* had as their unifying theme, "the actual application of economic theory and analytical techniques to important government policy issues, showing the lessons learned as a result of that application."[1] This, the second volume in the series, also draws on the experience of advisors who have been in the less developed countries under the auspices of the Development Advisory Service (DAS) of Harvard University. Like the first volume, this collection is intended to add to an understanding of the development process and to the methodology for its examination.

As the title implies, this volume draws generalizations from the experience of a single country where Harvard advisors have been working since 1954. It is *not,* however, intended as a comprehensive study of Pakistan's development. Except for the introductory chapter which provides a brief general summary of the Pakistan experience, the volume concentrates on specific economic issues that have proved particularly important and interesting. In this context, it builds on several general books on Pakistan recently published and has a strong methodological emphasis.

Most of the papers in this volume were originally presented and discussed at two conferences sponsored by the DAS in the fall of 1967 and 1968. We are grateful to the participants at both conferences for their critical comments, which substantially helped the authors with subsequent revisions. Besides the authors of papers in this volume, the following individuals took part in the two conferences:

Carl Anonsen	Dorris Brown
Sartaj Aziz	Robert Burns
Richard Barkey	Willem Bussink
Dwight Brothers	Hollis Chenery

1. Gustav F. Papanek, ed., *Development Policy: Theory and Practice* (Cambridge: Harvard University Press, 1968), p. vii.

David Cole
Emile Despres
Jakob Diddens
Christopher Dougherty
Eivind Erichsen
Just Faaland
William Gates
Lester Gordon
Edgar Gutierrez
Parvez Hasan
Warren Hogan
William Hollinger
Richard Mallon
Geoffrey Maynard
Leon Mears
Dick Netzer
Robert Pogson
Richard Porter
Lester Taylor
Antonio Urdinola
Raymond Vernon
Harold Wein
Louis Wells, Jr.

The revision of the papers in this volume was completed by 1969. The essays are concerned with Pakistan, its policies, and problems as of that date and do not take into account the major political and economic changes which took place subsequently.

All the conferees, and especially the authors, are indebted to Sophia Magoulias, Pamela Rowley, Belinda Burley and Wilma McCord, who helped manage these conferences and who saw this book through drafts and publication. Five of the essays were either written or revised in Cambridge under funds provided by the Agency for International Development to Harvard's Center for International Affairs. The authors are grateful for this support, although the views expressed are strictly personal, and are not necessarily those of AID. They are also grateful for the editorial assistance of Betsy Pitha and Marina S. Finkelstein.

There may be subsequent volumes in this series. Some may, like this one, cover a country or region; others may focus on a set of issues of importance primarily to less developed countries; still others may, like the first volume, include essays expected to contribute to a general understanding of methodology, policy, or programs. But whatever their focus, subsequent volumes will also consist primarily of essays by advisors, arising out of their work in less developed countries.

WPF
GFP

Contents

Tables

Figures

Development Policy II—The Pakistan Experience

1 Pakistan's Development: An Introductory Perspective[1]

Walter P. Falcon
and
Joseph J. Stern

Few countries that gained their independence after World War II started with greater handicaps than did Pakistan. Before the partition of British India, the two areas comprising Pakistan furnished raw jute, cotton, and surplus wheat to India, receiving manufactured goods in exchange. The severance of these ties by partition in 1947 seriously disrupted Pakistan's trade, commercial and industrial organization, channels of communication, and government. More than 6.5 million Muslim refugees came to Pakistan while 5.5 million Hindus and Sikhs emigrated. Only a few of the civil service elite, who had assisted the British administration of the subcontinent, were available for service in Pakistan. Refugees, concentrated in a few areas of West Pakistan, made up ten percent of the population. It is against this background of severe economic, social, and political stress, that Pakistan's development must be evaluated.

Economic Development

Prior to 1959–60 the performance of the economy was characterized by near stagnation in per capita income and by large year-to-year fluc-

1. Readers wishing a fuller statement of Pakistan's general development strategy are referred to several recent volumes: Stephen R. Lewis, Jr., *Economic Policy and Industrial Growth in Pakistan* (London: Allen and Unwin, Ltd., 1969); Stephen R. Lewis, Jr., *Pakistan: Industrialization and Trade Policies* (London: Oxford University Press, 1970); Gustav F. Papanek, *Pakistan's Development: Social Goals and Private Incentives* (Cambridge: Harvard University Press, 1967); and Joseph J. Stern and Walter P. Falcon, *Growth and Development in Pakistan, 1955–1969,* (Occasional Paper No. 23, Harvard Center for International Affairs, Cambridge, 1970). The latter source, in particular, contains full documentation for a number of points presented in Chapter 1.

tuations in the level of total output, largely as a result of fluctuations in agricultural production. The per capita income level in 1959–60 (about $65) barely exceeded that at Independence. In the 1960's, however, gross national product increased by over 5 percent annually, and the growth in agriculture was substantially above the rate of population increase. Whereas in the 1950's the impetus for the modest growth that did take place came from the industrial sector, in the 1960's both agriculture and industry contributed substantially to the overall development of the economy. (See Table 1.1.)

Pakistan's growth does not seem to have been inhibited generally by inadequate absorptive capacity or, until the late 1960's, by inflation. The performance in raising savings and export earnings was moderately good. Investment, in real terms, doubled every five years until 1964–65 when the ratio of gross investment to GNP reached a high of nearly 19 percent. (See Table 1.2.) Despite the rapid growth of investment, it appears that there was concurrent improvement in economic efficiency. The rapid increase in investment was made possible both by the government's ability to mobilize increased domestic savings and by the considerable inflow of external assistance. However, since 1964–65, both the savings rate and the level of external assistance have declined, although an

Table 1.1 Growth rates for GNP and major sectors[a] (percentage per annum)

Sector	1954–55 to 1968–69	1954–55 to 1959–60	1959–60 to 1968–69
1. Agriculture	2.9	1.4	3.4
1.a. Major crops	3.4	2.0	3.7
1.b. Other agriculture	2.2	0.1	3.0
2. Manufacturing	7.4	5.3	7.9
2.a. Large-scale manufacturing[a]	10.7	8.4	10.9
3. All other sectors	5.8	3.0	7.1
4. Total GNP	4.5	2.4	5.4
5. GNP/capita	2.0	–[b]	2.7

Source: Derived from the least-squares regression estimate $\log_e Y = a + b$ (time) with all values in constant 1959–60 prices. Calculated from: Government of Pakistan, Central Statistical Office, *Monthly Statistical Bulletin,* various issues.

[a] Large-scale manufacturing activities covers all firms employing 20 or more persons and using power.

[b] Not significantly different from zero.

Table 1.2. Investment, savings, taxation, import, and export ratios

Economic indicator	1954–55	1959–60	1964–65	1968–69
	(millions of rupees; current prices[b])			
Gross investment (I)	1,650[c]	3,840[b]	9,100[b]	10,521[d]
Gross savings (S)	1,425[c]	2,875[b]	6,085[b]	7,695[d]
Tax revenues (T)	1,304[c]	2,000[c]	4,008[b]	6,940[d]
Merchandise imports[a] (M)	1,103	2,461	5,374	4,870
Merchandise exports[a] (X)	1,223	1,843	2,408	3,240
GNP (market prices)	21,920[c]	32,679[b]	48,291[b]	72,060[d]
	Percent			
I/GNP	7.5	11.8	18.8	14.6
S/GNP	6.5	8.8	12.6	10.7
T/GNP	5.9	6.1	8.3	9.6
M/GNP	5.0	7.5	11.1	6.8
X/GNP	5.6	5.6	5.0	4.5

	1954–55 to 1959–60	1959–60 to 1964–65	1964–65 to 1968–69
Marginal savings rate	13.5	20.6	6.8
Marginal tax rate	6.5	12.9	12.3
Marginal import rate	12.6[e]	18.7	2.1
Marginal export rate	5.8[e]	3.6	3.5

[a]Government of Pakistan, Planning Commission, *Outline of the Fourth Five-Year Plan (1970–75)* (Islamabad, February 1970), p. 7.

[b]Government of Pakistan, Planning Commission, *Final Evaluation of the Second Five-Year Plan (1960–65)* (Karachi, December 1966), pp. 144, 154.

[c]Government of Pakistan, Planning Commission, *The Third Five-year Plan (1965–70)* (Karachi, June 1965).

[d]Government of Pakistan, Planning Commission, *Annual Plan 1969/70* (Islamabad, n.d.), pp. 9, 11.

[e]Import and export figures have not been adjusted for the change in the exchange rate after 1955, so these marginal rates must be interpreted with caution.

effective export promotion policy has helped to maintain the rapid rise in foreign exchange earnings.[2]

2. A fuller analysis of the export performance is provided by G. C. Hufbauer in Chapter 3.

The remarkable price stability that marked the Pakistan economy prior to 1965 was helped considerably by the increase in foreign assistance and in particular by foodgrain imports under the United States' P.L. 480 Program. The disruption of such foodgrain imports, the decline in aid, the increase in defense expenditures after the 1965 conflict with India, and the poor harvests of 1966 and 1967 caused prices to rise sharply. Following the dramatic agricultural production increase in West Pakistan in 1967–68, food prices were again stabilized in that province, although in East Pakistan prices continued to rise owing to a shortage of food.

The agricultural growth in the 1960's was in marked contrast to the stagnation of the earlier period. Beginning in 1959, government policy made wide use of market incentives. Prices were raised and, especially for foodgrains, stabilized under price-guarantee schemes. This was in sharp contrast to the earlier policy of direct controls over distribution and forced procurement at below-market prices. Subsidies on modern inputs—new seeds, fertilizers, pesticides—increased the willingness of the agriculturalists to abandon traditional practices for modern techniques. Technological change was particularly important in West Pakistan where the new seed varieties, in combination with other inputs, proved capable of increasing regional wheat and rice production by 50 percent over the period 1965–1970. One of the crucial inputs in this process was irrigation water, which increased substantially during the 1960's as a result mainly of the tubewell program.[3] West Pakistan agriculture also benefited from the foreign support provided under the Indus Basin Treaty, which rebuilt and improved a large part of the agricultural infrastructure and brought in over 2,500 man-years of technical assistance to help plan the entire water and power system. Unfortunately, no similar breakthrough has been achieved as yet for the monsoon agriculture of East Pakistan; however, a decentralized system for managing the widespread introduction of small pumps and wells promises an increased availability of water in the winter growing season and limited control over water during the monsoon floods.[4] Unless an appropriate rice-seed technology is developed, and unless rural organization problems are

3. The effectiveness of prices in influencing production, and the interaction of price policy and technological change, form the basis of Chapter 6 by W. P. Falcon and C. H. Gotsch. One aspect of power planning is presented by Henry Jacoby in Chapter 4.

4. Some of the problems of East Pakistan irrigation are dealt with in the essay by Robert Repetto, Chapter 5.

solved, rapid increases in agricultural production in East Pakistan are unlikely in the near future.

Rapid industrial growth was brought about in large part by specific government policies. Following the end of the Korean boom, the government found it necessary to curtail imports sharply. A highly protected market for consumer goods was established while imports of capital goods remained relatively cheap. With high prices for outputs, relatively low prices for capital goods, and low real wages, profits of 50 to 100 percent on investment were not unusual in the mid-1950's. While profit rates in some industries remain high there has probably been some general decline in the rate of return on investment. This decline has been partially offset by the increasing experience of Pakistani industrialists, by a decrease in administrative obstacles facing investors, by better prices for industrial exports and by an increase in the efficiency of financial and other institutions serving entrepreneurs.[5] At the same time continued liberal depreciation allowances, low direct tax rates, and an absence of anti-monopoly legislation continued to make industrial investments attractive. These factors also led to a highly concentrated pattern of industrial ownership. Although initial investments were largely in consumer goods industries and other manufacturing processes using relatively simple technology, more recent investments have encompassed the whole range of manufacturing, including capital-intensive and technically complex sectors.

Although Pakistan's industry is largely in the private sector, the rapid growth was not due to private initiative alone. Initially the government played an important role in providing the necessary incentives and infrastructure. Later it set up financial institutions to provide investment funds. Through the Pakistan Industrial Development Corporation (PIDC), the government undertook some industrial investment itself, especially in areas where private investors either were reluctant to invest because of the extreme risks or did not have the capital required. The government was also willing to permit the use of foreign technicians in both the public and private sectors, in effect importing the educational skills whose absence often hampers growth.

Although some of Pakistan's industrial development was high-cost—when international prices are used as the standard of comparison—the

5. Industrial development and the emergence of industrial entrepreneurs have been studied extensively by G. F. Papanek in *Pakistan's Development.* Further discussion of the characteristics and background of these industrialists is given in Chapter 8.

rapidly rising share of industry essentially from zero at partition to nearly 12 percent of GNP in 1968–69 represents a very impressive growth performance.

Social Development

In contrast to the generally successful growth policies followed in industry and agriculture, efforts to achieve economic equity and growth in the social sectors have made little progress. Part of this lack of progress stems from the fact that, despite recent growth, Pakistan remains one of the poorest countries in the world. It is estimated that 75 percent of the total number of households still receive a monthly income of less than Rs. 200 ($42). The daily calorie intake is around 2,100 per person, and the average diet is unbalanced. Eighty-five percent of the population cannot read or write, and medical services are scarce, with only one doctor for every 7,000 persons. Whichever social indicator one considers, Pakistan occupies a place near the bottom in comparison to other Asian countries—and Asia is the poorest continent. Even a completely equal distribution of present income and public services would not make for a "good" situation by international standards. In addition, the national response to equity problems in Pakistan has been inadequate. For example, over the entire period of planned development, that is, since 1954–55, the percentage allocation of development resources devoted to education never exceeded 6 percent; for health services only 2 percent; and for housing 20 percent (the latter even includes sizeable expenditures on the new capital at Islamabad and the second capital at Dacca).

Government policy and strategy itself significantly affected distributive justice (or injustice). On a variety of issues, including budget allocations and foreign exchange policy, West Pakistan was given favored treatment over East Pakistan.[6] The various license systems created large monopoly profits, which were either inadequately taxed or not taxed at all. The system of taxation, and the collection mechanism, probably made the tax system more regressive over time. Also, the failure to check the growth of the few industrial families, and to break their link with the major banks, helped to impede entry into the industrial field and created profitable monopolies. The government, too conscious of the need to

6. J. J. Stern examines the conflict between East-West equity and growth more rigorously in Chapter 2.

keep production going regardless of the social costs sometimes involved, discouraged and prohibited expressions of industrial conflict. Strikes were prohibited, labor unions suppressed, and punitive measures were taken against workers who tried to organize labor in an effort to improve their position. These factors, plus the large pool of unemployed labor, kept wages low in the face of rising productivity and high profits. In agriculture the large farmers benefited most from the introduction of new technologies and the subsidies on inputs, and their political power usually defeated attempts to tax their rising incomes.

During those years when the economy was growing rapidly, when a major portion of the cost of development was borne by the foreign aid donors, and when food prices were kept stable, such a situation was at least tolerated by most groups. But after 1965, when aid inflows declined, when an increasingly large proportion of revenues was devoted to defense expenditures, and when prices began to rise, the real incomes of the lower income groups declined and the weakness of the past development policy was clearly revealed. For example, serious deficiencies became apparent in the educational system. Over half of the primary-age school children were not attending school, and of those who did enroll, only 18 percent of the boys and 6 percent of the girls completed the first five years of schooling. Unemployment and underemployment were high, particularly in East Pakistan, where growth in the 1960's was insufficient to generate enough additional jobs to absorb the new entrants into the labor market.[7] All these factors contributed to the unrest that occurred in Pakistan in 1968–69. This unrest culminated in the resignation of President Ayub Khan and the reimposition of martial law under General Yahya Khan.

Pakistan's future development will be intimately linked with intra- and inter-provincial political events. No one in 1970 can be sure as to the form or direction that the latter will take; however, the biggest difficulty facing any future set of policy makers in the economic sphere will be in reconciling the simultaneous need for accelerated growth, better income distribution and improved quality of life.

7. One attempt to increase employment in East Pakistan—the Rural Public Works Program—is discussed by J. W. Thomas in Chapter 7.

2 Growth, Development, and Regional Equity in Pakistan

Joseph J. Stern

The stubborn persistence of regional income differences at various stages of economic development has long been recognized as a peculiar facet of economic growth. It would be unrealistic to expect equal economic growth in all regions of a state at the same time. Particular areas may have a special geographic advantage, a proximity to minerals or sources of power, naturally good communications, or be well suited for a special crop.

Although it is relatively simple to posit a variety of possible causes leading to spatial income inequalities, it is more difficult to explain their persistence. Since the economic interdependence among regions within a state can be expected to be much stronger than among nations, internal factor mobility should tend to eliminate interregional income differences unless transport costs are forbidding. But, because depressed areas and backward regions continue to exist, possibly internal factor flows do not occur rapidly enough to offset the dynamic conditions which further increase spatial inequalities. In some cases unequal rates of growth perpetuate themselves as investors are attracted to the dynamic region in the expectation of exploiting its potential external economies. It is difficult to be sure whether such externalities actually exist or whether investors, attracted by the aura of success surrounding the growing region, spend a

NOTE: An earlier version of this chapter was presented at the Sorrento Conference on development planning held under the auspices of the Development Advisory Service in 1967. Comments and suggestions by a number of readers, especially Professor Hollis B. Chenery, are gratefully acknowledged; responsibility for any errors and for the conclusions is my own. Portions of this research were supported by the Development Advisory Service and the Project for Quantitative Research in Economic Development, Harvard University, through funds provided by the Agency for International Development under Contract CSD-1543. The views expressed in this paper do not, however, necessarily reflect the views of AID.

great deal of time exploiting the opportunities around some "growth pole," neglecting others that may have arisen, or could be made to arise, elsewhere.

Although the problem is not limited to developing countries, regional income inequalities in such countries can produce severe repercussions. The development process often engenders political tensions. If economic differences between regions reinforce geographic, social, and linguistic differences, a growing disparity in regional welfare may severely strain the nation's political framework. A government program to ameliorate regional differences usually entails an effort to change patterns of resource flows in order to increase the share of total investment in the lagging region. A more active policy may include outright income transfer payments to the inhabitants of the backward region.[1]

Regardless of the policy, the need to consider the regional dimension adds a difficulty to the already complex problem of achieving rapid growth for the nation as a whole. A shift in investment resources from one region to another may well lead to a lower rate of growth of national income if the lagging region is characterized by less favorable economic conditions.[2]

Two obstacles usually restrict the scope of regional analysis: the difficulty in defining the physical boundaries of an economically meaningful area, and the lack of data relating to such an "economic development region."[3] Pakistan, divided into two noncontiguous regions, provides an opportunity to overcome these problems. East and West Pakistan are

1. Among the better known postwar regional development programs are those for southern Italy and northeast Brazil. For an analysis of the Italian situation see Hollis B. Chenery, Paul G. Clark, and V. Cao-Pinna, *The Structure and Growth of the Italian Economy* (Rome: Mutual Security Agency of the United States of America, 1953); and Hollis B. Chenery, "Development Policies for Southern Italy," *Quarterly Journal of Economics*, 86 (November 1962), 515–547. The Brazilian case is discussed in Werner Baer, *Industrialization and Economic Development in Brazil* (Homewood, Ill.: Richard D. Irwin for the Yale University Economic Growth Center, 1965), and Stefan H. Robock, *Brazil's Developing Northeast: A Study of Regional Planning and Foreign Aid* (Washington: The Brookings Institution, 1953). Additional references to regional planning and programs can be found in the extensive bibliography in John R. Meyer, "Regional Economics: A Survey," *Surveys of Economic Theory*, vol. II (New York: St. Martin's Press, 1965).

2. A less interesting case, where the dynamic region has grown solely because of favoritism on the part of the government, is not discussed. In such a situation the proper allocation of resources would not only ameliorate the regional problems but lead to a maximization of the potential national growth rate as well.

3. The term "economic development region" apparently was first used by Joseph Fischer, in "Concepts in Regional Economic Development Programs," *Papers and Proceedings of the Regional Science Association*, I (1955), W1–W20.

clearly defined, can readily be identified as "lagging" and "dynamic,"[4] and are areas for which specific development policies and objectives exist. Data on the economic performance of both provinces are available. Although a number of conceptual problems in allocating production by regions remain to be resolved and the regional data are likely to be even less reliable than the national accounts for all Pakistan,[5] the existing data provide the starting point for an analysis of the regional problem.

The objective of the present analysis is to highlight the regional growth problem and consider the possible effects a strict regional income equality target may have on the pattern of national development. First the background to the regional problem in Pakistan is presented. Then attention is focused on the long-term growth of the national and regional economies in a macroeconomic setting. Using the results of the macroanalysis an attempt is made to spell out the structural changes implied by alternative growth paths. Finally the policy alternatives open to the planners are discussed.

Growth and Structural Change in the Regional Economies, 1950–1965

Economic growth in Pakistan can be divided into two phases: the period from 1950 to 1960 (or perhaps 1959), one of relative stagnation;[6] and the years between 1960 and the present, when the economy has shown remarkable improvement in its development performance.

For the decade 1950 to 1960, gross national product in constant prices was estimated to have grown at 2.6 percent per annum, a rate just equal to the estimated growth of population. Over the period 1960 to 1965, national product, again at constant prices, has increased by more than 5.4 percent per annum, and per capita incomes have grown by 2.8 per-

4. This does not imply that there is economic homogeneity within each province. Indeed, it is likely that the intraprovincial differences in economic welfare are greater than the interprovincial differences. Nevertheless, the identification of East Pakistan as the "lagging" and West Pakistan as the "dynamic" region is valid as a generalization with considerable political importance.

5. Gustav F. Papanek, *Pakistan's Development: Social Goals and Private Incentives* (Cambridge: Harvard University Press, 1967).

6. Although Pakistan became independent in 1947, the statistical data for the first years are admittedly unreliable because they were heavily influenced by transient factors relating to the upheavals following partition. Consequently, they have been omitted from the analysis. It should also be noted that data in Pakistan cover July-through-June fiscal years. For convenience, reference is made to calendar years rather than to the more appropriate split fiscal years, i.e., 1959/60 will be written as 1960.

cent in a year.[7] Investment, as a percentage of GNP, had increased from 9.7 in 1960 to 17.3 in 1965, and the savings proportion rose from 6.5 to 10.5 percent over the same period.[8] Whereas at the start of Pakistan's First Five Year Plan the country was in the lower quartile of developing countries with respect to its investment, savings, and growth rate, by

Table 2.1a. Gross provincial product (1960 factor cost; millions of rupees unless otherwise noted)

Sectors	1950		1955		1960		1965	
	East	West	East	West	East	West	East	West
1. Agriculture	8,074	6,595	8,704	6,948	9,042	7,711	11,020	8,741
2. Mining	–	27	–	45	–	70	8	123
3. Manufacturing	472	961	651	1,569	912	2,018	1,532	3,179
4. Construction	58	179	126	289	224	427	900	1,021
5. Transport and communications	631	608	779	810	900	921	1,218	1,206
6. All others	3,139	3,721	3,556	4,445	3,894	5,320	5,242	6,797
7. Gross provincial product	12,374	12,091	13,816	14,106	14,972	16,467	19,920	21,067
8. Population (millions)	42.25	35.31	47.70	39.87	53.58	45.03	61.30	51.10
9. Gross regional product per capita (Rs.)	293	342	290	354	278	366	325	412

Sources: for 1950–1960, Taufiq M. Khan and Asbjørn Bergan, "Measurement of Structural Change in the Pakistan Economy: A Review of the National Income Estimates," *Pakistan Development Review,* 6 (Summer 1966); for 1965, Government of East Pakistan, Finance Department, *Economic Survey of East Pakistan, 1964–65* (Dacca, 1965); Government of Pakistan, Planning Commission, *Evaluation of the Second Five Year Plan, 1960–65.*

7. The figures used here are based primarily on official government data and suffer from a number of shortcomings. In addition, the use of a single terminal year to calculate annual growth rates can be misleading in an economy where one sector, agriculture, still predominates and may be subject to wide variations in its output level from year to year. Papanek, in *Pakistan's Development,* attempts to overcome this problem by substituting trend figures for actual output figures in the agricultural sector. Consequently, he shows a growth rate of 6.3 percent per annum for the period 1960–1965 for gross domestic product.

8. Taufiq M. Khan and Asbjørn Bergan, "Measurement of Structural Change in the Pakistan Economy: A Review of the National Income Estimates," *Pakistan Development Review,* 6 (Summer 1966), 163–208; Government of Pakistan, Central Statistical Office, Planning Commission, *Evaluation of the Second Five Year Plan, 1960–1965* (Karachi: Manager of Government Publications, 1966).

Table 2.1b. Percentage distribution of gross provincial product

Sectors	1950		1955		1960		1965	
	East	West	East	West	East	West	East	West
1. Agriculture	65.2	54.5	63.0	49.3	60.4	46.8	55.3	41.5
2. Mining	—	0.2	—	0.3	—	0.4	—	0.6
3. Manufacturing	3.8	7.9	4.7	11.1	6.1	12.3	7.6	15.1
4. Construction	0.5	1.5	5.6	5.7	6.0	5.6	6.1	5.7
5. Transport and communications	5.1	5.0	5.6	5.7	6.0	5.6	6.1	5.7
6. All others	25.4	30.9	25.8	31.6	26.0	32.3	26.5	32.3

the end of the Second Five Year Plan it had moved to the upper quartile.[9]

Overall Structure and Growth of the Regional Economies

Growth and structural change in the two regions have been far from uniform. The composition of production in East and West Pakistan is shown in Tables 2.1a and 2.1b. The agriculture sector continues to dominate both regional economies, but the share of agriculture in the gross regional product of West Pakistan has been declining rapidly. The share of manufacturing in the regional economies—and its rate of growth—is most striking.

At the time of partition both regions lacked any industrial base. Most of the early industrialization effort was concentrated in West Pakistan, with a variety of factors contributing to this spatial bias. The infrastructure in East Pakistan was, and continues to be, poor in comparison. Land cost is higher in East Pakistan and the physical presence of the central government in West Pakistan undoubtedly played a considerable role.[10] Although one may argue over the relative importance of these and other factors, the result has been the development of a rapidly expanding and diversified industrial sector in West Pakistan. Consequently, related factors such as banking and insurance have also favored West Pakistan, probably to an even greater extent than is reflected in Tables 1.1a and 1.1b, where the allocation of such service to regions has been made, in

9. Hollis B. Chenery and Alan M. Strout, "Foreign Assistance and Economic Development," *The American Economic Review*, 56 (September 1966), 679–733.

10. Gustav F. Papanek, "Pakistan's Industrial Entrepreneurs—Education, Occupational Background, and Finance," Chapter 8, this volume; Md. Anisur Rahman, *East and West Pakistan: A Problem in the Political Economy of Regional Planning* (Occasional Paper No. 20, Harvard Center for International Affairs, Cambridge, July 1968).

line with official Government of Pakistan procedure, on a fifty-fifty basis.

The patterns of sectoral growth within each region were also different during the 1950's and the early 1960's. From 1950 to 1960 both regional economies failed to exhibit any rapid growth, although the growth rate in East Pakistan was significantly lower in nearly all sectors than in West Pakistan. In the early 1960's all major sectors within each region experienced a higher rate growth than evidenced in the 1950's, and, significantly, East Pakistan's growth rate was such as to prevent further widening in the regional per capita product differences. Since 1965 the relative position of East Pakistan has worsened again—in part because of stagnation in its agricultural sector while West Pakistan enjoyed a rapid increase in agricultural production.[11]

The effect of the past growth pattern on regional per capita product is shown in Figure 2.1. Although a disparity in regional per capita product existed in 1950, it continued to increase until 1960. With East Pakistan as 100, the level of product per capita in West Pakistan stood at 116.7 percent in 1950, and at 131.7 percent, in constant prices, in 1960, declining to 126.8 percent in 1965. Although these data give some evidence of a reversal of the trend toward widening disparity, such evidence does not allow for any firm conclusion as to whether regional disparities are indeed being reduced. It is also important to note the more regular time path in West Pakistan's growth of per capita product since 1960 compared to that found in East Pakistan. This reflects the more diversified structure of West Pakistan's economy, and the crucial effect of weather on the level of agricultural output and hence on the growth of regional product in East Pakistan. This is made graphic in the sharp drop in the 1959 per capita product level in East Pakistan, when agricultural output declined precipitiously.

Foreign and Regional Trade

Perhaps no other aspect of the regional problem has involved more acrimonious debate, supported by fewer facts, than the question of net resource transfers between the two provinces. Exports from East Paki-

11. Given a number of unresolved conceptual problems and the lack of statistical information underlying the regional accounts, it is possible to reach alternative conclusions as to the level of disparity and its movement over time. The official national accounts estimates have probably, for political reasons, tended to underestimate the degree of interregional income differences. Papanek (*Pakistan's Development*, pp. 316–332) presents a less optimistic and perhaps more realistic analysis of the regional problem. The analysis of past regional performance confines itself to the period up to 1965. Recent evidence seems to indicate a further widening in the disparity level.

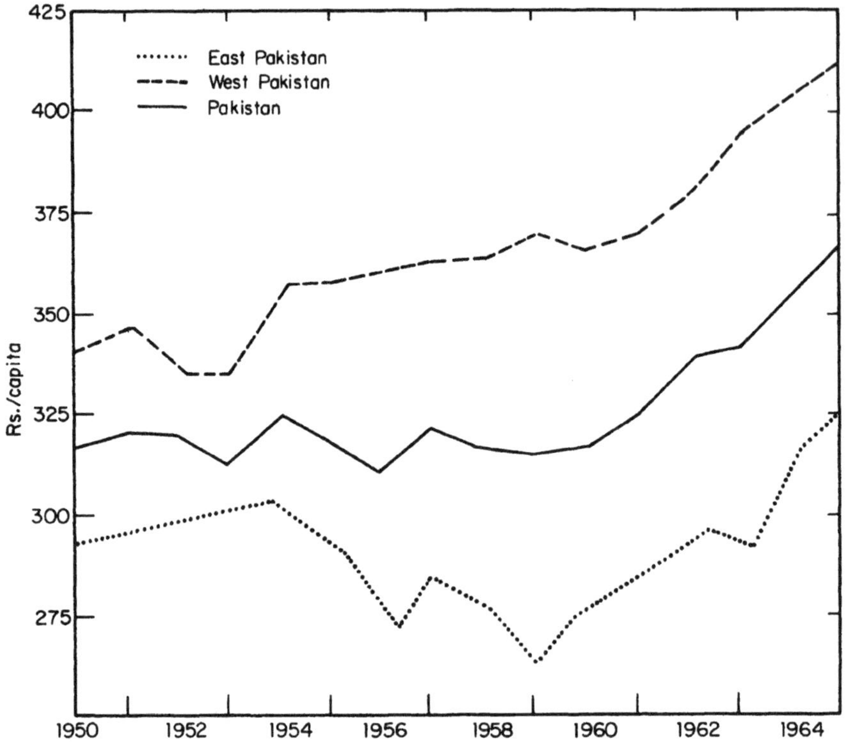

Figure 2.1. Per capita product

stan have earned the bulk of Pakistan's foreign exchange over the period from 1950 to 1965. At the same time the major share of foreign imports was destined for West Pakistan. In terms of regional commodity trade, East Pakistan has had a continued deficit on its current account, which until 1957 was less than its surplus on its foreign trade account; thus a net transfer of resources to West Pakistan was implied.[12] Haq estimates that such transfers amounted to Rs. 210 million per year from 1950 to 1955 and perhaps Rs. 100 million a year from 1956 to 1960.[13]

The mechanism for effecting such transfers was the combined operation of the exchange control and import licensing systems. Because exporters must surrender foreign exchange earned to the central govern-

12. Rahman, *East and West Pakistan.*

13. Mahbub-ul Haq, *The Strategy of Economic Planning: A Case Study* (Karachi: Oxford University Press, 1963).

ment, and as foreign exchange thus collected is licensed to importers in line with government policy, the volume of imports from abroad into each region can be controlled. Over time one might expect that the region's surplus in foreign trade balance would be offset by a deficit in its regional trade account. Exporters are paid in domestic currency which, if it cannot be used to buy foreign merchandise, will create inflationary pressures eventually resulting in a flow of goods from the lower-price region to the higher. This mechanism has not worked because shipping space for interregional trade has been limited and domestic currency transfers are unrestricted.

The precise measurement of such resource transfers is difficult, if not impossible, because of definitional questions and a lack of data relating to invisible trade and capital movements. Nevertheless, the total regional surplus on the commodity trade account, shown for East Pakistan in Tables 2.2a and 2.2b, was, certainly for the early period, of such a magnitude that even the inclusion of noncommodity transactions would not alter the conclusion that on balance a transfer of resources had taken place. Since the net inflow of foreign aid must equal a region's balance of

Table 2.2a. Foreign and regional commodity trade balances: East Pakistan (millions of rupees/current prices)

	Foreign account			Regional account			Total trade balance
Year	Exports	Imports	Surplus deficit (−)	Exports	Imports	Surplus deficit (−)	Surplus deficit (−)
1950	628	391	238	32	229	−197	41
1951	1,211	515	696	46	211	−165	531
1952	1,087	856	231	36	161	−125	106
1953	642	407	235	107	177	− 76	159
1954	654	311	334	131	370	−239	95
1955	732	332	400	181	293	−112	288
1956	1,041	376	665	221	319	− 98	567
1957	909	841	68	325	510	−185	−117
1958	988	748	240	264	690	−426	−186
1959	881	579	302	278	660	−382	− 80
1960	1,080	682	398	361	543	−182	216
1961	1,259	1,039	220	363	801	−438	−218
1962	1,301	899	402	401	832	−431	− 29
1963	1,249	1,059	190	469	918	−449	−259
1964	1,224	1,499	−275	511	844	−333	−608
1965	1,268	1,726	−458	542	857	−315	−773

Source: Government of Pakistan, Central Statistical Office, *Monthly Statistical Bulletin.*

Table 2.2b. Foreign and regional commodity trade balances: West Pakistan (millions of rupees/current prices)

	Foreign account			Regional account			Total trade balance
Year	Exports	Imports	Surplus deficit (−)	Exports	Imports	Surplus deficit (−)	Surplus deficit (−)
1950	565	930	−365	229	32	197	−168
1951	1,342	1,184	158	211	46	165	323
1952	922	1,504	−582	161	36	125	−457
1953	867	1,065	−198	177	107	76	−122
1954	641	845	−204	370	131	239	35
1955	491	801	−311	293	181	112	−198
1956	743	982	−240	319	221	98	−142
1957	698	1,525	−827	510	325	185	−642
1958	434	1,320	−866	690	264	426	−460
1959	444	1,036	−592	660	278	382	−210
1960	763	1,807	−1,044	543	361	182	−182
1961	540	2,181	−1,641	801	363	438	−1,203
1962	543	2,243	−1,700	832	401	431	−1,269
1963	998	2,086	−1,808	918	469	449	−1,359
1964	1,075	2,985	−1,910	844	511	333	−1,577
1965	1,151	3,674	−2,523	857	542	315	−2,208

payment deficit on its foreign and regional account, assuming no change in foreign exchange reserves, the data in Table 2.2 would tend to support the contention that West Pakistan has been the major recipient of foreign aid, even if one were to make a generous allowance for the effect of omitting invisible trade.

Investment and Savings

The caveats applied to the regional product accounts must be repeated in a comparison of savings and investment, shown in Table 2.3. Notwithstanding the shortcomings of the available investment series, they reveal a remarkable constancy in East Pakistan's share of total investment.[14] This constancy, despite the government's stated desire to increase the allocation of investment resources to East Pakistan, has generally been explained by a lack of "absorptive capacity" in that province. Although the causes of this "absorptive capacity" constraint were not specified, they have usually been considered to be a lack of technically skilled persons needed to implement new projects efficiently and an inability to utilize resources effectively because of inadequate infrastruc-

14. Haq, *The Strategy of Economic Planning;* Pakistan, Planning Commission, *The Second Five Year Plan, 1960–1965.*

Table 2.3. Regional savings and investment, 1961–1965 (millions of rupees/current prices unless otherwise noted)

	1961		1962		1963		1964		1965		Average 1961–1965	
	East	West	East	West	East	West	East	West	East	West	East	West
1. Gross regional product[a] (factor cost)	16,937	17,849	17,994	18,488	18,970	19,672	20,392	21,123	22,510	23,170	–	–
2. Indirect taxes/net of subsidies[b]	394	1,054	439	1,169	452	1,303	491	1,569	635	1,976	–	–
3. Gross regional product (market prices)	17,331	18,903	18,433	19,657	19,422	20,975	20,883	22,692	23,145	25,146	–	–
4. Gross regional investment[a]	1,355	3,205	1,963	3,837	1,818	4,433	2,420	4,790	2,929	5,401	–	–
5. Surplus (+)/deficit (–) total current account[c]	–246	–1,227	–117	–135	–363	–1,592	–674	–2,023	–753	–2,500	–	–
6. Gross regional savings	1,109	1,978	1,846	2,486	1,455	2,840	1,746	2,767	2,176	2,901	–	–
7. Investment as percentage of GNP	7.8	17.0	10.6	19.5	9.4	21.1	12.0	21.1	12.7	21.5	10.6	20.2
8. Savings as percentage of GNP	6.4	10.5	10.0	12.6	7.5	14.1	8.4	12.2	9.4	11.5	8.4	12.1
9. Percent of investment financed by own savings	81.8	61.7	94.0	64.8	80.0	64.1	72.1	57.8	74.2	53.7	79.5	59.9

[a]Government of Pakistan, Planning Commission, *Evaluation of the Second Five Year Plan, 1960–65.*
[b]Wouter Tims, *An Estimate of Regional Indirect Taxes, 1959/60–1964/65,* (mimeo, Karachi, 1966).
[c]Calculated from data in Table 1.2 and Joseph J. Stern, *Inter-industry Relations in East Pakistan, 1962/63* (Research Report No. 62, Karachi, 1968).

ture. The government presumably was unable to redress this pattern.

Though the concept of "absorptive capacity" is difficult to quantify, it is true that East Pakistan's development effort has at times been plagued with an inability to prepare a substantial "shelf of projects" which donors could aid. The admission that there are deterrents to the absorption of investment in no way removes the possibility that noneconomic factors played a role in the allocative decision-making process. The fact that the central government is located in West Pakistan and largely staffed by West Pakistanis undoubtedly had some effect.[15] Regardless of what emphasis is placed on the possible economic and political factors, the failure to substantially increase the share of investment in East Pakistan must be considered a major element in the inability to bring about any significant reduction in the level of disparity. The possibility that East Pakistan's economy is characterized by a lower absorptive capacity cannot be dismissed, and will be discussed more fully later.

Despite the caution with which one must interpret the data on savings, it appears from Table 2.3 that the average savings rate in East Pakistan is lower, and more variable, than that in West Pakistan. At the same time the marginal savings rate over the Second Plan period was 18 percent in East Pakistan and approximately 15 percent in West Pakistan. Although the government cannot precisely specify the national and regional savings rates, it can influence the savings rates greatly through adjustments in taxation and public savings. No definitive study has as yet been undertaken on the sources of central government tax revenues and expenditures by regions and their impact on regional savings and income. For the purpose of long-run regional analysis, however, it has been assumed that government policy will nearly equate the regional marginal savings rates and achieve a national marginal savings rate close to that projected over the Perspective Plan.[16] This implies that the two regions will share equally the burden of financing the domestic cost of development, even though government policy may distribute the benefits of economic growth unequally in line with its regional policy.

Although the regional per capita product[17] differences in Pakistan

15. Rahman, *East and West Pakistan.*

16. Government of Pakistan, Planning Commission, *The Third Five Year Plan* (Karachi: Government of Pakistan Press, May 1966).

17. It would be more appropriate to use regional income as a measure of welfare. However, because Pakistan does not provide estimates of national or regional income, regional product has been used as a proxy for regional income, although it should be noted that interregional income transfer payments can cause a divergence between the two.

appear to be smaller than those found in other developing countries,[18] a number of factors peculiar to Pakistan tend to exacerbate the regional problem. No other country consists of two noncontiguous regions, a situation which poses enormous obstacles to the mobility of capital and labor. And the fact that the central government plays a major role in the allocation of scarce resources provides a focal point for regional discontent. As a consequence of the political pressures generated by the disparity in regional welfare, the removal of all differences in regional per capita income levels has become a constitutional obligation. The Planning Commission has proposed that this goal be reached by 1985, the terminal year for the Perspective Plan.[19] In addition, Pakistan's long-term objectives call for a termination of net foreign aid inflows and a doubling of per capita incomes by 1985. Little analysis was undertaken to investigate the consistency of these objectives or to ascertain the opportunity cost of meeting the regional income parity target. The present analysis will, it is hoped, provide a clearer understanding of the possible effect which the regional objective might have on national development.

Regional Growth: The Macro-Economic Implications

Considerable insight into the development process is gained if it is analyzed in terms both of its dynamic relationships and of its related structural change, but the usual planning models either concentrate on the problem of planning over time, or, at the other extreme, emphasize sectoral analysis in a static setting. This is the result of the computational difficulties inherent in solving multisectoral, intertemporal models. If a regional dimension is added, the problem becomes even more complex.

Neither the dynamic nor the sectoral aspect of the development process can be omitted without considerable loss of information. The sectors of the economy should not be aggregated to such a degree that any technological differences in the production structures among sectors and regions is lost. Similarly, the disaggregation over time should leave scope for a gradual transition from one phase of the development process to the next rather than force abrupt changes such as would occur if the dynamic aspects of the problem were limited.

18. Jeffrey G. Williamson, "Regional Inequality and the Process of National Development," *Economic Development and Cultural Change,* 13.4 (July 1965), part 2, 1–84.

19. Pakistan, Planning Commission, *The Third Five Year Plan.*

The problem must be simplified even if it is difficult to decide what aspects of the analysis can be omitted with a minimal loss of information. One possible solution is to break the problem of planning over regions, time, and sectors into steps or stages, and solve each in succession.[20] Specifically, it seems appropriate to deal first with the problem of distributing production and income over time without regard to the composition of such output or expenditure. As a second stage the question of composition and structure can be analyzed. This means that first a macro problem is posited in which the changing relationships of the macro variables over time are given full attention, while at a later stage a micro problem, embodying the information previously obtained, is solved. Although such an approach has the obvious advantage of allowing considerable scope for the analyses of both the dynamic and sectoral aspects of regional growth, the method does have some limitations which are briefly discussed in the section on Regional Growth and the Structure of the Regional Economies.

The dynamic linear programming model used to analyze the time-phasing characteristics of the development path for the economy as a whole, and for the two regions, is an adaptation of the analytic framework developed by Chenery and MacEwan and Chenery and Dorfman.[21] Its primary feature is the realistic assumption of a permissible divergence between savings and investment, the gap being filled by foreign aid. Two sectors are specified, showing the capacity of the economy to transform domestic resources into foreign exchange. In addition to a "traditional" output-producing sector, a "trade-improving" production sector is specified which produces either "nontraditional exports" or import substitutes for foreign or regional trade. The resultant shift in production from the traditional to the trade-improving sector is presumed to cause a rise in the economy-wide capital output ratio reflecting the operation of the principle of comparative advantage. Trade-improving activities include both import substitution and export promotion, primarily in terms of developing new export commodities which to a considerable extent will come from the industrial sector. Hence both activities are likely to raise the capital output ratio. Only two scarce factors are considered—foreign

20. Jan Tinbergen and Hendricus Bos, *Mathematical Models of Economic Growth* (New York: McGraw-Hill Book Company, Inc., 1962).

21. Hollis B. Chenery and Arthur MacEwan, "Optimal Patterns of Growth and Aid: The Case of Pakistan," in Irma Adelman and Eric Thorbecke, eds., *The Theory and Design of Economic Development* (Baltimore: Johns Hopkins Press, 1966); Hollis B. Chenery and Robert Dorfman, "Optimal Growth Patterns in an Open Economy" (mimeo, Harvard Center for International Affairs, Cambridge, 1966).

exchange and capital. Any possibility of regional migration is omitted, since the distance and cost of interregional migration and the regional differences in language and social customs make it unlikely that population movements will be a major factor in Pakistan.

Specifically, the following function is to be maximized:

$$(1)\ \text{Max } W = \sum_{t=1}^{T} \sum_{j=1}^{J} \frac{C_{t,j}}{(1+i)^t} + \sum_{j=1}^{J} \sigma_j V_{T,j} - \gamma \sum_{t=1}^{T-n} \frac{F_t}{(1+i)^t}$$

where

$$\sigma_j = \delta(1 - \alpha_j) \sum_{t=1}^{\infty} \frac{(1 + \theta_j)^t}{(1 + r)^{T+t}}.$$

The objective function consists of three parts. The first term measures the discounted flow of consumption in each region during the period between 1965 and 1985. The discount rate is assumed to be equal for East and West Pakistan. The second term is an indicator of the discounted value of consumption in both regions in all the years following the Perspective Plan. The weight (σ_j) assumes that after year T, the final year considered by the model, the economy will achieve self-sustaining growth and the rate of growth of per capita income in the two regions will be equal. A higher discount rate is used for later years; this can be justified in terms of a diminishing marginal utility of rising per capita incomes. Finally, the last term represents the discounted value of foreign aid with a weight (γ) representing the price of foreign assistance. The supply of foreign aid is assumed to be infinitely elastic at price γ until year $T-n$, the last year of the Perspective Plan, at which time Pakistan's long-term objectives call for a termination of net aid inflows.[22] The definitions of all variables and parameters are given in Tables 2.7 and 2.8.

Definitional Equations

Gross regional product is defined as the sum of output of the regular production sector in each region and total trade-improving output, which is divided between the part whose foreign exchange earnings are used in the producing region ($V^1_{t,j,j}$) and the part which forms the physical counterpart of interregional transfer payments ($V^1_{t,j,k}$):

22. For a more complete discussion of this particular welfare function, see Chenery and MacEwan, "Optimal Patterns of Growth and Aid."

(2) $$V_{t,j} = V^0_{t,j} + V^1_{t,j.j} + V^1_{t,j.k}.$$

Similarly, total gross regional investment is the sum of investment in each sector:

(3) $$I_{t,j} = I^0_{t,j} + I^1_{t,j}.$$

Regional income is defined as gross regional product plus (minus) net regional transfer payments:

(4) $$Y_{t,j} = V_{t,j} \pm R_{t,j}$$

where such transfers are given by

(4a) $$R_{t,k.j} = V^1_{t,k.j} - V^1_{t,j.k}.$$

Regional expenditure is defined as:

(5) $$Y_{t,j} = C_{t,j} + I_{t,j} + E_{t,j} + e_{t,j.k} + V^1_{t,j.j} - M_{t,j} - m_{t,j.k}.$$

Savings, net of transfers, are equal to investment less the capital inflow:

(6) $$S_{t,j} - R_{t,j} = I_{t,j} - F_{t,j}.$$

The region's trade gap, which must be filled by the capital inflow, is determined by the region's export of traditional exports to the rest of the world, less imports and the current account balance for regional trade in terms of traditional goods, minus the trade-improving output destined for foreign trade:

(7) $$F_{t,j} = M_{t,j} + m_{t,j.k} - E_{t,j} - e_{t,j.k} - V^1_{t,j}.$$

Traditional exports, foreign and regional, are assumed to grow at an exogenously determined rate and are produced by the traditional sectors:

(8a) $$E_{t,j} = E_{0,j}(1 + \mu_j)^t$$
$$e_{t,j} = e_{0,j}(1 + \pi_j)^t.$$

Two further conditions are imposed. The regional exports from one region must equal the regional imports in the receiving region:

(8b) $$e_{t,j.k} = m_{t,k.j}$$

and the sum of the capital inflows into each region is equal to the foreign aid received by the nation as a whole:

(8c) $$F_t = \sum_{j=1}^{J} F_{t,j}.$$

Structural and Behavioral Constraints

Since labor is assumed to be in surplus, production in each sector is limited by the capital stock in that region. Thus, the capacity limit for regular production is given by:

(9) $$V^0_{t,j} \leq \frac{1}{k^0_j} K^0_{t,j},$$

and that for trade-improving production and transfers by:

(9a) $$V^1_{t,j,j} + V^{11}_{t,j,k} \leq \frac{1}{k^1_j} K^1_{t,j}.$$

While the model only considers two scarce factors, capital and foreign exchange, the fact that other resources not explicitly considered are also scarce leads to the assumption that the regional economies are characterized by diminishing returns to investment. The use of a "step" function to approximate, by linear segments, the diminishing productivity curve of investment necessitates a redefinition of investment:

(10) $$I^0_{t,j} = I^{01}_{t,j} + I^{02}_{t,j} + I^{03}_{t,j}$$

and

(11) $$I^1_{t,j} = I^{11}_{t,j} + I^{12}_{t,j} + I^{13}_{t,j}.$$

The total capital stock available for production in each region and each sector is given by:

(12) $$K^0_{t+1,j} = K^0_{t,j} + I^{01}_{t,j} + \beta_{2,j} I^{02}_{t,j} + \beta_{3,j} I^{03}_{t,j}$$

and

(13) $$K^1_{t+1,j} = I^{11}_{t,j} + \beta_{2,j} I^{12}_{t,j} + \beta_{3,j} I^{13}_{t,j}$$

where β_j defines the relative productivity of investment as the regional economies move downward on the marginal productivity of investment curve.

The exogenously specified limits on the regional economy's ability to absorb investment are introduced by adding a factor (φ_j) to the investment constraint and a factor (λ) which indicates that one-third of total investment may take place on each step of the marginal productivity curve:

(14) $$\begin{aligned} I^{01}_{t,j} + I^{11}_{t,j} &\leq \lambda_{1,j}(K^0_{t,j} + K^1_{t,j}) - \varphi_j \\ I^{02}_{t,j} + I^{12}_{t,j} &\leq \lambda_{2,j}(K^0_{t,j} + K^1_{t,j}) - \varphi_j \\ I^{03}_{t,j} + I^{13}_{t,j} &\leq \lambda_{3,j}(K^0_{t,j} + K^1_{t,j}) - \varphi_j. \end{aligned}$$

Maximum savings in any year are a function of base-year saving and increases in regional production:

$$(15) \qquad S_{t,j} \leq S_{o,j} + \alpha_j(V_{t,j} - V_{o,j}).$$

Demand for imports is a function of base-year imports and changes in regional production and investment:

$$(16) \qquad M_{t,j} + m_{t,j.k} \geq M_{o,j} + m_{o,j.k} + \eta_{o,j}(V_{t,j} - V_{o,j}) + \eta_{1,j}(I_{t,j} - I_{o,j}).$$

Although it is possible to incorporate most policy targets into the welfare function if the price associated with such a target were known a priori, it is usually easier to define certain additional policy targets as constraints to the model. Two objectives of the Pakistan Perspective Plan are introduced explicitly: foreign aid is to be terminated at some specified year and regional per capita incomes must be equalized by 1985 so that regional parity must be maintained in the future. Thus,

$$(17) \qquad F_t \leq 0 \qquad \text{for } t = T\text{-}n;\ T$$

and

$$(18) \qquad Y_{t,j}\left(\frac{1}{N_{t,j}}\right) = Y_{t,k}\left(\frac{1}{N_{t,k}}\right) \qquad \text{for } t = t\text{-}n;\ T.$$

In addition, unrealistic declines in per capita consumption and investment are ruled out:

$$(19) \qquad C_{t,j} \geq C_{t-1,j}(1 + o_j)$$

and

$$(20) \qquad I_{t+1,j} \geq I_{t,j}.$$

Similarly, declines in per capita regional income are considered an untenable possible alternative to solving the income disparity problem. Thus,

$$(21) \qquad Y_{t+1,j}\left(\frac{1}{N_{t+1,j}}\right) \geq Y_{t,j}\left(\frac{1}{N_{t,j}}\right).$$

Alternative Forms of the Model

Although a specific regional target is defined in the Pakistan Perspective Plan, three alternative patterns for regional growth can be specified. One possibility is to rule out any widening of the regional disparity over the level found in the base year:

$$Y_{t+1,j}\left(\frac{1}{N_{t+1,j}}\right) - Y_{t+1,k}\left(\frac{1}{N_{t+1,k}}\right) \leq Y_{t,j}\left(\frac{1}{N_{t,j}}\right) - Y_{t,k}\left(\frac{1}{N_{t,k}}\right). \tag{22}$$

Furthermore, it may, for political reasons, be necessary to restrict the permissible level of income transfer payment and eventually to terminate such payments after regional income differences have been eliminated. The first condition is given by:

$$R_{t,j} \leq q\, V_{t,j} \tag{23}$$

where q is an arbitrary constant representing the maximum percentage of regional production that is transferred. The second condition is given as:

$$R_{t,j} = 0 \qquad \text{for } t = T\text{-}n;\ T. \tag{24}$$

The Basic Solution

By using the basic model described above, the pattern of development can be forecast. Two important assumptions need to be stressed again before presenting the results. First, it has been posited here that the future marginal savings rates will be identical in both provinces. This is not an unreasonable assumption, despite the higher past marginal savings rate in East Pakistan, because historically the savings rates have been largely the result of severe import restrictions in East Pakistan that will need to be relaxed if a much higher growth rate is to be achieved without severe inflation. Second, it has been assumed that there is an absolute limit on East Pakistan's ability to absorb capital, given as an annual increase of 11 percent in investment. This assumption is crucial to the results. If this absorptive capacity constraint is raised to 16 percent, the cost of achieving regional per capita income equality is drastically reduced. The effect of relaxing this as well as other constraints is discussed in the sections following the discussion of the basic solution.

The growth of regional income and production in the basic solution is shown in Figure 2.2. (The values of all variables in the solution and their shadow prices are given in Tables 2.9 and 2.10.) By 1971, which corresponds approximately to the end of the Third Five Year Plan, the difference in regional per capita income has been reduced to 26 percent from a level of 30 percent in 1965, falls to 20 percent by 1974, and is elimi-

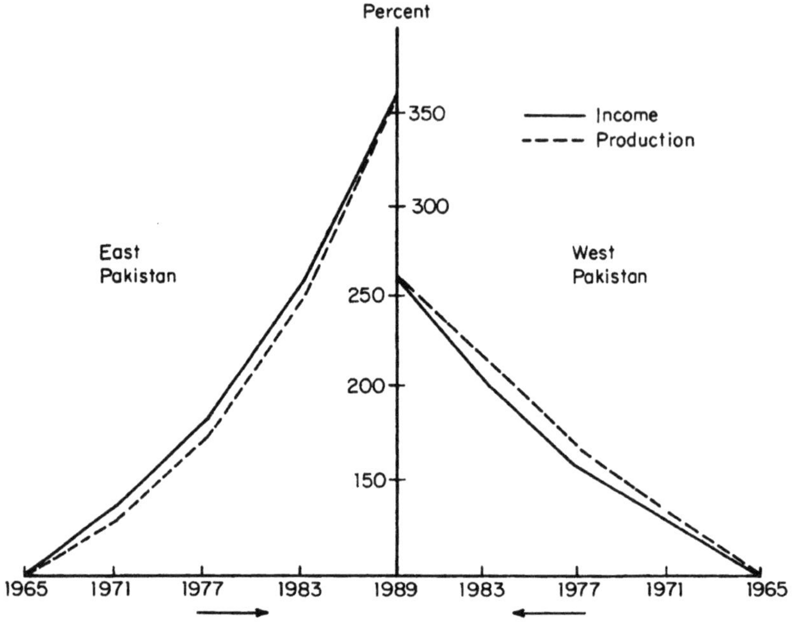

Figure 2.2. Index of income and production in the basic solution

nated by 1986.[23] This pattern of diminishing per capita income differences corresponds, at least for the early years, closely to that projected by the Planning Commission. The primary difference between the model results and the Perspective Plan projections is the Planning Commission's assumption that there will be a sharp drop in the level of disparity between 1975 and 1980, whereas the model solution postpones the major decrease in disparity till the later period, 1980–1985.

The process by which the regional incomes are equated is through the combination of a high growth rate in East Pakistan, as high as permitted by the absorptive capacity stipulated for that province, and the redistribution of income and resources from West Pakistan, used either for an increase in investment or consumption in East Pakistan. The result

23. The model was run for eight periods, each scaled to represent three years, in an effort to reduce the computational time required per solution. Thus $T = 0$ is equivalent to plan year 1965, $t = 1$ to 1968, $t = 2$ to 1971, and $t = 8$ to 1989. Consequently, there is no direct correspondence between the model time periods and the initial years of each successive five year plan encompassed in the Perspective Plan.

is a terminal year per capita income level of Rs. 640 in both regions. For the entire period, income grows in East Pakistan at an annual compound rate of 5.5 percent and at 4.0 percent in West Pakistan, implying an annual growth rate of 4.9 percent for the economy as a whole.

This rate of growth for the national economy is well below that indicated in the Perspective Plan, where a growth of 7.2 percent per annum is forecast. Although no attempt has been made to choose precisely those parameters which would reproduce the Planning Commission's long-term growth pattern, it is of some interest to see what effect the regional considerations have had on the model results. When using the parameters that characterize the basic solution, but eliminating all regional considerations, a growth rate of 6.8 percent per annum appears feasible. This result is brought about by the more favorable conditions posited for West Pakistan, especially the higher absorptive constraint, and because the objective function values consumption equally in both regions. As a result, once the constraint on regional parity is removed, the value of discounted consumption is maximized if both regions grow at the highest rate permitted by the parameters. In terms of regional equity this goal implies a sharp increase in the level of disparity. Per capita income in this solution is Rs. 633 for East Pakistan and Rs. 1208 for West Pakistan. A failure to implement a positive regional policy will leave the income level in East Pakistan in 1985 only slightly lower, and that in West Pakistan considerably higher, as compared to the basic solution. It thus becomes apparent that, given the conditions postulated on the model, the major burden in equalizing regional income will be borne by West Pakistan, with but a minor increase in the welfare of East Pakistan.

The patterns of investment and foreign aid inflow for each province differ (see Figures 2.3, 2.4, and 2.5). In East Pakistan, the maximum growth of investment constraint is binding through 1980, while in West Pakistan the minimum investment constraint is operative. The combination of the high savings rate and the low level of investment in West Pakistan permits that province to finance its own investment needs and regional transfers. Regional savings in East Pakistan rise as rapidly as possible, given the marginal rate of savings, so that by the terminal year of the analysis, the regional savings-investment gap is closed, as is the regional income-production difference. This autarchic requirement imposes a severe constraint on the pattern of regional growth. As long as there is an insistence on equating regional production and regional income by 1989, the terminal income level is set primarily in terms of East Pakistan's own productive potential. The growth rate in West Pakistan

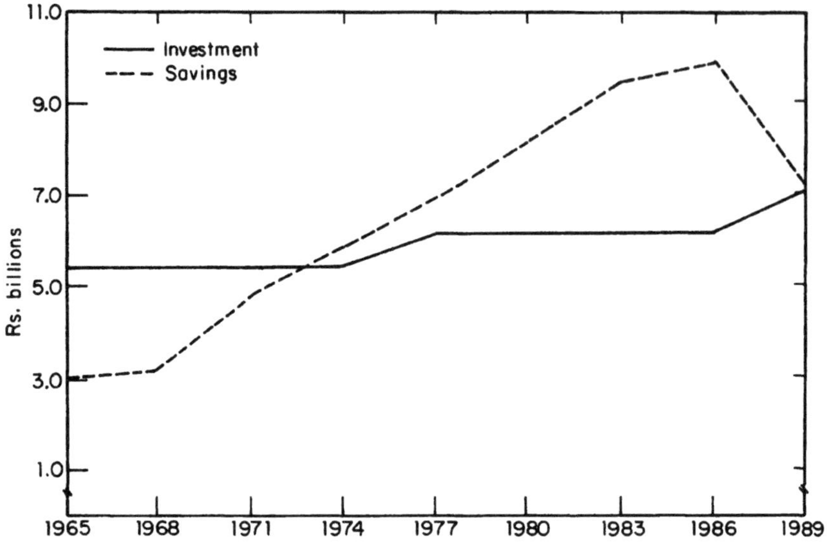

Figure 2.3. Investment and savings in West Pakistan (basic solution)

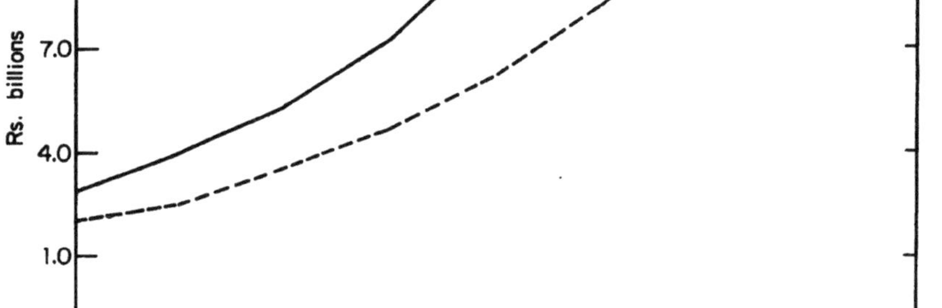

Figure 2.4. Investment and savings in East Pakistan (basic solution)

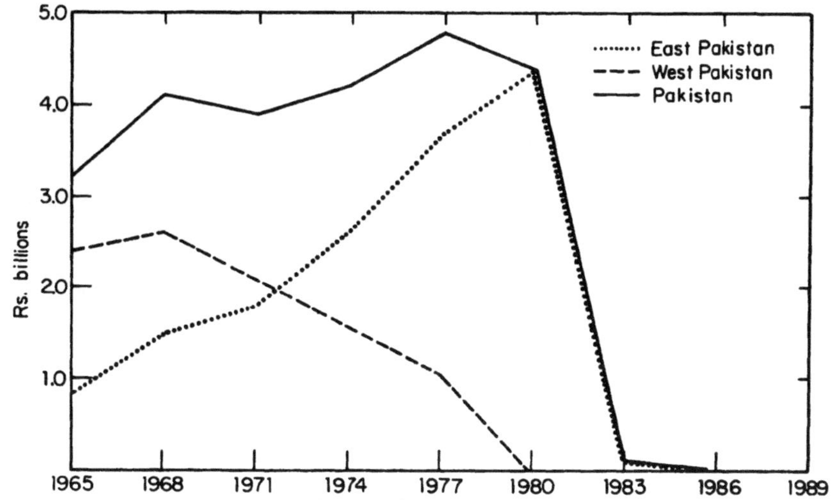

Figure 2.5. Foreign aid in the basic solution

can merely adjust itself to this level. Finally, as regards the regional allocation of foreign aid, a sharp reduction in the aid inflow to West Pakistan is observed, so that, after 1974 all foreign aid is destined for East Pakistan.

Alternative Patterns of Growth

Although it is clear from the basic solution that Pakistan's policy of equalizing regional per capita incomes by 1985 is feasible, at least in terms of the specification of the economic structure presented in this chapter, the cost of such a policy to the economy is more clearly brought out by a consideration of alternative growth paths.

Maintaining the equal income target but permitting regional transfers beyond 1989 yields an increase of nearly 10 percent in the terminal income level,[24] an increase brought about as follows: the higher growth of production in West Pakistan generates a higher level of savings and hence permits an increase in interregional transfers; the limit on such transfers is now West Pakistan's ability to mobilize savings, and the terminal income level is no longer set by East Pakistan's own production capability.[25]

If, in addition to the relaxation on the regional production-income gap, a temporary deterioration in the level of disparity is permitted, a further

24. See Table 2.11.

25. The effects on the regional growth rates and income levels by varying the policy constraints are summarized in Table 2.11.

increase in the terminal income levels of both regions is possible. Such an alternative involves a rapid rate of growth of income in West Pakistan so that in 1977 this province reaches a level of per capita income of Rs. 703. There is no subsequent growth of per capita income. This rapid initial growth of income makes possible the generation of a higher level of savings which can be used to eliminate the regional income differences rather rapidly through high levels of interregional transfers. Two factors should be noted. The level of disparity rises to 50 percent before beginning to decline, and such a level may create an intolerable strain on the national fabric, even though disparity would be eliminated by the end of the Perspective Plan period. Finally, the fact that the regional transfers are condensed into a relatively short period, and hence form 6 percent of West Pakistan's income for the period 1983 to 1989, may indicate that such a redistributional policy is unlikely to be implemented or be feasible.

To a considerable extent the dissatisfaction in East Pakistan which led to the large-scale disturbances in that province beginning in 1968 was caused by the failure further to reduce interregional disparity. At the same time there has been a growing recognition in West Pakistan that the cost to that province of rigid adherence to a policy that would remove all interregional income differences by 1985 could be extremely high. The conflict between regional development and interregional equity has been most apparent in West Pakistan's desire to export its growing agricultural rice and wheat surplus rather than use these resources to meet the food deficit in East Pakistan. And in discussions regarding the size of the Fourth Plan (1970–1975) and its regional allocation, West Pakistan strongly resisted any major increase in the national tax effort since it was clear that such resources would be raised largely in West Pakistan but be expended in East Pakistan. There is growing evidence therefore that the failure to reduce interregional income differences has weakened the possibility ofmoving vigorously toward regional equity in the future.

In the final case considered the redistributional effect is limited to a level below that made feasible by regional savings. In the basic solution such interregional transfers rise to 6.0 percent of West Pakistan's income in 1974, and for the period as a whole, average 4.8 percent of income in that region. Such a redistributional effort may be politically intolerable and administratively unfeasible.[26] Arbitrarily limiting such

26. Precise estimates on the effects of redistributional policies carried out elsewhere are difficult to secure. A comparison of transfer payments as a percentage of national income for the period 1956–1961 shows that they averaged 6.2 in the United States, 7.8 in the United Kingdom, and 18.7 in France. Wallace C. Peterson, "Transfer Expenditure, Taxes, and Income Distribution in France," *Quarterly Review of Economics and Business,* 5 (Fall 1965), 5–23; C. Westrate, "An Estimate of the Magnitude of Income Redistribution in New Zealand," *Economic Record,* 33 (April 1957), 97–102.

transfers to 3 percent of income in West Pakistan reduces terminal income levels in both regions to Rs. 634, as compared to Rs. 640 in the basic solution. Thus, if the regional parity target is maintained but the implied redistribution effort is limited, the result will be a lower level of welfare for the population as a whole. And for the alternative solutions considered above, where regional transfers play an even greater role, the cost in not implementing a regional transfer policy results in an even greater loss of potential income. The effect of a number of such alternative regional policies on the terminal income level is shown in Figure 2.6.

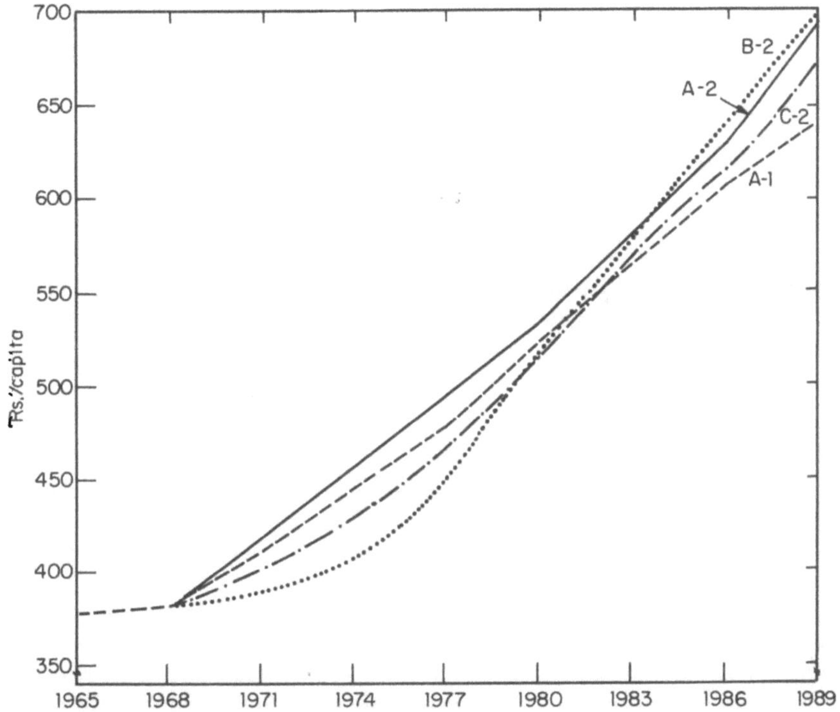

Figure 2.6. Growth of per capita income in East Pakistan under alternative regional policies

A-1 Basic solution
A-2 Regional transfer in terminal year
B-2 No time path for removal of disparity specified
C-2 Regional transfers limited

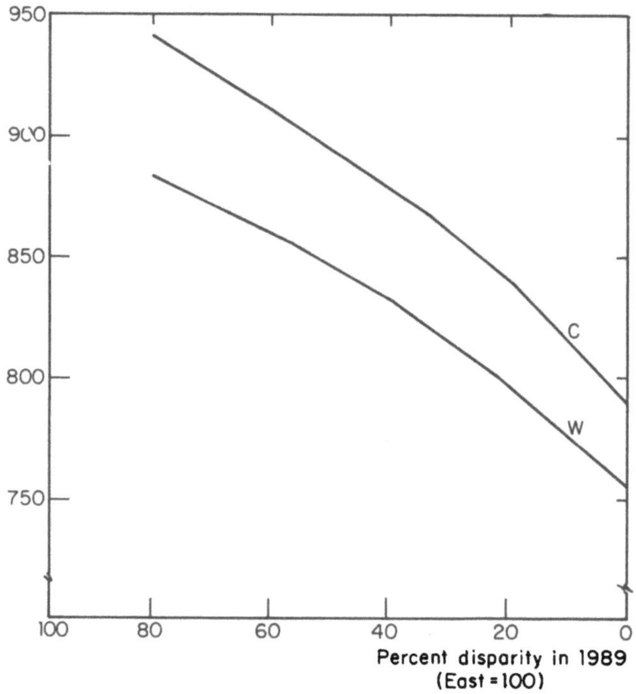

Figure 2.7. Effect of alternative regional targets
W. Value of welfare function
C. Discounted consumption stream (all Pakistan)

Alternative Regional Growth Targets

This chapter so far has concentrated on alternative policy choices, all of which were assumed to operate within the framework of meeting the constitutional requirement of equating regional per capita incomes by 1985. It may be, however, that once the economy is confronted with a clearer consideration of the opportunity cost of implementing such a policy, political considerations may force a postponement of the target date for achieving parity. Although the extreme solution where regional equity considerations are omitted entirely presents a result, in terms of regional disparity, that is likely to be politically unacceptable, a more realistic target might be to equate regional per capita growth rates. This implies that the present level of disparity in percentage terms, would remain constant, at least over the Perspective Plan.

Such an equal per capita growth rate target can be considered as one end of a spectrum of regional growth targets with the equal per capita income solution at the other extreme. By solving the model for the equal regional growth rate target and then parametrically varying downward the permissible level of disparity, a curve is generated which shows the trade-off between national (and regional) income levels and the level of disparity (see Figure 2.7). Thus, with a 5 percent difference in regional per capita incomes in 1989, the per capita income in East Pakistan increases by 1 percent (see Table 2.11) over the strict parity solution. If the target is to equate per capita growth rates in the two provinces, an increase of nearly 6 percent in per capita income in East Pakistan is possible as compared to the basic solution.

The alternatives open to the policymakers provide for the possibility of considering political trade-offs. In return for a relaxation of the regional disparity constraint presently imposed on the Planning Commission, East Pakistan can be offered the possibility of a higher level of future income. For West Pakistan the choice is also for a higher income level, but at the cost of underwriting a considerable redistribution of income over time. Such bargaining situations are stated more appropriately in terms of probable outcomes rather than absolute certainties. Though it is possible to show that both regions can achieve higher per capita income levels once the absolute parity constraint is relaxed, given the simplistic structure of the model, the attractiveness of such alternative regional targets will depend, perhaps crucially, on the degree of certainty with which the policymakers of each province view these alternatives. The primary purpose of presenting such alternatives is to permit consideration of a wider choice in framing regional policies in terms of the cost to the nation as a whole of the present restrictive regional policy.

Variations in Absorptive Capacity

An analysis of the results presented above indicates that the major barrier to meeting both the regional welfare target and achieving a high rate of growth for the national economy is the absorptive capacity constraint. Since, at the same time, this parameter reflects a largely arbitrary judgment, it is worthwhile to consider the effect of variations on the results implied by changes in this constraint.

Raising the absorptive capacity constraint in East Pakistan from an 11 to a 13 percent increase in investment per year, equal to that in West Pakistan, results in a rise of the terminal year per capita income level to Rs. 715 as compared to Rs. 640 in the basic solution. The level of disparity is eliminated more rapidly than in the basic solution, although absolute parity in the levels of per capita income still is not reached until 1986. The effect of positing an equal absorptive capacity for both regions is to eliminate nearly all differences in the growth potential of the two regions. This solution is therefore inconsistent with the hypothesis that the difference in the past growth performance of the regions reflects a basic difference in their economic potential.

The sensitivity of the results to the absorptive capacity constraint is more clearly brought out by raising the limit on new investment in East Pakistan to a 16 percent increase per annum. At this level for the absorptive capacity constraint the "shadow price" on the regional parity equation falls to Rs. 50.1 million or only 6 percent of the shadow price found in the basic solution, indicating that at such a rate of growth of investment parity in incomes per capita between the two regions can be obtained at relatively little cost in terms of growth foregone. The rate of growth of per capita income is 2.7 percent in East Pakistan and 2.5 percent in West Pakistan. Apparently a similar assumption about the possibility of raising investment in East Pakistan at such a high rate underlies the projections on regional growth prepared by the Pakistan Planning Commission. The terminal income level of Rs. 891 per capita for both regions is close to that forecast in the Perspective Plan.[27]

There is little a priori reason for rejecting such a high rate of investment for East Pakistan. Nevertheless, its acceptance should be placed in a somewhat broader perspective. A rate of increase of investment of 16 percent per annum would place the performance of East Pakistan above the historically observed maximum rate of growth of investment for fifty countries.[28]

Appeal to the historical experience of other countries cannot be used to rule out a more dynamic development pattern in Pakistan. Indeed, over the period 1950 to 1965 the rate of increase in investment in Pakistan was close to 20 percent per annum.[29] This, however, is measured from an extremely small base and gives little support to the possibility of maintaining such a rapid pace over the next twenty years. If absorptive capacity is defined as that amount of investment, or that rate of gross domestic investment expressed as a proportion of GNP, which can be made at an

27. Part of the difference found in the present analysis and that of the Planning Commission can be explained by the slightly higher rate of population growth used here. Pakistan, Planning Commission, *The Third Five Year Plan*.

28. Hollis B. Chenery and Alan M. Strout, "Foreign Assistance and Economic Development," *The American Economic Review*, 56 (September 1966), 679–733.

29. Papanek, *Pakistan's Development*, p. 8.

acceptable rate of return with the supply of co-operant factors considered as given in the short run, then any judgment as to a reasonable limit on future investment must consider the factors that made the past increases possible. Pakistan made judicious use of foreign technical assitance to supplement its own scarce skilled labor supply. The preponderant proportion of such imported skilled manpower was used in West Pakistan where nearly 2,500 man years of technical assistance were made available over an eight-year period to assist in the preparation of projects for water and power sectors. The massive use of such technical assistance undoubtedly raised the absorptive capacity of West Pakistan province, and a study on a similar scale dealing with the Ganges-Brahmaputra River basin in East Pakistan would undoubtedly permit equally vast and profitable investment projects to be undertaken there. Until the factors that inhibit the rate of growth of investment are specified and policies to overcome these constraints are delineated, it is difficult to resolve the question as to what a reasonable limit to the future growth of capital formation might be. Nevertheless, alternative investment patterns can be considered.

Rapid increases in investment often are accompanied by rising trends in the capital-output ratios. Positing an absorptive capacity ceiling of 16 percent but coupling this with a rising capital coefficient yields a terminal year per capita income level only 6 percent over that found in the basic solution. An additional alternative considers the possibility that the ability to absorb investment is a dynamic aspect of development likely to respond to past growth rates. That is, insofar as the absorptive capacity bottleneck reflects a lack of skilled labor, managerial talent, and organizational ability, these factors are likely to become less scarce after a period of rapid increase in the investment level. A precise specification of such an absorptive capacity function is beyond the scope of this chapter, but it can be approximated by letting the investment limit vary upward over time in East Pakistan from its initial level of 11 percent in 1965 to 16 percent in 1980. The result is an increase in the terminal income level to Rs. 733 per capita, an increase of 12 percent over that found in the basic solution.

Although the discussion of the absorptive capacity constraint brings into focus the critical role this parameter has on the possibility of achieving regional parity at a minimum cost to the national economy, its specification must be considered unsatisfactory. Without a more precise study of the specific factors that determine the limit on efficient capital accumulation it is only possible to conclude that, unless investment growth in East Pakistan can be stepped up dramatically, the present regional parity target will have severe repercussions on the national growth rate.

Regional Growth and the Structure of the Regional Economies

It is desirable to quantify the sectoral structure implied by alternative solutions of the macroeconomic model, although it may introduce some inconsistencies into the analysis. Before describing the sectoral model, therefore, it is necessary to spell out some of the difficulties.

There is no great difficulty in specifying a consistent set of initial conditions for both the macro and the sectoral model. It is more important to ensure comparability over time in the two. The main divergence which is likely to occur is in the relation of the sectoral capital-output ratios and the aggregate capital coefficients for each of the regions used in the aggregate model. As an initial condition the aggregate capital coefficient for each region can be calculated from the sectoral composition of regional output and sectoral capital coefficients. Over time, however, the weighted sum of the sectoral capital coefficients will change as the relative output levels of the various sectors change. Neither the direction nor the magnitude of such changes can be estimated a priori. One possible solution is to solve the "time-path" model using a constant capital coefficient and then, by means of these results, specify a number of exogenous variables in the sectoral model. The sectoral output levels thus derived will, in turn, imply changes in the aggregate regional capital coefficients. The sensitivity of the dynamic model to such changes in the capital coefficients can then be tested. If the time-path model is highly sensitive to such changes, a recursive procedure should be adopted until a set of coefficients is generated whose value over time approximates that derived from the changes in the sectoral composition of output.

A second difference between the time-path model and the sectoral model is that the regional economies have been characterized by diminishing returns to investment in the aggregate model. The sectoral model will have no such apparent characteristic. This difference reflects the need to represent in a highly aggregated model the reallocation of resources to exchange earning and savings activities, in which their productivity is progressively lower, until equilibrium is reached. In a two-sector model such a reallocation procedure is best represented by assuming diminishing returns to capital as the amount of investment is increased. For the sectoral model this reallocation of resources is made a function of the need to meet a minimum level of output for each sector and to allocate investment to more than one trade-improving activity. That is, although a specific sector may be most attractive in terms of its relative saving of scarce resources in producing output, demand considerations force the economy to shift to the next most attractive sector. Finally, a problem arises from the use of separate terminal conditions for the two models. While each stage of the analysis yields an optimal solution, there is no simple way of assuring that precisely the same optimal path would be chosen if the entire problem were solved in one intricate model.

It is apparent that the relation between the two models is far from straightforward and that some inconsistency may be introduced into the analysis. This cost should, however, be weighed against the additional insights to be gained by analyzing the dynamic as well as structural changes of the growth process.

In order to allow for a considerable degree of disaggregation, the sectoral model is limited to a static analysis covering two time segments, 1965–1974 and 1974–1986.[30] The constraints of the sectoral model, by

Table 2.4. Sectoral model equations

Set number Equation	Constant or controlled variables	Number of equation
1. *Output determination*		
${}_kX_i - \sum_{j=1}^{n} {}_ka_{ij}\,{}_kX_j - {}_kI_i - {}_kR_i - {}_{kl}r_i + {}_kM_i + {}_{lk}r_i$	$\geq {}_kC_i + {}_kE_i + {}_{kl}1_i - {}_{lk}m_i$	(42)
2. *Investment demand*		
(a) $\sum_{i=1}^{m} {}_kI_i + i = \sum_{m}^{n} + 1\ {}_kI_i + MI$	$= {}_kI$	(2)
(b) $\tau_k I_i - \sum_{j=1}^{m} {}_kb_{ij}\,{}_kX_j + \sum_{j=m}^{n} + 1\ {}_kb_{ij}\,{}_kX_j$	≥ 0	(12)
(c) $\tau_k MI - \sum_{j=1}^{m} {}_kz_j\,{}_kX_j - \sum_{j=m}^{n} + 1\ {}_kZ_j\,{}_kX_j$	$= 0$	(2)
3. *Demand for foreign imports*		
(a) $\sum_{i=1}^{n} {}_k\overline{M}_i + {}_kMI + \sum_{j=1}^{m} {}_kp_j\,{}_kX_j + \sum_{j=m}^{n} + 1\ {}_kp_j\,{}_kX_j$	$= {}_kE + {}_kR + {}_kF - {}_kMC$	(2)
(b) ${}_k\bar{M}_i$	$\leq \bar{\varphi}_i\, X_i$	(12)
4. *Import substitution*		
(a) ${}_kR_i$	$\leq {}_k\varphi_k R$	(16)
(b) $i = \sum_{m+1}^{n} {}_kR_i$	$\leq {}_kR$	(2)
(c) ${}_kr_i$	$\leq {}_k\lambda r_k$	(16)
(d) ${}_{lk}r_i - (1 + \theta_i)\ {}_{kl}r_i$	$= 0$	(16)
(e) $i = \sum_{m+1}^{n} (1 + \theta_i)\ {}_{kl}r_i$	$\leq {}_kr$	(2)

30. These unequal time segments result from the use of three-year time periods in the macroeconomic model.

Table 2.5. Variable and parameter definitions for the sectoral model

Variables

X_i = output of sector i
I_i = investment good output of sector i
R_i = output from sector i for foreign trade-improving or import substitution
r_i = output from sector i for regional trade-improving
C_i = consumption of good i
E_i = foreign traditional exports of good i
e_i = regional traditional exports of good i
$\bar{M}_j$ = competitive imports of good i
MI = investment good imports
MC = consumer good imports
m_i = traditional regional imports
E = total traditional exports
F = net inflow of foreign aid

Parameters

a_{ij} = input coefficient
b_{ij} = capital coefficient for regular production
$\hat{b}_{ij}$ = capital coefficient for trade-improving production ($\hat{b}_{oj} > b_{ij}$)
z_j = imported capital coefficient for regular production
$\hat{z}_j$ = imported capital coefficient for trade-improving production
p_j = noncompetitive import coefficient for regular production
$\hat{p}_j$ = noncompetitive import coefficient for trade-improving production
φ = upper bound on import substitution for foreign trade in sector i
$\hat{\varphi}$ = upper bound on competitive imports for foreign trade in sector i
λ = upper bound on import substitution for regional trade in sector i
θ = transport cost coefficient for regional trade of good i
τ = terminal weights (stock-flow conversion factor) for investment

Subscripts

i, j = sectors, where $i = 1$ to $i = m$ are traditional output producing sectors and $i = m + 1$ to $i = n$ are trade-improving output sectors[a]
k, l = regions, where $k = 1, 2$
$l = 1, 2$

[a]The symbol ^ is used to indicate that the sectors referred to are trade-improving sectors.

groups, with the exogenous variables appearing on the right-hand side, are given in Table 2.4, and the definitions of the variables and parameters in Table 2.5. A brief description of the various equations follows.

Output Determination. Twenty-one commodity balances are identified for each region. Total consumption, exports, and traditional regional imports are set at levels determined by the time-path model. Consumption of each commodity is given by the change in consumption expenditure and the relevant regional expenditure elasticities. The commodity structure of traditional exports is derived from the commodity composition in the base year, except that account is taken of the probably inelastic demand for raw jute and jute products.

The interindustry coefficients (a_{ij}) are derived from separate input-output tables for East and West Pakistan. Separate sectors are identified for traditional and trade-improving output. Although characterized by higher capital coefficients, the nontraditional sectors presumably have the same input structure as the traditional output-producing sectors.

Investment Demand. Equation (2a) is definitional. Total capital resources are specified exogenously in line with the results from the time-path model. Equations (2b) and (2c) relate investment demand to output changes through a capital-coefficient matrix. The factor τ, wherever it appears, is a necessary terminal condition for conversion of the flow of investment over the decade to capital stock.

Foreign Imports. Equation (3a) is definitional. Total demand for foreign imports consists of competitive imports, investment goods imports, and noncompetitive imports of intermediate goods. Consumer goods imports are given exogenously. The balance of payments constraint again is derived from the time-path model. Equation (3b) limits competitive imports into any one sector to a certain level ($\bar{\varphi}$) of total demand.

Import Substitution. The total amount of nontraditional production is set exogenously. The sectoral composition of such output is determined by the relative cost in terms of the scarce factors (capital and foreign exchange) required to produce various trade-improving commodities. In addition, an upper bound must be placed on the trade-improving production produced by any one sector, or the linearity of the model would result in the choice of only one trade-improving sector.

Equations (4c) and (4d) refer to regional nontraditional output which forms the physical counterpart of the interregional income transfers. Equation (4d) defines the imports of nontraditional, regionally traded commodities as the production of such a good in West Pakistan plus the transport cost associated with moving this good. Equation (4e) ensures that the sum of such exports is, if feasible, at least equal to the regional transfers called for by the time-path model.

The primary purpose of the sectoral model is to provide an indication of the optimal production structure in a static setting, given the constraints imposed by the time-path model. The objective function is taken as the maximization of regional product. This interpretation, in reality, comes close to a feasibility or consistency test of the macroeconomic values previously generated. The primary question to be addressed to this model is: given the aggregate targets to be met for a specific regional policy and the regional allocation of resources, is such a set of final demands feasible given the production structure of the regional economies?

The Composition of Output and Structural Change

Two solutions have been used to constrain the sectoral model. The first, the equal per capita income solution, represents the most orthodox interpretation of the regional objective; the second, the equal growth rate solutions, is taken as representative of a realistic alternative to the present regional target. The composition of output under these two alternatives is given in Tables 2.12, 2.13, 2.14, and 2.15.

For East Pakistan the results of both solutions are broadly similar. This similarity reflects the fact that in the macro-model East Pakistan's growth rate is always at the maximum permissible rate given its absorptive capacity. As investment continues to rise sharply in East Pakistan over the entire period, the highest sectoral growth rates are found for the investment goods sectors and those sectors closely related to creation of new capacity. The relatively low growth rates for the textile sectors are a result of the assumption that export demand for raw and manufactured jute is limited. Agricultural output increases at a rate slightly below that for regional product as a whole. Nevertheless, judged by the past performance of the agriculture sector in East Pakistan, this will still call for a substantial improvement in the agricultural performance.

The sectoral growth rates for West Pakistan revealed by the two solutions bring into sharp focus the cost of adhering to the strict parity target. In the equal income solution, which posits a reduction in the regional growth rate for West Pakistan in the later period, the result is a sharp reduction in the growth rate for the investment goods sectors and such related sectors as metal products and nonmetallic minerals. In addition, the effect of restraining growth in West Pakistan has a dramatic effect on the agriculture sector. Agricultural output increases by 5.2 percent in the early period and 6.0 percent in the later period. While these growth rates are still below that forecast by the Planning Commission, they are admittedly high. Although few countries have sustained a growth rate for agricultural output as high as 6 percent for any length of time, there is widespread optimism among agricultural economists familiar with the Pakistan situation that a dramatic increase in the agricultural growth rate in West Pakistan is likely. Consequently, adherence to a strict regional income parity policy would have the effect of foregoing the possible benefits expected as a result of the past structural changes that have taken place in the rural economy of West Pakistan.

Table 2.6 brings out the structural changes implied by the equal growth rate solution. Both regional economies show a similar trend, that is, a decline in the share of the agriculture sector and an increase in the share of manufacturing in regional product. The implied change for East Pakistan is dramatic. The share of manufacturing nearly triples, while the share of agriculture declines from over half of regional product to less

Table 2.6. Percentage of structural change in the Pakistan economy

Sector	1955	1960	1965	1974	1986
		East Pakistan			
1. Agriculture	63.0	60.4	55.3	48.3	43.3
2. Manufacturing	4.7	6.0	7.6	16.3	19.9
3. Others	32.3	33.5	37.1	35.4	36.8
Gross regional product	100.0	100.0	100.0	100.0	100.0
		West Pakistan			
1. Agriculture	49.3	46.8	41.5	35.5	33.2
2. Manufacturing	11.1	12.3	15.1	26.3	29.2
3. Others	39.6	40.9	43.4	38.2	37.6
Gross regional product	100.0	100.0	100.0	100.0	100.0
		Pakistan			
1. Agriculture	56.1	53.3	48.2	41.1	37.6
2. Manufacturing	8.0	9.3	11.5	21.9	25.1
3. Others	35.9	37.4	40.3	37.0	37.3
Gross national product	100.0	100.0	100.0	100.0	100.0

Sources: for 1955–1965, Khan and Bergan, "Measurement of Structural Change in the Pakistan Economy"; for 1974–1986, based on equal regional growth rate solution.

than 44 percent by 1986. In part this rapid rise in the share of manufacturing reflects the relatively small base from which East Pakistan began in 1965. But to a considerable extent the rapid structural change is an inevitable result of the continued high rate of investment growth implied by the macro-solution. For the economy as a whole the expectation is that its structure will become fairly diversified by 1986, relying for only about one-third of national product on the agricultural sector and having a substantial manufacturing base.

Regional Growth: The Policy Implications

Two clear goals in Pakistan's long-term development plans can be identified: to raise the level of well-being for the population as a whole as rapidly as possible, and to do so while ensuring an equitable regional distribution of income. In isolation the first objective would maximize the growth of the national economy with little or no attention to regional welfare. Though economically sound, such an alternative runs the risk of endangering national unity.

At the other extreme is the present policy of equating regional per capita income levels by 1985. On the assumptions embodied in this analysis such a policy would appear to sacrifice a considerable amount of growth to achieve the regional equity target. Nevertheless, the present strict parity target is likely to have a certain appeal to East Pakistan since the attainment of equality in per capita incomes depends primarily on each region's capacity to generate income and relies only to a minimal extent on a redistribution of income from West to East Pakistan. Given the past alleged regional bias on the part of the central government, East Pakistan may well feel that any policy that looks toward an amelioration of the regional income differences through an active redistribution policy is unrealistic. In fact, East Pakistan may decide that any deviation from the present regional target will only result in a more rapid rate of growth of income in West Pakistan which will not be offset by a redistribution of income. It seems unlikely, however, that the present policy can be carried out if, as the results of the present analysis indicate, the implication is for a sharp reduction in the growth rate in West Pakistan. Not only are there serious doubts about the possibility of actually implementing the policies necessary to frustrate the dynamism of this region, but such a policy entails considerable political risks as well.

A realistic assessment of alternatives indicates that there is a need for a regional policy falling somewhere between these extremes. One alternative is to equate regional growth rates over the Perspective Plan period (1965–1985), thus maintaining the approximate initial 30 percent difference in regional product per capita but using a redistribution policy to reduce the income per capita differences to one-third the 1965 level. In effect this policy postpones a complete removal of disparity to some time after the end of the Perspective Plan.[31] One critical element in assessing this policy is to judge the feasibility of implementing the distributional aspect of this solution. For the period as a whole the transfer payments form 7.5 percent of factor incomes in West Pakistan in the equal growth rate solution identified as (F-2) in Table 2.11. Such a level of transfer payments is relatively large, although over the period 1956–1961, transfer payments averaged 6.2 percent of national income in the United States and 7.8 percent in the United Kingdom.[32] Redistributive

31. It seems likely that, once growth is accelerated in East Pakistan, the demands for absolute parity in per capita income levels will become less strident.

32. Peterson, "Transfer Expenditure, Taxes, and Income Distribution in France"; Findley Weaver, "Taxation and Redistribution in the United Kingdom," *The Review of Economics and Statistics,* 32 (August 1950), 201–213.

expenditures usually take the form of pension payments, family allowances, expenditures on health and education, and other subsidies. One form of subsidy in the Pakistan situation might be related to agricultural development in West Pakistan. The rapid increase in agricultural output in that province could be used to subsidize food expenditures in East Pakistan. Although such policies must be considered in greater detail than is possible here, it is not unreasonable to foresee a surplus food program for East Pakistan based, not on surplus food imports supplied by the United States, but on interregional trade in food grains. Although the level of redistributive payments is not inconsequential, it does not appear to be of such magnitude that this type of solution need be rejected outright.

Brief mention should be made of the likely impact of alternative policies on the aid-giving countries. Regardless of which regional target is adopted, the economy will continue to depend on external assistance for some time. Yet donor countries and agencies increasingly have allocated aid to recipients whose past performance indicates a high return on such assistance. If Pakistan is to attract the required level of foreign aid, it must adopt a set of regional policies consistent with a high national growth rate. The substitution of a policy based on equal per capita regional growth rates for the present policy of equating regional income levels appears to be a realistic alternative open to the government. Not only would it allow for an increase of welfare in both regions and utilize more fully capacity in West Pakistan, but it is likely to be the regional policy with the greatest possibility of successful implementation.

The consideration of alternative regional growth targets may lead to a further evaluation of this policy in Pakistan. It is necessary, however, to recall again that all the alternatives considered reveal the critical role played by the absorptive capacity limit on investment especially in East Pakistan. Any policy aimed at raising the level of investment that can be efficiently employed in that province will tend to ameliorate the regional growth problem. A long-run development strategy for Pakistan should consider what factors might inhibit a rapid pace of capital formation in East Pakistan and promote policies that will remove such obstacles. Unless it is possible to step up the rate of investment in East Pakistan to a level considerably above that in West Pakistan, a solution to the regional equity problem is likely to result in a reduction in the national growth rate.

Appendix

Table 2.7. Definition of variables and parameters in the macro-model

Variables

V = gross regional product
V^0 = regular production
V^1 = production for nontraditional trade
I = total gross investment
I^0 = investment for regular production
I^1 = investment for nontraditional production
Y = regional income
R = regional transfers
S = savings
F = foreign capital inflow
M = traditional imports, foreign trade[a]
m = traditional imports, regional trade[a]
E = traditional exports, foreign trade[a]
e = traditional exports, regional trade[a]
C = consumption
N = population
K = capital stock
k_o = capital-output ratio, regular production
k_1 = capital-output ratio, nontraditional production

Parameters

i = rate of discount
γ = cost of foreign exchange
σ = weight for terminal year income
δ = weight on post-plan consumption
α = marginal rate of savings
θ = post-plan growth rate
r = rate of discount on post-plan consumption
μ = exogenous rate of growth for foreign exports
π = exogenous rate of growth for regional exports
β_2 = relative productivity of "fair" (type 2) investment
β_3 = relative productivity of "bad" (type 3) investment
λ_1 = limit to increase of "good" (type 1) investment
λ_2 = limit to increase of "fair" (type 2) investment
λ_3 = limit to increase of "bad" (type 3) investment
φ = absorptive capacity limit
η_0 = marginal import rate on regional income
η_1 = marginal import rate on regional investment
ρ = rate of population increase

[a]Traditional imports and exports are those imports which would be imported and those exports which could be sold if the structure of the economy remained unchanged from the base year.

Table 2.7. Definition of variables and parameters in the macro-model *(Cont.)*

Subscripts
t = time
j,k = regions, where $j = 1,2$; $k = 1,2$
T = terminal year of analysis

Table 2.8. Values of variables and parameters, 1965 (1965 prices; millions of rupees)

		East Pakistan	West Pakistan
Variables[a]			
1. Gross regional product	V_0	22,659	24,578
2. Saving	S_0	2,072	3,020
3. Investment	I_0	2,819	5,413
4. Imports (foreign)	M_0	1,922	4,240
5. Imports (regional)	m_0	965	550
6. Exports (foreign)	E_0	1,590	1,432
7. Net capital inflow	F_0	747	2,393
8. Consumption	C_0	20,587	21,558
9. Capital stock	K_0	56,648	73,734
10. Capital-output ratio: regular production	k_0	2.5	3.0
11. trade improving	k_1	4.0	4.0
12. Population (millions)		61.3	51.1
13. Income per capita (Rs.)		370	481
Parameters			
1. Marginal rate of savings	α	0.25	0.24
2. Rate of growth of traditional exports: foreign	μ	4.0	5.8
regional	π	4.0	3.0
3. Marginal rate of imports: on income	η_0	0.20	0.25
on investment	η_1	0.40	0.30
4. Size of each step of the marginal productivity of investment curve	λ	0.33	0.33

[a]Trend values derived from least squares regression fitted to actual data, 1960–1965. Data: Khan and Bergan, "Measurement of Structural Change in the Pakistan Economy"; Government of Pakistan, Central Statistical Office, *Monthly Statistical Bulletin*, various issues.

Table 2.8. Values of variables and parameters, 1965 (1965 prices; millions of rupees) *(Cont.)*

5. Relative productivity of:			
"good" investment	β_1	1.00	1.00
"fair" investment	β_2	0.75	0.75
"poor" investment	β_3	0.50	0.50
6. Absorptive capacity limit	φ	0.11	0.13
7. Population increase:[b]			
1965–1970	ρ	3.2	2.9
1970–1975	ρ	2.9	2.7
1975–1980	ρ	3.0	2.8
1980–1985	ρ	3.0	2.8
1985–1990	ρ	2.8	2.7
8. Rate of discount	i	0.08	0.08
9. Rate of discount, post-Perspective Plan	r	0.10	0.10
10. Cost of foreign exchange	γ	2.0	2.0
11. Relative valuation of post-plan consumption	δ	1.0	1.0
12. Post-plan growth rate	θ	7.3	7.1
13. Weight for terminal year income	σ	3.6	3.2
14. Terminal year of analysis	T	24	24
15. Terminal year for foreign aid	T-n	21	21
16. Terminal year for removal of disparity	T-n	21	21
17. Terminal year for regional transfers	T	24	24

[b]James W. Brackett and Donald S. Akers, *Projections of the Population of Pakistan by Age and Sex: 1965–1985* (Washington, June 1965).

Table 2.9. Summary of variables in the basic solution (billions of rupees)

Plan year	Income	Consumption	Investment	Foreign trade[a] Exports	Foreign trade[a] Imports	Regional trade Exports	Regional trade Imports	Savings	Capital inflow
				East Pakistan					
1965	22.7	20.6	2.8	1.6	1.9	0.6	1.0	2.1	0.8
1968	25.3	22.8	3.9	1.8	2.8	0.6	1.1	2.5	1.5
1971	30.1	26.5	5.3	2.3	3.5	0.7	1.2	3.5	1.8
1974	34.9	30.3	7.2	2.8	5.0	0.8	1.3	4.7	2.6
1977	41.0	34.8	9.9	3.6	6.8	0.9	1.4	6.2	3.7
1980	48.6	40.3	13.5	4.5	9.3	1.0	1.5	8.2	5.3
1983	57.3	46.6	14.2	5.7	8.6	1.1	1.7	10.7	3.4
1986	71.3	59.0	14.2	7.2	8.5	1.3	1.8	12.2	1.9
1989	81.7	64.9	16.8	9.0	8.5	1.4	1.9	16.8	–
				West Pakistan					
1965	24.6	21.6	5.4	1.4	4.2	1.0	0.6	3.0	2.4
1968	27.0	23.9	5.4	1.7	4.8	1.1	0.6	3.2	2.6
1971	30.8	27.5	5.4	2.5	5.1	1.2	0.7	3.3	2.1
1974	34.8	30.9	5.4	3.2	5.1	1.3	0.8	3.9	1.6
1977	39.7	34.7	6.1	4.0	5.1	1.4	0.9	5.0	1.1
1980	45.8	38.8	6.1	5.1	4.7	1.5	1.0	7.0	(−0.9)
1983	52.5	43.0	6.1	6.4	3.5	1.7	1.1	9.5	(−3.3)
1986	56.3	48.3	6.1	8.0	6.6	1.8	1.3	8.0	(−1.9)
1989	64.2	57.1	7.1	10.1	10.7	1.9	1.4	7.1	–
				Pakistan[b]					
1965	47.3	42.2	8.2	3.0	6.1	–	–	5.1	3.2
1968	52.3	46.7	9.3	3.5	7.6	–	–	5.7	4.1
1971	60.9	54.0	10.7	4.8	8.6	–	–	6.8	3.9
1974	69.7	61.2	12.6	6.0	10.1	–	–	8.6	4.2
1977	80.7	69.5	16.0	7.6	12.4	–	–	11.2	4.8

Table 2.9. Summary of variables in the basic solution (billions of rupees) *(Cont.)*

Plan		Con-	Invest-	Foreign trade[a]		Regional trade			Capital
year	Income	sumption	ment	Exports	Imports	Exports	Imports	Savings	inflow
1980	94.4	79.1	19.6	9.6	14.0	-	-	15.2	4.4
1983	109.8	89.6	20.3	12.1	12.1	-	-	20.3	0.03
1986	127.6	107.3	20.3	15.2	15.2	-	-	20.3	-
1989	145.9	122.0	23.9	19.1	19.1	-	-	23.9	-

	Investment by type					Capital stock		Production		
									Nontraditional	
Plan year	Regular	Trade improving	"Good"	"Fair"	"Bad"	Regular	Trade improving	Regular	Foreign	Regional
					East Pakistan					
1965	2.8	-	2.8	-	-	56.6	-	22.7	-	-
1968	3.2	0.7	1.3	1.3	1.3	62.9	-	25.3	-	-
1971	4.6	0.7	1.8	1.8	1.8	69.5	2.3	27.9	0.6	-
1974	6.1	1.1	2.4	2.4	2.4	79.4	4.3	31.8	1.1	-
1977	8.5	1.4	3.3	3.3	3.3	92.3	7.7	37.0	1.8	-
1980	8.5	5.0	4.5	4.5	4.5	119.4	11.8	44.3	3.0	-
1983	8.2	6.0	6.2	6.1	1.8	126.2	26.4	50.6	6.7	-
1986	8.0	6.2	8.2	5.9	-	148.0	39.8	58.9	10.5	-
1989	9.3	7.5	10.7	6.2	-	166.5	59.2	66.9	14.8	-
					West Pakistan					
1965	5.4	-	5.4	-	-	73.7	-	24.6	-	-
1968	1.0	4.4	2.6	2.6	0.2	85.9	-	27.0	-	-
1971	3.2	2.3	3.7	1.7	-	88.8	11.8	29.4	1.4	1.5
1974	3.6	1.8	4.9	0.5	-	96.5	18.3	32.2	2.6	1.9

1977	3.5	2.6	6.1	–	–	107.0	23.7	35.7	4.0	1.9
1980	3.6	2.5	6.1	–	–	117.4	31.4	39.1	6.6	1.2
1983	4.7	1.4	6.1	–	–	128.2	38.8	42.7	9.7	–
1986	4.7	1.4	6.1	–	–	142.5	42.7	47.5	8.8	1.9
1989	5.8	1.4	7.1	–	–	160.6	42.7	53.5	10.7	–
					Pakistan[b]					
1965	8.2	–	8.2	–	–	130.3	–	47.3	–	–
1968	4.2	5.1	3.9	3.9	1.5	148.8	–	52.3	–	–
1971	7.8	3.0	5.5	3.5	1.8	158.3	14.1	57.3	2.0	1.5
1974	9.7	2.9	7.3	3.9	2.4	175.9	22.6	64.0	3.7	1.9
1977	12.0	4.0	9.4	3.3	3.3	199.3	31.4	72.7	5.8	1.9
1980	12.1	7.5	10.6	4.5	4.5	227.8	43.2	83.4	9.6	1.2
1983	12.9	7.4	12.3	6.1	1.8	254.4	65.2	93.3	16.4	–
1986	12.7	7.6	14.3	5.9	–	290.5	82.5	106.4	19.3	1.9
1989	15.1	8.9	17.8	6.2	–	327.1	101.9	120.4	25.5	–

[a]Trade-improving production was allocated to foreign exports until the growth rate of exports reached 7.9 percent, the growth rate given in the Perspective Plan. The remainder was allocated to import substitution.

[b]Totals may not add up because of rounding.

Table 2.10. Shadow prices in the basic solution

	Foreign trade constraint		Productive capacity constraint					
			Regular trade		Regular trade		Savings constraint	
t	East	West	East		West		East	West
1	0.81	0.81	32.06	31.15	2.06	2.90	–	–
2	0.52	0.13	25.32	25.32	1.92	1.92	0.13	0.52
3	0.42	0.10	20.05	20.05	1.50	1.50	0.10	0.42
4	0.34	0.08	15.88	15.88	1.16	1.16	0.08	1.34
5	0.27	0.07	12.56	12.56	0.92	0.92	0.06	0.27
6	0.16	0.09	9.93	9.93	0.71	0.71	0.11	0.18
7	0.15	0.14	8.93	8.93	0.43	0.43	–	–
8	4.21	–	8.46	8.43	0.18	0.32	6.59	–

	Investment constraint							
t	"Good"	"Fair" East	"Bad"	"Good"	"Fair" West	"Bad"	Minimum investment growth constraint	
1	24.19	17.86	11.53	0.96	0.48	–	–	0.28
2	19.07	14.05	9.04	0.37	–	–	–	0.19
3	15.08	11.11	7.14	0.29	–	–	–	0.10
4	11.92	8.78	5.64	–	–	–	–	0.00
5	9.42	6.93	4.45	–	–	–	–	0.13
6	4.47	2.23	–	–	–	–	–	0.21
7	2.11	–	–	–	–	–	4.02	0.15
8	–	–	–	–	–	–	8.46	0.18

	Disparity constraints		
t	Maximum disparity	Removal of disparity	Aid termination constraints
1	278.46	–	–
2	192.87	–	–
3	138.81	–	–
4	89.05	–	–
5	43.70	–	–
6	–	–	–
7	–	23.06	7.47
8	–	920.57	2.14

Table 2.11. Summary of solutions using alternative targets, policies, and parameters

Solution	Characteristic of Solution	Terminal year income (Rs./capita)	Rate of growth of income: East	West (percent)	Pakistan
I. *Basic parameters*					
A-1	Equal per capita income[a]	640	5.5	4.1	4.8
A-2	Equal per capita income	695	5.7	4.4	5.2
B-2	Equal per capita income; disparity widens first	700	5.9	4.5	5.4
C-1	Equal per capita income; regional transfers limited to 3 percent of income of West Pakistan	634	5.3	4.0	4.8
C-2	Equal per capita income; regional transfers limited to 3 percent of income of West Pakistan	678	5.6	4.4	5.1
D-	No regional income constraints	633 (East) 1208 (West)	5.4	7.4	6.8
E-1	Disparity reduced to 5 percent	640 (East)	5.5	4.3	5.1
E-2	Disparity reduced to 5 percent	703 (East)	6.0	4.7	5.3
F-1	Equal per capita growth rates	640 (East)	5.5	5.3	5.4
F-2	Equal per capita growth rates	740 (East)	6.2	5.9	6.0
II. *Alternative parameters*					
H-1	Absorptive Capacity East Pakistan 13 percent	730	6.1	4.7	5.4
I-1	Absorptive Capacity East Pakistan 16 percent	891	7.0	4.5	6.3
I-1a	Absorptive Capacity East Pakistan 16 percent Capital Output Ratio 3.75	684	5.6	4.4	5.1
J-1	Marginal rate of savings East Pakistan 18 percent	625	5.4	4.0	4.7
K-1	Marginal rate of savings West Pakistan 18 percent	620	5.3	3.9	4.6
L-1	Capital output ratio rises by 10 percent	614	5.3	3.9	4.6
M-1	Absorptive Capacity East Pakistan Rises to 16 percent	733	6.1	4.7	5.4

Table 2.11. Summary of solutions using alternative targets, policies, and parameters (*Cont.*)

Solution	Consumption discounted (billions of rupees)	Foreign Aid: Discounted (billions of rupees)	Foreign Aid: Undiscounted (billions of rupees)	Shadow price regional target (billions of rupees)
I. *Basic parameters*				
A-1[a]	731.63	34.6	64.0	326.65
A-2	776.83	44.7	61.7	67.57
B-2	780.62	57.8	115.7	141.77
C-1	729.47	53.6	112.4	310.29
C-2	774.51	54.3	109.6	281.20
D-	941.39	65.2	125.6	-
E-1	738.43	50.7	176.4	314.25
E-2	745.66	59.8	120.3	295.19
F-1	781.64	59.2	117.7	139.61
F-2	815.35	62.0	136.2	78.43
II. *Alternative parameters*				
H-1	865.49	48.2	98.2	240.53
I-1	951.78	72.6	162.2	50.10
I-1a	745.82	61.9	132.4	361.72
J-1	768.87	49.6	96.7	330.46
K-1	760.29	44.5	86.7	124.16
L-1	625.81	42.2	84.0	339.26
M-1	812.20	45.6	95.1	296.20

[a]Numeral (1) refers to condition where regional transfers are terminated in terminal year while numeral (2) indicates an absence of this constraint.

Table 2.12. Composition of regional production, East Pakistan. (based on equal income per capita solution)

Sector	Production (billions of rupees) 1965	1974	1986	Rate of growth (percent) 1965–74	1974–86
1. Agriculture	11.41	16.05	30.22	4.1	5.4
2. Mining	0.08	0.13	0.35	5.5	8.6
3. Food processing	1.16	2.12[a]	5.56[a]	7.0	8.4
4. Cotton textiles	0.29	0.41[a]	0.92[a]	3.9	6.9
5. Jute textiles	0.40	0.49	0.65	2.3	2.4
6. Other textiles	0.14	0.23	0.49	5.6	6.5
7. Wood products	0.04	0.06	0.18	4.6	9.5
8. Paper products	0.15	0.26[a]	0.87[a]	6.3	10.5
9. Leather products	0.03	0.04	0.10	3.3	7.9
10. Rubber products	0.05	0.08[a]	0.18[a]	5.4	7.0
11. Fertilizer	0.02	0.07	0.27	14.9	11.9
12. Chemicals	0.13	0.24[a]	1.26[a]	7.0	14.8
13. Nonmetallic minerals	0.16	0.36	0.96	9.4	8.5
14. Metals	0.20	0.38	0.95	7.4	8.0
15. Machinery	0.08	0.20	0.59	10.7	9.3
16. Transport equipment	0.14	0.26	0.65	7.2	7.9
17. Miscellaneous	0.23	0.25	0.30	1.0	1.5
18. Construction	1.11	2.00	4.55	6.7	7.1
19. Electricity	0.12	0.25	0.71	8.5	9.1
20. Transport services	1.22	2.03	4.29	5.8	6.4
21. Other services	5.44	7.33	15.05	3.4	6.1
Gross regional product	22.60	33.24	69.20	4.4	6.3

[a]Includes nontraditional output for foreign trade.

Table 2.13. Composition of regional production, West Pakistan (based on equal income per capita solution)

Sector	Production (billions of rupees) 1965	1974	1986	Rate of growth (percent) 1965–74	1974–86
1. Agriculture	9.54	13.36[b]	19.13	4.0	3.1
2. Mining	0.20	0.41	0.82	8.1	5.7
3. Food processing	1.58	2.84[a,b]	4.90[a,b]	7.1	4.4
4. Cotton textiles	1.12	2.08[a,b]	2.99[a]	7.1	3.1
5. Jute textiles	—	—	—	—	—
6. Other textiles	0.18	0.39	0.62	8.9	4.0
7. Wood products	0.03	0.05	0.09	5.8	5.0
8. Paper products	0.09	0.16	0.31	6.6	5.7
9. Leather products	0.11	0.20	0.27	6.9	2.6

Table 2.13. Composition of regional production, West Pakistan (based on equal income per capita solution) *(Cont.)*

10. Rubber products	0.07	0.21[a,b]	0.43[a,b]	13.0	6.1
11. Fertilizer	0.04	0.11	0.29	11.9	8.4
12. Chemicals	0.43	1.17[a,b]	2.72[a,b]	12.8	7.3
13. Nonmetallic minerals	0.10	0.31	0.79	13.4	8.1
14. Metals	0.36	1.06	2.54[b]	12.8	7.6
15. Machinery	0.32	0.77	2.02[b]	10.2	8.4
16. Transport equipment	0.30	0.49	0.89	5.6	5.1
17. Miscellaneous	0.22	0.49[a]	0.81[a]	9.3	4.3
18. Construction	1.38	2.19	3.46	5.3	3.9
19. Electricity	0.22	0.54	1.19	10.4	6.8
20. Transportation	1.26	1.74	2.65	3.7	3.5
21. Other services	7.03	9.13	12.08	3.1	2.1
Gross regional product	24.58	37.70	59.00	5.0	3.7

[a] Includes nontraditional output for foreign trade.
[b] Includes nontraditional output for regional trade.

Table 2.14. Composition of regional production, East Pakistan (based on equal regional growth rate solution)

	Production			Rate of growth	
	(billions of rupees)			(percent)	
Sector	1965	1974	1986	1965–74	1974–86
1. Agriculture	11.41	16.05	30.02	4.1	5.3
2. Mining	0.08	0.13	0.36	5.5	8.6
3. Food processing	1.16	2.13[a]	4.17[a]	7.1	5.8
4. Cotton textiles	0.29	0.57[a]	1.15[a]	7.1	6.5
5. Jute textiles	0.40	0.51	0.84	2.8	4.3
6. Other textiles	0.14	0.25	0.65	6.7	8.3
7. Wood products	0.04	0.05	0.19	4.6	10.1
8. Paper products	0.15	0.28[a]	0.90[a]	7.2	10.2
9. Leather products	0.03	0.04	0.09	3.3	7.0
10. Rubber products	0.05	0.07[a]	0.16[a]	3.8	6.9
11. Fertilizer	0.02	0.07	0.37	14.9	12.9
12. Chemicals	0.13	0.26[a]	1.37[a]	8.0	14.8
13. Nonmetallic minerals	0.16	0.37	1.05	9.8	9.1
14. Metals	0.20	0.34	0.90	6.1	8.5
15. Machinery	0.08	0.19	0.60	8.7	11.5
16. Transport equipment	0.14	0.25	0.77	6.6	10.7
17. Miscellaneous	0.23	0.26	0.45	1.2	4.7
18. Construction	1.11	2.03	4.87	7.0	7.5
19. Electricity	0.12	0.24	0.73	8.5	9.7
20. Transport services	1.22	2.04	4.37	5.9	6.6
21. Other services	5.44	7.35	15.34	3.4	6.3
Gross regional product	22.60	33.26	69.24	4.4	6.3

[a] Includes nontraditional output for foreign trade.

Table 2.15. Composition of regional production, West Pakistan (based on equal regional growth rate solution)

	Production (billions of rupees)			Rate of growth (percent)	
Sector	1965	1974	1986	1965–74	1974–86
1. Agriculture	9.54	15.05[b]	30.31	5.2	6.0
2. Mining	0.20	0.42	1.03	8.6	7.9
3. Food processing	1.58	3.01[a,b]	7.04[a,b]	7.4	7.3
4. Cotton textiles	1.12	2.27[a,b]	4.36[a,b]	8.2	5.6
5. Jute textiles	—	—	—	—	—
6. Other textiles	0.18	0.42	0.92	9.9	6.8
7. Wood products	0.03	0.06	0.14	8.0	7.3
8. Paper products	0.09	0.19	0.43	8.7	7.1
9. Leather products	0.11	0.22	0.47	9.9	6.5
10. Rubber products	0.07	0.23[a,b]	0.61[b]	14.1	8.5
11. Fertilizer	0.04	0.13	0.38	14.0	9.5
12. Chemicals	0.43	1.28[a,b]	3.03[a,b]	12.9	7.4
13. Nonmetallic minerals	0.10	0.38	1.05	16.0	8.9
14. Metals	0.36	1.15[a,b]	2.88[a,b]	13.7	7.9
15. Machinery	0.32	0.89[a]	2.49[a,b]	12.0	9.0
16. Transport equipment	0.30	0.69	1.59	9.7	7.2
17. Miscellaneous	0.22	0.55[a]	1.33[a]	10.7	7.6
18. Construction	1.38	2.98	6.88	8.9	7.3
19. Electricity	0.22	0.71	1.89	13.9	8.5
20. Transportation	1.26	2.04	5.01	5.5	7.7
21. Other services	7.03	10.03	19.50	4.1	5.7
Gross regional product	24.58	42.41	91.34	6.3	6.6

[a] Includes nontraditional output for foreign trade.
[b] Includes nontraditional output for regional trade.

3 West Pakistan Exports: Effective Taxation, Policy Promotion, and Sectoral Discrimination

G. C. Hufbauer

First, using Marshallian tools, I have forged a concept of effective export taxation. Effective taxation is the mirror image to effective protection against imports. Both bear a simple relationship to the resource cost of foreign exchange, if questions of internal income distribution and foreign market elasticity are overlooked. The Marshallian analysis of taxation and resource cost inevitably neglects those dynamic aspects of trade and industrial efficiency that have commanded much attention in the recent literature.

Second, Pakistan's program of export incentives not only overcomes the bias against industrial exports arising from the typical developing nation system of tariffs, quotas, and taxation. It also provides generous incentives for the export of manufactured commodities. Pakistan may be one of the few developing countries that affords its industrial sector the double advantage of substantial protection against imports and substantial incentives for exports.

Third, the export incentive program almost certainly suffers from an excessive number of policy tools. Apart from the bonus voucher system,

NOTE: At the time I wrote this chapter, I was attached to the Planning and Development Department, Government of West Pakistan, Lahore, as a member of the Harvard Development Advisory Service, on leave from the University of New Mexico. (I have since returned to the University of New Mexico.) The views expressed do not reflect the views of either the West Pakistan Government or the Harvard Development Advisory Service. I am grateful to Marvin Rosen, Emile Despres, Hollis Chenery, Stephen Guisinger, and Joseph Stern for comments.

four minor schemes and six mini-schemes were also in operation during 1968. This uncoordinated profusion may distort incentives within the manufacturing sector, for example by encouraging the use of imported inputs or by promoting the export of goods with low value added. At the least, the present approach obstructs administrative efficiency and obscures any rational economic analysis of the program.

Fourth, the estimated structure of effective subsidies within the industrial sector gives the misleading impression that Pakistan's comparative advantage rests with branded consumer goods and heavy industrial products (receiving low export incentives) rather than with textiles (receiving high export incentives). However, the incentives for nontextile industrial exports, other than leather goods, are presently too small to stimulate volume exports; and for statistical reasons it seems likely that textile incentives have been overstated relative to other incentives.

Fifth, the promotion policies seem to have exercised a plausible differential impact on commodity export growth. Even over the long run, however, the connection is rough. Within a broad middle ground, little distinction can be drawn between export growth associated with subsidies of 30 percent and growth connected with subsidies of 90 percent. The subsidies have been important, but in this range other factors have made a greater impact on differential export expansion.

Sixth, very high prices are being paid at the margin for foreign exchange. Additional manufactured exports may cost Rs. 18 or more per dollar earned (compared with an official exchange rate of Rs. 4.75 per dollar), and foreign exchange saved through industrial import substitution may have nearly the same cost. These costs are in line with the value of foreign exchange in marginal uses, but they substantially exceed the resource cost of foreign exchange earned through increased agricultural production.

Seventh, any evaluation of import-export efficiency must take into account two major functions of trade controls—to mold the internal distribution of income, particularly property income; and to direct the economic structure into avenues supposedly favored by infant industry considerations. A trade system irrational from the static resource viewpoint may be justified by political or dynamic growth considerations. With this in mind, the major export distortions favoring industry and discriminating against agriculture might be justified by strong appeals to political "costs" and infant industry arguments. It seems equally probable, however, that Pakistan's policy makers have slid unaware into distortions of the present magnitude.

Effective Taxation of Exports

West Pakistan has what every developing country wants: fast-growing exports of industrial goods.[1] Between 1955 and 1967–68,[2] while raw cotton exports dipped substantially and then regained their 1955 level, and rice and miscellaneous primary exports showed modest growth, cotton textiles, leather goods, and other manufactured exports blossomed. (See Table 3.1. For convenience, all tables appear in Appendix A.) This chapter looks at the cost of West Pakistan's notable success with manufactured goods.

In common with many developing countries, West Pakistan has a highly protective industrial policy, and an internal revenue system largely dependent on indirect taxation of industrial goods and services.[3] Unless appropriately modified, the combination of these features can greatly retard manufactured exports. As counterweights, the Government of Pakistan operates one major export incentive scheme (the bonus voucher plan), four minor schemes, and six mini-programs.

1. This desire has accompanied the disenchantment with "excessive" import substitution. See United Nations, *Toward a New Trade Policy for Development,* Report by the Secretary-General of the United Nations Conference on Trade and Development (New York, 1964); D. M. Schydlowsky, "From Import Substitution to Export Promotion for Semi-Grown-Up Industries: A Policy Proposal," *Journal of Development Studies,* 3 (July 1967), 405–413; A. Urdinola and R. Mallon, *Policies to Promote Colombian Exports of Manufactures* (Report No. 75, Harvard Development Advisory Service, Cambridge, September 1967); A. O. Hirschman, "The Political Economy of Import-Substituting Industrialization in Latin America," *Quarterly Journal of Economics,* 82 (February 1968), 89–99. Also see the study by Jack Baranson, *Manufacturing Problems in India: The Cummins Diesel Experience* (Syracuse: Syracuse University Press, 1967), for a case analysis of the problems encountered by intensive import substitution in the subcontinent. The notion that fast-growing exports are connected with rapid overall economic growth finds support in the statistical work of R. F. Emery, "The Relation of Exports and Economic Growth," *Kyklos,* 20 (1967), 470–484. Using an orthogonal regression equation on international data, Emery found that a 1.0 percent increase in exports is associated with a 0.4 percent increase in GNP. Also see B. A. de Vries, *Export Experiences of Developing Countries,* IBRD Occasional Papers (Baltimore: Johns Hopkins University Press, 1967).

2. Since 1960, Pakistan trade statistics, together with other economic data, have been compiled on a fiscal year basis. Thus, 1967–68 refers to the period from July 1, 1967, through June 30, 1968.

3. In 1966–67, total central taxes collected in West Pakistan came to about Rs. 3,380 million, and total provincial taxes amounted to some Rs. 480 million. (Both figures exclude charges for services rendered, for example, post office receipts and irrigation revenues.) Of these sums, approximately Rs. 2,780 million and Rs. 210 million respectively were accounted for by customs duties, sales taxes, excise taxes, and miscellaneous taxes against industrial goods and services. Thus, about 77 percent of central and provincial tax receipts raised in West Pakistan were derived from indirect levies.

With so many policies, some framework is needed to assess their overall impact, both on total exports and on each export activity. The framework used here is based on the concept of "effective taxation" or "effective subsidization" (negative taxation) of exports. This concept relates the value of all disincentives and incentives affecting an export industry to the factor payments (value added) contributed by that industry. This "effective taxation" measure is similar to the domestic resource cost of foreign exchange. A little additional manipulation therefore yields an idea of the exchange rate paid for dollars earned by different export activities.

After estimating effective taxation and resource cost of foreign exchange, I ask: How rational is the structure of export incentives? The answer turns on the logic of discrimination between industry and agriculture.

The "Effective Taxation" Framework

"Effective taxation" of exports is the mirror image of "effective protection" against imports. The rate of "effective protection" or "effective tariff," a concept developed as an accurate measure of the shield against foreign competition,[4] differs from the ad valorem tariff rate in two principal ways. First, it expresses customs duties and duty-surrogates (quotas, licenses, etc.) as a percentage of value added rather than as a percentage of price. When land, labor, and capital contribute only 10 percent of the selling price, the industry enjoys more protection from a given ad valorem duty than when these basic factors contribute 50 percent of the selling price. Second, the effective tariff reflects protection on purchased inputs. This protection is a double-edged sword. An industry with 10 percent ad valorem protection which buys half its inputs

4. See H. G. Johnson, "Tariffs and Economic Development: Some Theoretical Issues," *Journal of Development Studies,* 1 (October 1964), 3–30; R. Soligo and J. J. Stern, "Tariff Protection, Import Substitution and Investment Efficiency," *Pakistan Development Review,* 5 (Summer 1965), 249–270; B. Balassa, "Tariff Protection in Industrial Countries: An Evaluation," *Journal of Political Economy,* 73 (December 1965), 573–594; G. Basevi, "The U.S. Tariff Structure: Estimates of Effective Rates of Protection of U.S. Industries and Industrial Labor," *Review of Economics and Statistics,* 48 (May 1966), 712–729; W. M. Corden, "The Structure of a Tariff System and the Effective Protective Rate," *Journal of Political Economy,* 74 (June 1966), 221–237; H. G. Grubel and H. G. Johnson, "Nominal Tariffs, Indirect Taxes and Effective Rates of Protection: The Common Market Countries 1959," *Economic Journal,* 77 (December 1967), 761–776; A. H. H. Tan, "Differential Protection, Economic Indices, and Optimal Trade Policies" (Ph.D. thesis, Stanford University, May 1968); S. Naya and J. Anderson, "Substitution and Two Concepts of Effective Rate of Protection," *American Economic Review,* 59 (September 1969), 607–612.

from suppliers who enjoy 20 percent protection is no better off than under a regime of free trade.

The effective protection concept has been further refined to express value added at world prices; to recognize the special position of non-traded inputs; to accommodate an overvalued exchange rate; and to reflect the possibility of input substitution rather than fixed coefficients.

Effective taxation, like effective protection, is related to value added. It takes account of tariffs, taxes, scarcity premiums, and subsidies which, by raising the cost of inputs or lowering the cost of export output, hinder or help overseas sales. (For reference, Appendix B presents analogous effective protection and effective taxation formulas, and their counterpart formulas for determining domestic resource plus political "cost" per marginal unit of foreign exchange saved or earned.)

A few simple examples will illustrate the calculation of effective protection and taxation rates. A more detailed example appears in Appendix B.

Suppose an industry with pre-tariff value added of 10 percent per unit of output receives ad valorem tariff protection of 20 percent, but simultaneously its inputs are protected by a 15 percent duty. The effective protection against imports enjoyed by this industry is:

Output price of one unit after tariff	Intermediate input cost for one unit after tariff	Output price before tariff	Input cost before tariff

$$\frac{[1(1 + 0.20) - 0.90(1 + 0.15)] - [1 - 0.90]}{[1 - 0.90]} = 65 \text{ percent.}$$

Value added before tariff

Alternatively, effective protection or taxation could be related to value added after the tariff (this alternative is used in the subsequent empirical exercises).

Suppose an export industry with pre-taxation value added of 30 percent per unit of output must pay 25 percent ad valorem duty on all its inputs. The effective taxation of this industry's exports is:

Export price of one unit before tariff	Intermediate input cost for one unit before tariff	Export price after tariff	Input cost after tariff

$$\frac{[1 - 0.70] - [1 - 0.70(1 + 0.25)]}{[1 - 0.70]} = 58 \text{ percent.}$$

Value added
before tariff

Finally, suppose that the same export industry now receives a subsidy of 40 percent on each unit exported. Then:

Export price of one unit before subsidy	Intermediate input cost for one unit before tariff	Export price after subsidy	Input cost after tariff

$$\frac{[1 - 0.70] - [1(1 + 0.40) - 0.70(1 + 0.25)]}{[1 - 0.70]}$$

Value added
before tariff

$= -75$ percent.

In other words, the industry enjoys an effective subsidy of 75 percent on exports (a subsidy is the same as a negative tax).

Fixed Input Coefficients

In both Appendix B and the empirical calculations, fixed input coefficients have been assumed. Naya and Anderson show, in a paper seen too late for reflection here, that estimates of effective protection made under a fixed coefficients assumption will overstate the true rate if input substitution exists.[5] By extension of the Naya-Anderson analysis: fixed coefficient estimates of effective subsidization of exports will overstate (and fixed coefficient estimates of effective taxation will understate) the true rates if substitution characterizes the production structure.

These last propositions may be readily illustrated. Let a_{ij} represent the value input coefficient, prior to the imposition of the tariff, of commodity j used in the production of one unit of good i; let a'_{ij} represent the input coefficient after the tariff; let t_j represent the ad valorem tariff on input j; and let ${}_xs_i$ represent the ad valorem export subsidy. Consider an export commodity, i, with two inputs, a_{im} on which a duty is levied, and a_{ix} with no tariff or subsidy. The effective subsidy formula, distinguishing between input coefficients before and after the subsidy, then becomes:

$$\frac{[1 - a_{im} - a_{ix}] - [1(1 + {}_xs_i) - a'_{im}(1 + t_m) - a'_{ix}]}{[1 - a_{im} - a_{ix}]}.$$

5. Naya and Anderson, "Substitution and Two Concepts of Effective Rate of Protection."

Letting:

$$da_{im} = a'_{im} - a_{im},$$

$$da_{ix} = a'_{ix} - a_{ix},$$

and consolidating terms, this expression becomes:

$$\frac{[da_{im} + da_{ix}] - {}_x s_i + a'_{im} t_m}{[1 - a_{im} - a_{ix}]}.$$

If any degree of substitution exists between inputs, then, because input m has become relatively more expensive:

$$da_{ix} > 0.$$

Furthermore, if da_{im} is negative and if the inputs are less than perfect substitutes for one another:

$$|da_{im}| < |da_{ix}|.$$

From these premises, it follows that the substitution term $[da_{im} + da_{ix}]$ is positive. A positive substitution term reduces the magnitude of an effective export subsidy (shown by a negative value for the whole expression) or enhances the magnitude of an effective tax (shown by a positive value) compared to those estimates obtained when $[da_{im} + da_{ix}]$ is ignored. Since the estimates in this chapter adhere to the fixed coefficients assumption, thereby neglecting the substitution term, they overstate subsidies and understate export taxes.

Relationship between Foreign and Domestic Prices

Fundamental to all the effective protection and taxation formulas is the effect of tariffs, indirect taxes, licensing premiums and export subsidies on the relationship between domestic and foreign prices. One way of determining this effect is by empirical observation, along the lines pioneered by Pal and Alamgir, and employed (in modified form) by Balassa in a study of effective tariff rates among industrial countries. Another way is to rely on a theoretical determination of the relationship between domestic and foreign prices, drawing on postulates from competitive market behavior. This method was used by Soligo and Stern to analyze industrial efficiency in Pakistan, by Basevi to study United States effective tariffs, and more recently by Johnson and Grubel to examine

European Common Market protection.[6] The empirical approach may give more reliable results since deviations from competitive market behavior are common, especially in developing countries. However, the theoretical method nicely illuminates the impact of policy measures. Because statistical information is lacking on price differentials between foreign and domestic markets (data which the statistical authorities should collect as a matter of routine), the theoretical method has been chosen here. (Since this chapter was written, two studies using the empirical approach have appeared. See footnote 58.)

For importable goods, the relationship between domestic and foreign price is assumed to be given by:

$$(1) \qquad {}_{m}P_{hi} = {}_{m}P_{fi}(1 + t_i)(1 + p_i).$$

(For convenience, all parameters and variables are defined in the glossary of Appendix B.) Equation (1) says that, for importable goods, the home price equals the foreign price at the official exchange rate marked up by customs charges, and marked up again by any scarcity premium arising from licensing restrictions. In this context, the scarcity premium includes the premium cost of bonus vouchers required for importation of the commodity. The left side of (1) represents the home price, and the right side represents landed cost plus scarcity premium on competitive imports.

For exportable goods, it is assumed that the relationship between domestic and foreign prices is given by:

$$(2) \qquad {}_{x}P_{hi}/(1 + {}_{h}e_i)(1 - {}_{h}s_i) = {}_{x}P_{fi}(1 - {}_{x}e_i)(1 + {}_{x}s_i).$$

Equation (2) says that, for exportable commodities, the home price, discounted by home indirect taxes and increased by home subsidies, equals the foreign price decreased by indirect taxes levied on foreign sales and increased by the export subsidy. This formulation implies that producers are content to obtain the same *net* receipts per unit of output on both domestic and overseas sales, regardless of the level of tariff protection or the stringency of licensing. The left side of (2) represents

6. M. L. Pal, "The Determinants of Domestic Prices of Imports," *Pakistan Development Review,* 4 (Winter 1964), 597–622, and "Domestic Prices of Imports in Pakistan: Extension of Empirical Findings," *Pakistan Development Review,* 5 (Winter 1965), 547–585; M. Alamgir, "The Domestic Prices of Imported Commodities in Pakistan: A Further Study," *Pakistan Development Review,* 8 (Spring 1968), 35–73; Soligo and Stern, "Tariff Protection"; Basevi, "The U.S. Tariff Structure"; Grubel and Johnson, "Nominal Tariffs." B. Balassa, "Tariff Protection," essentially used Benelux input-output coefficients to represent free market conditions for the industrial countries in his study, on the ground that Benelux prices are close to world prices.

the producer's net receipts from home sales, and the right side the producer's net receipts from export sales ("net" means exclusive of indirect taxes and inclusive of subsidies). Competitive behavior is presumed.

Despite the widespread belief that monopolies rule Pakistan's industrial structure, competitive behavior offers a reasonable model for cotton textiles, leather goods, and simple metal products—West Pakistan's principal export industries. The section on Impact of Promotional Policies examines in a general way the consequences if export price formation is not governed by the rules of competitive behavior.

One obvious constraint controls the values of t, p, e, and s. If $(1 - {}_xe_i)(1 + {}_xs_i)(1 + {}_he_i)(1 - {}_hs_i)$ exceeds $(1 + t_i)(1 + p_i)$ for any commodity by more than international transport charges, then the country will find itself importing goods for re-export, losing foreign exchange on every transaction. To avoid this outcome, the values of t, p, e, and s must be governed by Condition (3):

$$(3) \qquad (1 - {}_xe_i)(1 + {}_xs_i)(1 + {}_he_i)(1 - {}_hs_i) \leq (1 + c_i)(1 + t_i)(1 + p_i)$$

In the analysis of effective taxation in Pakistan, I assume that Condition (3) always applies, though it may be enforced through potential exchange control measures rather than through actual tariffs or scarcity premiums.

The empirical work here is based on the 1962–63 Rahman Khan-MacEwan (RKM) input-output table.[7] The sectoral classification in the RKM table is sufficiently broad that imports and exports appear in most sectors. This poses a problem: Should the sectors be catalogued as "importables," with price relations determined by Equation (1), or as "exportables," with price relations determined by (2)? A compromise was adopted.

Home prices for rice (sector 1), cotton (4), miscellaneous agriculture, forestry, and fishery (sector 6), cotton textiles (11), and leather goods (15) are assumed to be governed by the exportable relationship. In other words, home prices of inputs from these five sectors presumably equal world prices plus any export subsidies and any indirect taxes selectively levied on home output. The five exportable sectors sell substantial quantities abroad, and have moderately homogeneous products. Export conditions therefore, probably determine their domestic prices.

Prices for all other goods (designated importable sectors) are assumed to be determined in two ways. Exports are governed by the exportable relationship. But inputs to other sectors are regulated by the importable

7. A. Rahman Khan and A. MacEwan, *Regional Current Input Output Tables for the East and West Pakistan Economies 1962/63* (Research Report No. 63, Pakistan Institute of Development Economics, December 1967).

relationship. These importable sectors manufacture mostly nonhomogeneous goods. Exports comprise only a small portion of output, and that portion is generally distinct from both imports and production for the home market. Import conditions, therefore, probably determine prices charged to other domestic sectors.

These assumptions mean that home-foreign price relationships of rice, cotton, miscellaneous primary goods, cotton textiles, and leather goods may be derived by appropriate application of Equation (2). Export prices of other goods will also be given by (2), but domestic prices of inputs from the importable sectors are determined by Equation (1). This dual treatment of importable sectors seems the least damaging compromise.

Potential Effective Export Taxation

Now that these observations on price formation have been made, the potential effective taxation of West Pakistan exports, which would exist in the absence of any export promotion measures, may be analyzed using Equation (4). The same equation, with appropriate redefinition of the underlying variables, can be used to analyze the actual effective taxation or subsidization when some or all the export incentive measures are taken into consideration. The equation is:

(4) $$T_i = \frac{{}_xW_i - {}_xV_i}{{}_hV_i}.$$

Equation (4) says that effective taxation is the difference between value added if the product were sold on world markets free of domestic taxation and all traded inputs were bought at world prices, and value added gained from export sales under actual conditions with respect to taxation and input purchases, this difference being expressed as a percentage of value added received on home sales. Given the assumptions of Equation (2), value added on foreign sales is the same as value added on home sales. The underlying definitions of value added, based on price relationships (1) and (2), are set forth in Appendix B.

A major defect of the effective taxation-protection approach is the assumption that relationships between the factor prices for land, labor, and capital are unaffected by tariffs, subsidies, and other market imperfections. This assumption may be plausible when the distortions are marginal in character, but when the distortions approach the massive nature of those in Pakistan, the assumption becomes highly suspect.[8]

8. This point was made by Emile Despres at the 1968 Sorrento Conference of the Harvard Development Advisory Service.

Table 3.2, Appendix A, ignoring these conceptual difficulties and making use of Equation (4) and selective data on the West Pakistan economy, illustrates the potential effective taxation in the absence of all export incentive schemes. Appendix B gives a sample calculation of effective tax rates.

Table 3.2 is suggestive rather than definitive. The sectoral classification and technical coefficients are those of the 1962–63 RKM input-output table. The customs charges, indirect taxes, and export subsidies appearing in Table 3.2 are rough guesses. Tax and tariff parameters are based on 1965–67 collections; export subsidy values are based on rough presumptions about the operation of the incentive system under the 1968 structure of rates and rules. Most importantly, the calculations embody a number of assumptions which, if altered, could materially change the estimated rates.

Despite the approximate nature of the underlying parameters, Table 3.2 shows that in the absence of export incentives, the Pakistan system of protection and taxation would heavily penalize industrial exports. The effective tax rates often exceed 100 percent, mainly because of the heavy system of indirect taxation on industrial production.

Pakistan has implemented five important policies to reverse this potential bias against industrial exports. For rough comparison Table 3.3 records the approximate value of each policy measure, based on the 1966–67 pattern of exports. The total value of these measures came to about Rs. 677 million in 1966/67, or almost 80 percent of FOB export receipts from the sales of manufactured goods.

In addition to these five policies and the usual "jawbone" campaign, the government has implemented numerous mini-schemes: it guarantees export credits (since May 1962); it exempts export profits from corporation tax (since July 1963); it grants tax holidays running from two to six years, depending upon location, to every industry with "an appreciable export potential" (since June 1964); it discounts export bills at a rate 1 percent beneath the ordinary discount rate (since 1967); it allows concessional railway freight rates on some 50 export commodities (since 1960); and it permits the import of textile looms from the Soviet Union and Eastern Europe without surrender of bonus vouchers.[9] The quantitative magnitude of these mini-schemes is unknown.

9. The major, minor, and mini-policies are all briefly described by M. R. Khan, Officiating Secretary, Chamber of Commerce and Industry, "Export Incentives," *Trade Journal* (May-June 1968). (*Trade Journal* is the organ of the Pakistan Chamber of Commerce and Industry.)

Export Promotion Policies

Tax Exemption

The most obvious incentive measure is to exempt exports from sales and excise taxes. In the context of Equation (2), tax exemption means that the foreign price of exports differs from the domestic price by the extent of indirect taxes; previously both prices were equal. The change serves to reduce effective taxation by diminishing the difference between ${}_xW_i$ and ${}_xV_i$. Table 3.3 indicates that the present system of exemptions saved exporters some Rs. 62 million during 1966–67.

The central government has recently shifted the excise tax obligation of several industries from a production basis to a capacity basis.[10] Cement, sugar, vegetable oil, and cotton textiles have so far been affected by the change. Under the new system, tax exemption depends on the ratio of exports to assessed capacity. Since actual capacity ordinarily exceeds assessed capacity, this provision should prove at least as favorable as the present system of exemptions.

The exemption system covers central indirect taxes, but provides no relief from provincial and local levies. Among these the most serious is the octroi tax on goods moved by truck. Such taxes are ignored in the calculations of Table 3.2, which therefore understate in a minor way the effective taxation and overstate the effective subsidization of exports.

Tax Rebates

A second incentive measure, closely related to tax exemption, is the rebate of central sales taxes, excise taxes, and customs duties, on inputs used directly in the manufacture of exports. The rebate practice, approved by GATT, enjoys a widespread following among industrial countries. Tariffs and indirect taxes *paid by the enterprise* are, however, only partly responsible for the bias against industrial exports.

The rebate of tariffs tends to bring the cost of "importable" inputs actually purchased from abroad into line with world prices. The rebate of indirect taxes on domestic output tends to bring the cost of "exportable" inputs into line with world prices. But the rebate system offers only partial relief from the higher price of importable inputs *actually purchased from*

10. Under the capacity taxation system, excise levies depend not on actual production but rather on assessed capacity. Capacity assessments are made by a high-level team visiting each factory; presumably, these assessments will remain fixed for some period of time unless capacity is increased by new units or major expansions. Capacity taxation was introduced to combat irregularity in the excise and sales tax administration, but it should also stimulate production.

domestic sources. The extent of relief is limited by the indirect taxes paid on the competitive domestic product. If domestic taxation is low compared to the tariff rate, either the relief will be inadequate or the exporter will choose to use imported inputs rather than domestic supplies. The latter solution, of course, defeats the intent of a protective system.

In estimating the relief afforded by the Pakistan rebate system, I assumed that rebates are paid on inputs from sectors 7 through 29; that 60 percent of inputs from these sectors are indigenous and 40 percent foreign; and that the respective average rates of indirect taxation are 5 percent and 30 percent. Hence, the assumed rebate rate per unit of output valued at domestic prices equals 15 percent of inputs from sectors 7 through 29.

The rates were converted to a foreign valuation basis through application of Equation (2). For this calculation, ${}_{x}s_{i}$ was defined to include export performance licenses and bonus vouchers, but not rebates themselves. As Table 3.2 shows, the estimated rebates sometimes exceed 15 percent of the FOB export price. The 1966–67 value of rebates as theoretically calculated would amount to about Rs. 67 million. The Central Board of Revenue estimates that actual rebates were roughly Rs. 64 million during that year, of which Rs. 43 million were customs charges (see Table 3.3, Appendix A). In 1967–68 total rebates reached Rs. 93 million, largely because of a jump in customs refunds. Perhaps exporters are turning more to imported inputs in order to gain full advantage from the present rebate system.

Export Performance Licensing

The third export incentive measure, and at one time the most important, is export performance licensing (EPL). Export performance licenses are intended to insure that exporters receive an "adequate" supply of imported raw materials. In the context of Equation (4), this means eliminating the scarcity premium on importable inputs, a premium which otherwise would cause value added at world prices to exceed value added received on export sales.

The recommendation that exporters receive preferential treatment in the award of import licenses originated from the 1952 Pakistan Export Promotion Committee.[11] The recommendation was implemented two

11. The institutional description here comes from W. E. Hecox, *The Use of Import Privileges as Incentive to Exporters in Pakistan* (Research Report No. 30, Pakistan Institute of Development Economics, 1965). Also compare two papers by the same author, prepared under the auspices of the U.S. Agency for International Development, Pakistan:

years later when the collapse of the Korean export boom and the resulting import squeeze made import licenses extremely valuable. In 1954, import licenses equal to 30 percent of FOB exports, unrestricted as to use, were awarded for overseas sales of selected primary and manufactured commodities.

Since June 1954, the scheme has been variously amplified, contracted, and modified with each six-month "shipping period."[12] The scope of EPL has been changed by altering the list of eligible exports, by offering different licensing privileges for different exports, by restricting licenses to imports actually used in the production of exports, and by raising and lowering the rate of import entitlements per unit of FOB exports. At times, explicit schedules relating FOB exports to import license entitlements have been announced; at other times, the licensing authorities have been admonished to give exporters special treatment and to penalize firms not meeting their export potential. Formerly, EPL awards were very liberal. From 1962 to 1964 some goods were allowed licenses equal to 100 percent of FOB exports; as late as 1966, many manufactured goods were receiving licenses at a 50 percent rate. Recently, the scheme has been construed less liberally. In 1968, a top rate of 30 percent was set on EPL. (Meanwhile, the irrelevant debate continues as to whether, because of the overlap between regular licensing and EPL, exporters receive imports twice for the same volume of production.)[13]

The EPL system has always had critics. Frank Child maintains that "export performance licensing is an administrative nightmare of such horrendous complexity as to break the spirit of the ablest bureaucrat. . . . It should be abandoned forthwith."[14] (Despite such complaints, other

"A Note on Export Performance Licensing Scheme, FOB Export Rates and their Determination" (mimeo, June 1968), and "A Note on Incentives and Implicit Exchange Rates for Selected Industries under the Export Bonus Scheme and Export Performance Licensing" (mimeo, June 1968).

12. The two "shipping periods" are January-June and July-December. The shipping periods correspond not to any natural phenomena, but rather to the distressing frequency of alterations in government import and export policy.

13. This debate misses the point. The regular licensing system is simply a vehicle for arbitrary distribution of windfall profits. The EPL system, on the other hand, links the distribution of windfall profits to export performance, thereby bringing the exporters' costs in line with world prices. Whether a producer is licensed once, twice, or three times for a given volume of production, the only license that counts for export *incentive* purposes is the license linked to export performance. The others simply represent gratuitous assignment of rent.

14. Frank Child, "Impact of the Trade and Payments Control System on Economic Development in Pakistan" (mimeo, Third Economic Development Seminar, sponsored by West Pakistan Industrial Development Corporation, Karachi, March 1968), p. 11.

countries have embarked on similar schemes. In 1961, for example, Colombia activated the Plan Vallejo.[15] This plan permits exporters to obtain imported raw materials, even prohibited commodities, by a scheme similar to EPL, with exemption from import duties and prior import deposits. Like the equivalent Pakistani schemes, however, the Plan Vallejo is administered on an ad hoc basis, apparently without systematic ground rules.)

Much administrative complexity and many needless changes in Pakistan export performance licensing have resulted from a failure to appreciate the scheme's proper role, which is either to exempt exporters from the payment of scarcity premiums on importable inputs or to compensate them for such payment.

It is immaterial whether these scarcity premiums accrue to license holders or are absorbed in a bonus voucher or auction system; nor does it matter whether the EPL scheme provides imports for the direct use of exporters, or merely provides compensation, via resale of licenses, for the use of high-priced indigenous inputs. In calculating EPL rates, therefore, it should make no difference whether the importable inputs are purchased from abroad or are obtained locally.[16] The exporter may purchase his inputs locally, but these inputs will reflect any scarcity premiums on competitive imports. The problem is completely analogous to the rebate of indirect taxes.

To determine licensing percentages—again on the proviso that the EPL scheme must operate within the licensing framework—it would suffice to have a recent input-output table and an up-to-date comparison of international and domestic prices. The input-output table would give importable inputs per unit of domestic sales. The price comparison list would identify importable inputs carrying scarcity premiums, and it would indicate the value of FOB exports per unit of domestic sales. This latter ratio is needed, in conjunction with the input-output table, to translate importable inputs per unit of domestic sales into importable

15. See the description in A. Urdinola and R. Mallon, *Policies to Promote Colombian Exports of Manufactures*.

16. Thus an EPL-type scheme should grant licenses in an amount approximately equal to the amount of importable inputs carrying scarcity premiums per unit of FOB exports. The direct use or sale of the licenses would roughly compensate for inflated industrial costs. The compensation would not be exact, since scarcity premiums vary from commodity to commodity. The premiums on the exporter's inputs might be low, but he might use the licenses to import, and resell, goods with high premiums. EPL rates would need to differ among commodities in order not to penalize "processed" exports, such as synthetic textiles, metal goods, and miscellaneous manufactures, which combine domestic labor with a high content of importable inputs.

inputs per unit of export sales, and thus to determine appropriate EPL rates.

The contribution of the EPL scheme toward reduced taxation of exports is equal to the EPL rate times the average scarcity premium times the average landed cost of importable inputs. For the calculations here, the average tariff is taken to be 30 percent and the average scarcity premium or markup on landed cost is set at 35 percent for all industries. Under these assumptions, the value of EPL ranges up to 13 percent of FOB export receipts. A scarcity premium of 35 percent may be too conservative, but since effective taxation rates in Table 3.2 were also calculated with conservative premiums, the "tax" and the "relief" are on much the same footing.

Table 3.3 indicates that the 1966/67 value of the scheme, assuming a 50 percent rather than a 35 percent premium, reached approximately Rs. 59 million. This was less than the value of tax rebates. The relative importance of EPL has gradually diminished during recent years, because of the reduction of rates, the imposition of higher tariffs, and, most importantly, the advent of the bonus voucher system. (In January 1970, the EPL system was abolished.)

Pay-As-You-Earn

The fourth policy designed to ameliorate export taxation is the "pay-as-you-earn" scheme (PAYE). This scheme and related programs attempt to play the same role for capital goods as EPL did for industrial raw materials; unfortunately, they are experiencing virtually the same cycle of expansion, contraction, and modification that has marked the EPL scheme.

In Pakistan, the Comprehensive Industrial Investment Schedule, drawn up at the beginning of the Five Year Plan and revised annually, nominally controls the composition, location and volume of private investment.[17] The schedule is enforced by the government investment banks which allocate the bulk of foreign exchange loans for imported capital equipment.

Invariably, there are more applicants than investment funds, because of an unrealistic official exchange rate, low interest rates, and modest

17. The word "nominally" is well chosen. The annual changes in the schedule seem generally to meet the demands of private investors for increased sanctions in the high-yielding industries and locations, rather than to force investment into low-yielding industries or backward areas. This responsiveness to market forces (albeit slowed by some bureaucratic friction) should be regarded as a virtue, not a vice.

customs charges on imported capital equipment.[18] To alleviate the shortage of investment funds, the PAYE scheme was adopted in 1963.[19] It permits the exporter to negotiate a foreign supplier's credit for purchase of capital equipment. Applicants for the PAYE scheme are screened by two government agencies. The terms of repayment are then subject to approval from the State Bank of Pakistan, which generally insists on a repayment period of at least eight years with interest no higher than 8 percent.

Until 1967, the exporter's entire foreign exchange earnings were available for repayment of PAYE credits, within the terms approved by the State Bank. Since the exporter was benefiting simultaneously from the performance license and bonus voucher schemes, his direct use of foreign exchange might well exceed his earnings. In 1967 the amount of foreign exchange available for repayment was limited to 10 percent of annual foreign exchange earnings. If, with this limitation, the exporter's foreign exchange earnings are insufficient to meet the repayment schedule, he supposedly must cover the deficit by surrender of bonus vouchers.

The impact of PAYE is much bigger on paper than in reality. The PAYE applications sanctioned by government agencies since 1963 are tallied in Table 3.4. Of the 115 authorized applications, less than 20 show any signs of implementation. The main difficulty is the State Bank's insistence on comparatively long repayment periods and modest interest rates, given the absence of any repayment guarantees.

Owing to the shortcomings of the PAYE scheme, the 1968 Comprehensive Industrial Investment Schedule was drawn up with liberal provision for so-called export-oriented industries. Unfortunately, a label does not guarantee exports. This twist echoes the earlier attempts to accommodate exporters' raw material needs by combining exhortation with regular import licensing. A more promising policy initiative was the 1968 stipulation that down payment on government investment bank loans be made in bonus vouchers. This step toward market allocation of capital should afford an edge to the export industries.

In evaluating the effective taxation of exports, I ignored tariffs and scarcity premiums on imported capital equipment. This source of taxa-

18. In January 1968 the government took two important steps toward use of the market mechanism to ration foreign exchange for investment purposes. The first was a 10 percent surcharge on imported capital equipment. The second was a requirement that applicants for government investment bank loans of foreign exchange make the down payment in the form of bonus vouchers.

19. The description of PAYE is based on information supplied by Mr. R. A. Zuberi, economist at the Investment Promotion and Supplies Department.

tion could be incorporated by treating the annual depreciation of capital equipment like any other current input (Appendix B). Since the analysis in Table 3.2 of effective taxation says nothing about capital equipment, and since PAYE has had a very limited impact, no attempt is made to quantify the value of this scheme on a commodity basis. On a generous estimate of implementation, the benefits of PAYE could not have exceeded Rs. 5 million in any recent year (Table 3.3).

Export Bonus Vouchers

The well-known bonus voucher system provides a flexible exchange rate for sales of industrial exports and purchases of selected imports, thereby transferring to exporters the licensing profits otherwise created by an overvalued exchange rate. The system has been amply described elsewhere.[20]

The January 1968 trade policy set three rates. Exporters of raw wool and jute manufacturers, exporters of semiprocessed goods, and exporters of finished manufactures could collect vouchers equal to 20, 30, and 40 percent of FOB sales respectively. (These percentages were raised in 1970, and, in addition, raw jute and cotton were given a 10 percent rate.) The worth of bonus vouchers per unit of FOB exports is derived by multiplying the bonus rate by the bonus market premium.

The yield from bonus vouchers is tabulated in Table 3.2. The figures demonstrate that the voucher system provides substantial incentive for industrial exports. The subsidy rates on FOB exports reach 64 percent, given a bonus voucher issue rate of 40 percent and a premium of 160 percent. As Table 3.3 shows, the premium value of bonus vouchers, at 1968 rates on 1966–67 exports, comes to about Rs. 488 million, a much greater sum than the combined value of the minor schemes.

To a limited extent, however, the bonus voucher system, like any export incentive measure, also has a negative effect on industrial exports. When an export is subsidized, its home price is driven up, thereby adversely affecting those exports which employ it as an input. Gross export gains among newly favored commodities are partly offset by losses among existing exports. The West Pakistan cotton handloom industry, for ex-

20. H. J. Bruton and S. R. Bose, "The Export Bonus Scheme: A Preliminary Report," *Pakistan Development Review*, 2 (Summer 1962), 229–268; H. J. Bruton and S. R. Bose, *The Pakistan Export Bonus Scheme* (Research Report No. 11, Pakistan Institute of Development Economics, 1963). Q. K. Ahmad, "The Operation of the Export Bonus Scheme in Pakistan's Jute and Cotton Industries"; R. Soligo and J. J. Stern, "Some Comments on the Export Bonus, Export Promotion, and Investment Criteria"; R. F. Mallon, "Export Policy in Pakistan"; all in *Pakistan Development Review*, 6 (Spring 1966), 1–79.

ample, has complained that the high price of cotton yarn—a result of the bonus voucher system—retards handloom exports.[21]

Impact of the Promotion Policies

What effect do the five promotion policies have on the subsidization of industrial exports? What connection is there between incentives and export growth? Most importantly, are the incentives too generous or not generous enough?

The effective taxation or subsidization of exports is found by applying Equation (4), when ${}_xW_i$ and ${}_xV_i$ are defined to encompass tax exemption of exports and export subsidies. In the short run, taxes and subsidies are presumably shifted forward to the exporting industry, which faces a temporarily fixed foreign price. In the long run, however, export sales should expand or contract, causing a forward adjustment in FOB prices and a backward adjustment in domestic costs, until export profits approach the returns obtainable elsewhere. Thus, the effective taxation and subsidization estimates derived from Equation (4) indicate the short term effect of the fiscal system on export profits, and the long term incentive given the export industries to expand or contract.

For illustrative purposes, effective tax and subsidy rates are calculated in two steps. In the first calculation, only tax exemption and minor incentives are considered. As column 10 of Table 3.2 shows, these features convert the high taxes on industrial exports into modest subsidies.

In the second calculation, all incentive measures are considered; in other words, bonus vouchers are added to the minor incentives. Bonus vouchers substantially increase the subsidies on industrial exports. This is shown by column 13 of Table 3.2. Total subsidy rates often exceed 100 percent of home value added. Such results may be exaggerated and inaccurate, owing to the overstatement of benefits, the theoretical approach to price formation, and the use of outdated and imperfect data, particularly an input-output table for a period (1962–63) different from that for which export benefits are measured (1966–1968).[22] Nevertheless, export subsidies on some manufactures, including cotton textiles, are so high that—under equilibrium price conditions—value added at world prices would be very small or negative.

21. This issue was raised in the West Pakistan Provincial Assembly, May 13–18, 1968. See the *Pakistan Times* for that period.

22. On the theoretical possibility of rates exceeding 100 percent, see S. E. Guisinger, *Negative Value Added and the Theory of Effective Protection* (Report No. 95, Harvard Development Advisory Service, Cambridge, April 1968).

Effect of Subsidies on Exports

Has the wide disparity of export incentives, especially between agricultural and industrial goods, exerted any differential impact on the growth of various West Pakistan exports? A lag usually occurs between changes in effective tax or subsidy rates and export growth. Even this lag would be obscured by the effects of technology, foreign demand, and other influences. Nevertheless, a comparison between the broad sweep of export growth since 1955 and absolute levels of effective taxation circa 1966–1968 is legitimate. Prior to 1955, little of the present tax and subsidy apparatus existed. Hence, the absolute 1966–1968 effective tax and subsidy rates crudely represent the changes in rates, from approximately zero levels, during the years since 1955.

Figure 3.1, based on the data in Table 3.1, draws the comparison. Compound rates of export growth since 1955 are contrasted with effective export subsidies (taxes are indicated as negative subsidies) circa 1966–1968. The tax and subsidy rates are usually averages based on the findings of Table 3.2. However, when the 1967–68 export policy involved a radical departure from prior practice—for example, the award of bonus vouchers for wool exports—an appropriate ad hoc adjustment was made.

Figure 3.1 shows that subsidy rates are related to export growth. The relationship is not precise; over shorter periods than twelve years, a very haphazard connection would probably emerge. The relationship in Figure 3.1 consists largely of a band between three clusters of observations: agricultural commodities at one extreme, textiles at the other extreme, and everything else in between. This relationship indicates that the incentive system devised in the late 1950's and expanded in the 1960's has molded export growth in the direction of manufactures, particularly textile goods.

Despite the substantial incentives and their stimulation of manufactured exports, excess capacity characterizes most branches of West Pakistan industry.[23] The export promotion program has not entirely succeeded in joining idle hands and idle machines at the task of making goods for foreign markets. Establishments in the metal industries typically operate fewer than 200 shifts per year; producers of leather goods usually work about 300 shifts; only in textiles and cement are production rates of 900 shifts (continuous operation) attained with reasonable frequency.[24] A policy of reducing excess capacity by expanding export sales

23. W. P. Hogan, *Capacity Utilization in Pakistan Manufacturing Industry* (Report No. 84, Harvard Development Advisory Service, Cambridge, September 1967).

24. G. C. Hufbauer, "Exports, Establishment Size, and Shifts Worked" (mimeo, Harvard Development Advisory Service, Lahore, May 1968).

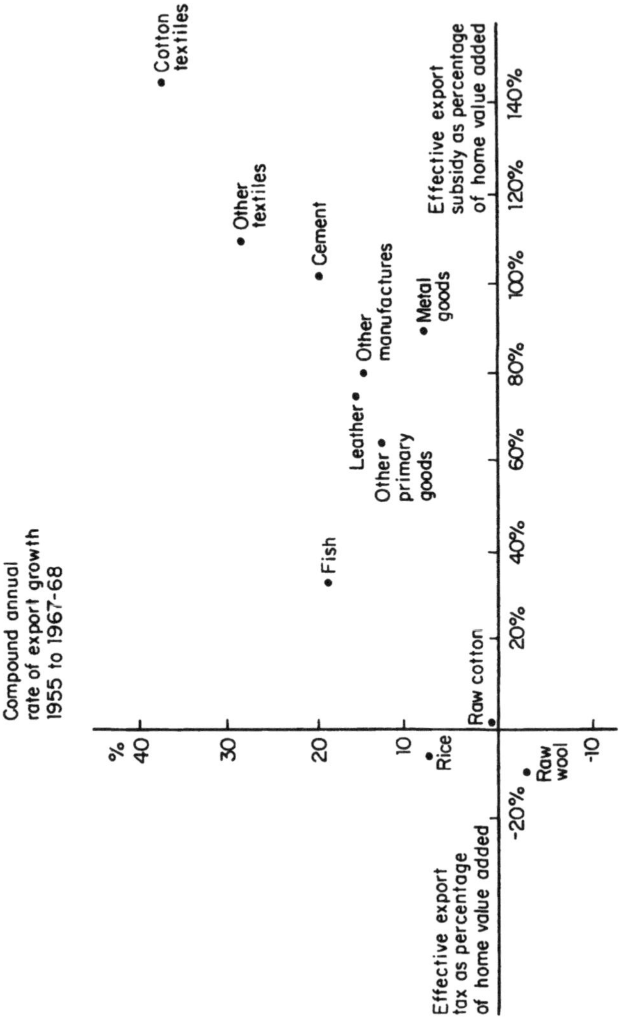

Figure 3.1. Relation between export growth and effective subsidies

is appealing. To implement the policy, it may require export incentives even more generous than those presently awarded.

Level of Export Subsidies

Are subsidies too generous or not generous enough? The question has at least three dimensions. First, considerations of cost: Is the marginal cost of foreign exchange earned through export production excessive by contrast with the cost of import substitution or the value of foreign exchange to the economy? Second, the issue of differentials: Could foreign exchange be earned more efficiently by shifting resources to agricultural production? Third, subsidy rates approaching 100 percent of home value added: Are these aberrations of data or are they genuine cases of uneconomic export production? In subsequent sections, I examine the first two dimensions. Here I discuss subsidy rates in the neighborhood of 100 percent.

Earlier it was pointed out that the export price equation presumes competitive behavior. Net receipts, from homes sales, however, may be substantially higher than net receipts from foreign sales. As one observer notes: "The Export Promotion Bureau used to have so-called pledging sessions at which each industry, through its representatives, would stand up and publicly declare its exports for the next fiscal year."[25] Faced with these pressures, the larger firms might accept lower profits on export sales in order not to jeopardize their standing. Likewise, the mini-schemes involving profits tax exemption, complete tax holidays, and special export credits—all of which were ignored in the foregoing analysis—could lead to smaller *gross* profit margins on export sales than on home sales, consistent with the same *net* profit in both markets. In both cases, value added on exports would be less than value added on home sales, contrary to the assumptions made previously and in Appendix B. FOB export prices would be lower, vis-à-vis home prices, than the relationship stipulated by Equation (2). Hence, value added at world prices, the first term in the numerator of (4), would be less than the calculations allow. Subsidy rates might be correspondingly larger than those given in Table 3.2.

The converse possibility should be considered. Firms which are seriously involved in the export business might earn bigger profits abroad than at home. Manufactured exports grew 20 percent per year between 1964–65 and 1967–68, a pace which is hard to explain entirely by the administrative stick. Furthermore, a substantial proportion of cotton textile exports go to Western European and North American markets

25. Marvin Rozen, Pakistan Institute of Development Economics, private correspondence.

which are limited by quota restrictions. Pakistan's quota is divided among the big textile firms in cartel fashion rather than auctioned to the highest bidder. If, for these and other reasons, foreign sales earn especially high profits, then the effective subsidy rates of Table 3.2 would be exaggerated.

The same relation between home and export profits need not characterize all industries. Some, like cotton textiles, with a standardized product and quota markets abroad, may enjoy especially high profits on foreign sales. Others, like simple machinery, with acute marketing, feedback, and quality problems, may accept very low profits while penetrating foreign markets. A close look at selected exporting firms is needed not only to sort out this particular issue but also to refine other elements in the effective subsidy calculation.

Several other complications must be mentioned, especially because they uniformly indicate lower subsidies than the rates calculated in Table 3.2.

1. In the 1962–63 input-output table employed in the computation of 1967–68 subsidy rates, the ratio of gross value added to manufacturing sales (both large- and small-scale firms) was 27 percent. By 1965–66, when prices had risen 5 percent, the ratio for large-scale firms was 32 percent. Prices rose another 10 percent between 1965–66 and 1967–68.[26] If the higher price levels since 1962–63 have resulted in substantially greater value added per unit of sales, then effective subsidy rates would be lower than those calculated.

2. In the same vein, Stern suggests that industrial inputs as a share of total output have probably been exaggerated in the vintage 1962–1964 input-output tables because of the estimation of consumption as a residual.[27] Papanek further suggests that industrial profits may be consistently understated in the statistical reports, especially for highly profitable industries like cotton textiles.[28] Again, an appropriate correction would reduce the subsidy rates of Table 3.2.

3. In West Pakistan, as in most countries, the large, highly profitable firms contribute a disproportionate share of industrial exports. *Average* input-output coefficients understate the value added proportion for these firms. As before, an understated value added leads to an overstated subsidy estimate.

26. Government of Pakistan, Central Statistical Office, *Monthly Statistical Bulletin* (July 1968). Government of Pakistan, Bureau of Statistics, *Census of Manufacturing Industries: 1965–66* (preliminary release, February 1968).

27. J. J. Stern, *An Evaluation of Inter-Industry Research in Pakistan* (mimeo, Harvard Development Advisory Service Conference, Sorrento, Italy, September 1968).

28. G. F. Papanek, private correspondence.

4. The theoretical calculations in Table 3.2 could exaggerate the minor incentive schemes since, as Papanek points out, these are administered with considerable delay and occasional irregularity.[29] For example, the exporter collects the tariff rebate on incorporated foreign materials only upon shipment of his goods to an overseas port. This may be six months after the duty was paid; even then the rebate may be subject to ad hoc negotiation.

5. If extensive substitution, rather than fixed coefficients, characterizes the production structure, then, as the Naya-Anderson analysis shows, the fixed coefficient estimates overstate the true subsidy levels.

Many of these complications relate to the value added proportion of output. Table 3.5 therefore crudely analyzes the possible impact of profit rate differentials and value added errors on the effective subsidy rates given in Table 3.2, and gives a weighted average subsidy rate for the major manufactured exports specified in Table 3.1. The absolute subsidies are expressed both as a percentage of export value added (the base for the calculations in Table 3.2, under the assumption that export and home value added are the same) and as a percentage of export value added plus the cost of nontraded inputs.[30] Details of the sensitivity analysis are given in the notes to Table 3.5.

The findings of Table 3.2, labeled "original results" in Table 3.5, indicate an average effective subsidy of 95 percent on export value added. The figure rises to 122 percent or drops to 82 percent, depending on the profit relationship between home and foreign sales.

However, if price increases since 1962–63 have greatly expanded the wage and profit portion of output, or if for some other reason profits are higher and interindustry deliveries are smaller than reflected in the input-output data, then effective subsidies fall in the lower range of 69 percent to 86 percent of export value added. If absolute subsidies are related to value added *plus* the cost of nontraded inputs, (Base 2), the rates decline to about 60 percent.

These exercises and the related qualifications suggest certain tentative conclusions. First, Pakistan's export policies seem to avoid the gross error of providing such generous subsidies that manufactured goods are sold abroad at prices insufficient to recover the world market cost of traded inputs. This may happen occasionally, but the phenomenon is probably not widespread, especially given a reasonable allowance for

29. G. F. Papanek, private correspondence.

30. Export value added is the same as home value added when profit rates on foreign and domestic sales are the same. When profit rates differ, export value added is the more meaningful base for expressing subsidy rates.

conceptual difficulties in the price equations and deficiencies in the input-output data. Indeed, on the assumption that the use of nontraded inputs imposes no direct or indirect pressure on the balance of payments (only an approximate assumption for transport, electricity, and gas services), a reasonable margin may exist between the average foreign exchange cost and earnings of manufactured exports.

Second, the findings recommend a closer look at the meaning of fast export growth rates. The rate of export expansion plays a key role in any assessment of overall economic progress, prospective independence from foreign assistance, and future capacity to service international loans. The fast growth of manufactured exports (e.g., cotton textiles), however, may take place at the expense of export growth in commodities used as inputs (e.g., raw cotton). Furthermore, a difference may exist between the growth of *gross* export earnings and the growth of *net* export earnings after deducting the cost of imports directly and indirectly required to produce the exports. If the composition of exports shifts toward low value added items, toward items with fewer nontraded inputs, or toward items on which high subsidies are given, then net earnings may grow more slowly than gross earnings. It would be interesting to contrast the two rates, both for Pakistan and for other developing countries.[31]

Third, no important conclusions should be drawn from the apparent intra-industry structure of effective subsidies. According to the estimates, cotton and other textiles are subsidized at the highest rates, while metal goods, cement, and other manufactures receive lower incentives. This comparison might lead to the erroneous conclusion that West Pakistan's comparative advantage rests with heavy industry and brand-name consumer goods rather than textiles. Possibly, however, textile subsidy rates have been overstated because of relatively high export profits, and subsidy rates on other goods have been understated because of relatively low export profits. Furthermore, exports of heavy industrial goods are presently small and exports of branded consumer goods are nil. Much larger subsidies than are presently enjoyed by the textile sector might be required to move these goods abroad in any volume. Apart from production cost considerations, the marketing of such goods demands a large and risky outlay to cultivate foreign buyers, enlarge the staff, and modify the production specifications. Unless short-run profits are generous or long-run assurances of continuing incentives exist, firms will resist the necessary expenditure to develop foreign sales.[32]

31. See N. Islam, "Commodity Exports, Net Exchange Earnings, and Investment Criteria," *Pakistan Development Review,* 8 (Winter 1968), 582–605.

32. These considerations were suggested by G. F. Papanek and Raymond Vernon.

Fourth, even on the strongest modification of the original findings, effective subsidy rates for manufactured goods as a whole remain generous enough to raise serious questions about cost and efficiency vis-à-vis agriculture. In early 1970, raw jute and cotton exports were awarded a 10 percent bonus voucher rate; but the rates for manufactured goods were also increased, so the effective discrimination between industry and agriculture remains. The magnitude of discrimination is shown in Table 3.3, note (f), which indicates that the aggregate value of bonus vouchers and the four minor schemes comes to about 80 percent of FOB receipts from subsidized exports, mainly manufactured goods. To be sure, haphazard and probably meaningless incentive differentials exist within the manufactured sector. Within agriculture, the cropping pattern has been badly distorted with sugarcane and wheat selling well above world import prices when cotton and high quality (basmati) rice are selling at or beneath export prices. But the important incentive differentials are those which divide industry from agriculture. I now turn to questions of cost and efficiency between industry and agriculture.

Resource and Political Costs of Foreign Exchange

There are at least three theoretical reasons for tax and subsidy discrimination between export commodities.

First, home prices may not accurately reflect social costs because of imperfect markets or infant industry situations. The infant industry argument commands high esteem in the developing world. Appeals to the argument, however, are rarely quantified. Proper evaluation of this argument would require considerable knowledge about sectoral productivity and price trends set in a sophisticated economic framework.[33] The Paki-

33. Elsewhere, I have offered a partial technique for evaluating the infant industry argument as applied to a single activity (G. C. Hufbauer, "The Infant Industry Argument: Its Evolution and Applications" [unpublished, January 1967]). M. Bruno has developed a much more comprehensive technique for simultaneous evaluation of many sectors ("Development Policy and Dynamic Comparative Advantage," in R. Vernon, ed., *The Technology Factor in International Trade,* [A Conference of the Universities-National Bureau Committee for Economic Research, Columbia University Press: New York, 1970]). N. Islam has gathered data from Tariff Commission Studies which cast doubt on the assumption—crucial to the infant industry dogma—that the *length* of production experience in Pakistan reacts favorably on relative unit costs (domestic vs. foreign) ("Comparative Costs, Factor Proportions, and Industrial Efficiency in Pakistan," *Pakistan Development Review*, 7 [Summer 1967], 213–246). Islam's data, however, do not include the important jute textile and cotton textile industries. G. F. Papanek argues that in these industries a distinct infant industry phenomenon can be observed (*Pakistan's Development—Social Goals and Private Incentives* [Cambridge: Harvard University Press, 1967]).

stan package of export policies may contain large doses of infant industry rationalization, but because of data and computational limitations, not to mention conceptual difficulties, I shall ignore the argument in analyzing export discrimination.

A second, more tangible, reason for discrimination is that the elasticity of foreign demand may be smaller for some commodities than for others. A smaller elasticity means fewer foreign exchange receipts at the margin, since additional offerings exercise a greater adverse impact on the price of previous units sold. For this reason, goods with lower foreign demand elasticities should presumably receive fewer export incentives.

The third reason for discrimination between commodities is that the government may adopt policies which implicitly depress the price of key export goods. For example, the government may choose to promote cost-of-living stability. If primary exports play a prominent role in the wage budget, as for example meat in Argentina, these goods may be kept cheap and plentiful on the home market at the expense of foreign sales. Or the government may have a policy of limiting agricultural rents, either to curtail the power of big landowners, or to enhance economic growth by shifting property incomes toward more dynamic groups.[34]

Whatever the policy, the analytic outcome is the same. Additional exports, when stimulated by higher prices, may produce windfall income gains which run counter to some aspect of domestic policy. These gains must be treated, not as mere transfers of income, but as a political "cost" or adverse redistribution effect of promoting exports. The total cost of producing an extra unit of output for export therefore equals net domestic resources consumed plus the political "cost" of windfall income gains. Of course, in some circumstances the windfall gains may count as a political "benefit" to be deducted from the resource cost of export production. In short, the manipulation of foreign trade provides a powerful tool for controlling the domestic economic structure and the internal distribution of income. The consequences of raising and lowering export prices thus reach far beyond the resource cost of foreign exchange.[35]

34. A Ricardian model, in which the landlords clash with the industrial and commercial classes for property income, underlies this policy. In the Ricardian model, the stable cost-of-living policy merely represents an intermediate device for concentrating property incomes in the industrial and commercial groups. Higher cost-of-living for the working population would ultimately be passed along to the urban property owners.

35. In a full-blown linear economic model, these political costs could be treated as constraints—a point verbally noted by H. B. Chenery. See also J. O'Connell, "An International Adjustment Mechanism with Fixed Exchange Rates," *Economica*, 35 (August 1968), 274–282.

Do these arguments relating to elasticity of supply and demand and political cost justify the present bias against West Pakistan exports of cotton, rice, and (potentially) wheat? This question can be reformulated: To what extent does the ratio between net marginal domestic cost, including political cost, and net marginal foreign exchange earned differ between commodities? If the ratio is higher for one commodity than another, then foreign exchange could be secured more cheaply, in terms of minimizing domestic resource and political cost, by stimulating exports of the cheaper commodity.

Different authors have defined the ratio between domestic costs and foreign exchange earnings in different ways.[36] Most of the variations differ as to which costs are domestic and which are foreign in nature. For present purposes, a general expression of the resource cost ratio is:

$$ {}_{x}R_i = \frac{{}_{x}MC_i}{{}_{x}MR_i}. \tag{5} $$

In the following empirical work, (5) is interpreted to include the cost of nontraded[37] inputs among domestic resource costs of the industry in question.[38]

The political costs or benefits of greater export production are represented in (5) as a percentage, presumably between +100 percent and −100 percent, of windfall income resulting from higher export prices. At worst, windfall transfers to a sector might be totally wasted compared with their alternative use (cost = 100 percent); at best, those trans-

36. The formulation of the problem offered here is based on the work of W. Liepe, "Notes on the Derivation of Optimal Tariff Expressions" (manuscript, University of New Mexico, April 1967). See also A. Krueger, "Some Economic Costs of Exchange Control: The Turkish Case," *Journal of Political Economy,* 74 (October 1966), 466–480; M. Bruno, "The Optimal Selection of Export-Promoting and Import-Substituting Projects," in United Nations, *Planning the External Sector: Techniques, Problems, and Policies,* Report on the First International Seminar on Development Planning (New York, 1967); B. Balassa and D. M. Schydlowsky, "Effective Tariffs, the Domestic Cost of Foreign Exchange, and the Equilibrium Exchange Rate," *Journal of Political Economy,* 76 (May—June 1968), 348–360.

37. In the calculations of Tables 3.6 and 3.7, miscellaneous manufactures are regarded as traded inputs, although, as G. F. Papanek has pointed out in private correspondence, this sector may partly serve as a residual dumping ground for advertising, legal, and other business services.

38. Alternatively, the ratio could be defined to exclude nontraded as well as traded inputs. The economic underpinnings of this alternative seem more doubtful; if used, the resource cost of most West Pakistan manufactured exports would appear much higher than the ratios cited in Table 3.6.

fers could be entirely productive (benefit = 100 percent). If the costs or benefits somehow exceed 100 percent, the question arises: Why have those passing political judgment not already taxed or subsidized the sector's income?

The ratio between costs and benefits in Equation (5) may be expressed as so many domestic monetary units per unit of foreign exchange. In this form it reflects the rate of transformation between immobile domestic factors, services, and political costs on the one hand, and foreign exchange earnings on the other.

In the numerical exercises, it is assumed that traded inputs are perfectly elastic in demand and supply. This important assumption leads to an understatement of net earnings if the foreign demand for exports used as inputs is less than perfectly elastic; conversely it results in an overstatement of net earnings if the foreign supply of importables used as inputs is less than perfectly elastic.

The assumption of perfect elasticity seems unobjectionable for imported commodities. But for locally manufactured inputs, imperfectly elastic export markets are probably the rule. Indeed, because they are crude, nonstandardized, or inadequately marketed, such inputs may have no foreign demand.[39] In principle, assigning realistic demand elasticities to exportable inputs would solve this problem, but in practice the calculations assume infinite elasticities.

When all elasticities of foreign demand are infinite, and either political costs are zero or the elasticity of home supply is infinite, the measure defined by (5) bears a simple relation to the effective taxation of exports.[40]

$$T_i = \frac{1}{{}_xR_i} - 1. \tag{6}$$

If elasticities of demand and supply were all infinite, then the ranking of industries according to static desirability of expansion would be the

39. This point was verbally made by H. B. Chenery.

40. As Balassa and Schydlowsky point out, ("Effective Tariffs") the Bruno-Krueger measures ("The Optimal Selection" and "Some Economic Costs") of resource cost of import substitution are not so easily related to the index of effective protection. This is so because the Bruno-Krueger measures *include* the domestic resource cost of traded inputs in the cost of producing an extra unit of output. The inefficiency of supplying sectors is thereby attributed to the industry under consideration, a procedure which seems inappropriate when distinguishing between industries. On the other hand, Bruno and Krueger state in rebuttal that they did not intend an across-the-board inclusion of indirect costs. Furthermore, they argue that the inclusion or exclusion makes no difference. See A. Krueger, "Evaluating Restrictionist Trade Regimes: Theory and Measurement" (mimeo, St. Paul, Minnesota), and M. Bruno, "Domestic Resource Costs and Effective Protection: Clarification and Synthesis," (revised, mimeo, Hebrew University, Jerusalem, January 1970).

same using either the effective taxation statistic or the resource ratio. Because elasticities differ, a measure other than effective taxation is needed to determine foreign exchange and investment strategy (infant industry considerations make the problem even more complex).

Falcon and Gotsch have done some careful work on supply elasticities in West Pakistan agriculture. Their findings indicated lagged *relative* price responsiveness of 0.29 (±0.08), 0.16(±0.09), and 0.06(±0.03), for cotton, rice, and irrigated wheat acreage respectively.[41] Evidently, when the price of one agricultural good increases, land is diverted from other uses. Price responsiveness of this sort suggests that gains in one crop through higher export prices are largely offset by losses elsewhere.

But that conclusion understates the total price reaction for two reasons. First, the use of inputs which enhance yield per acre, particularly tubewell water, improved seed, and fertilizer, is probably responsive to price changes vis-à-vis the industrial sector. Because tubewells and fertilizer are comparatively new phenomena, at least on a large scale, because weather and poor reporting greatly affect yield and yield statistics,[42] and because heretofore the use of new inputs has been governed more by supply constraints and subsidy policy than by variations on the demand side,[43] it has been impossible to measure the responsiveness of yields to industrial-agricultural price changes. The magnitude of this response is not known for the United States, much less for any of the developing countries. Furthermore, as Falcon and Gotsch have shown, the optimal short-run use of additional water is often the cultivation of new acreage and double-cropping, rather than heavier application on existing irrigated land.[44] Hence, the acreage response to price change reflects "generated"

41. W. P. Falcon and C. H. Gotsch, *Relative Price Response, Economic Efficiency, and Technological Change: A Study of Punjab Agriculture* (Report No. 11, Harvard Development Advisory Service, Cambridge, February 1967). Chapter 6, this volume.

42. Cf. G. C. Hufbauer, "Cereal Consumption, Production, and Prices in West Pakistan," *Pakistan Development Review*, 8 (Summer 1968), 288–297.

43. In other words, physical limitations on the supply of fertilizer (determined in part by government subsidy and foreign exchange policy), improved seed varieties (determined by the biological rate of multiplication), and tubewell connections (determined by funds allocated to the Water and Power Development Authority for distribution lines, and by the alacrity of the WAPDA staff), have heretofore principally determined the pace of utilizing new inputs. See W. P. Falcon and C. H. Gotsch, *Agricultural Policy and Performance in the Punjab: A Comparative Study of India and Pakistan* (Report No. 96, Harvard Development Advisory Service, Cambridge, May 1968).

44. W. P. Falcon and C. H. Gotsch, *Agricultural Development in Pakistan: Lessons from the Second-Plan Period* (Report No. 6, Harvard Development Advisory Service, Cambridge, 1966); C. H. Gotsch, *A Programming Approach to Agricultural Policy Planning in West Pakistan* (Report No. 77, Harvard Development Advisory Service, Cambridge, 1967).

as well as "diverted" crop land. With these considerations in mind, I arbitrarily assume that the long-run net response (after allowing for reduced output of other crops) of cotton and rice output to price changes vis-à-vis the industrial sector is no less than 0.2 and no greater than 0.5. These elasticities are presumed to apply either to overt changes in the price of agricultural or industrial output, or to covert changes via subsidized industrial inputs for agriculture.

I assume that the long run supply elasticities of industrial output, although probably large, are not a matter of concern because windfall income transfers to the industrial sector are not regarded as a political cost. In fact, since industry is preferred by many planners, windfall gains to industry might be seen as a political benefit. Nevertheless, in a simplistic Ricardian two-sector economy, double-counting occurs if agricultural windfalls are treated as a cost and industrial windfalls as a benefit. Because larger agricultural rents mean smaller industrial profits, the sort of dual treatment mentioned above would result in counting the same windfall transfer twice.

Foreign demand elasticities for Pakistan exports, apart from jute and jute goods, have not been estimated. The long-run elasticities of demand for homogeneous primary commodities, such as rice and cotton, of which Pakistan supplies a small portion of world consumption, may be as high as 10. On the other hand, the elasticities of demand for standardized manufactured goods, like cotton textiles and leather, and also for simple machinery, sporting goods, and toys, are probably less than 5.[45] The assumption of a high demand elasticity, however, partially compensates for the fact that traded inputs which otherwise would be exported face imperfectly elastic foreign markets.

Putting these arbitrary elasticity assumptions in Equation (5), together with the appropriate tax and subsidy rates, gives the ratios presented in

45. H. B. Junz and R. R. Rhomberg found no long-run demand elasticity estimates exceeding 5.0 in their study of total manufacturing exports from eleven industrial countries. ("Prices and Export Performance of Industrial Countries, 1953–1963," *International Monetary Fund Staff Papers,* 12 [July 1965], 224–269.) Examining one-digit SITC groups, M. E. Kreinin found elasticity estimates of 1.6 for chemicals (SITC 5), 1.7 for machinery and transport equipment (SITC 7), 4.5 for other manufactures (SITC 6 and 8) ("Price Elasticities in International Trade," *Review of Economics and Statistics,* 49 [November 1967], 510–516). Raymond Vernon has pointed out verbally that such elasticities are probably overstated because a queueing effect gets mixed up with price effects in the estimating procedure. Rising prices in industrial countries reflect full capacity utilization. In these circumstances export orders go to the end of the queue and hence exports decline. However, the *whole* decline is attributed to rising relative prices. Furthermore, the fact that cotton textile exports face quota markets means that their price elasticity is lower than for similar standardized commodities.

Table 3.6. These ratios show the high resource plus political cost of foreign exchange and the critical issues underlying any strategic choice between industrial and agricultural exports. Appendix B gives a sample calculation of the resource plus political cost of foreign exchange.

Critical Issues Between Industry and Agriculture

Pakistan's planners generally accept a shadow foreign exchange price of 1.75 times the official exchange rate (Rs. 4.75 equals $1.00). The appropriate foreign exchange rate for evaluating policy and project alternatives is thus thought to be about Rs. 8.3 per $1.00. This shadow price may reflect the exchange rate at which licensing restrictions could be lifted, and an even lower shadow price may be appropriate for project aid, since such assistance is politically confined to fairly narrow uses.[46] But for some planning purposes, the marginal cost and value of foreign exchange may have more relevance than either the general equilibrium exchange rate or the special equilibrium rate needed to clear the project assistance market.[47] The findings in Table 3.6 suggest a much higher marginal resource cost of net foreign exchange earnings than Rs. 8.3 per $1.00 for industrial exports. The figure, shown in Case 1 of Table 3.6, is at least Rs. 18 per $1.00; for some important goods, including cotton textiles, the cost may be infinitely large. Even if export profits are one-third larger than home profits, and value added as a fraction of sales has risen since the 1962–63 RKM table, the resource cost of manufactured exports is only 15–20 percent lower than the costs indicated by Table 3.6 (see Table 3.5).

Do these findings justify an upward revision in the appropriate shadow price of foreign exchange for planning purposes? The answer depends on three considerations.

46. Cf. H. A. Adler, "The Shadow Price of Foreign Exchange and the Discount Rate for the Appraisal of Projects" (mimeo, Pakistan Planning Commission memorandum, August 7, 1968).

47. The marginal cost and the marginal value of foreign exchange often exceed the equilibrium exchange rate that would prevail in the absence of licensing restrictions. On the cost side this happens because foreign markets are not perfectly elastic; hence part of the "cost" of additional foreign exchange earnings takes the "hidden" form of lower prices on existing exports. The logical way to price foreign exchange at its marginal cost is to impose customs charges equal to the differential between marginal and average cost at the point of intersection between the marginal cost curve and the demand curve. If this is done, then on the value side the equilibrium exchange rate is lower than the market worth of foreign exchange because imported goods have been marked up by duties on their way to the final customer. If all external transactions took place at the equilibrium rate without paying import tariffs, then the volume of trade would expand, but the terms of trade would worsen.

One consideration is the value to the economy of a marginal unit of foreign exchange. One way of assessing this value is to look at the purchaser's outlay for the most costly import (inclusive of customs charges) brought in under full bonus. This outlay suggests the value of foreign exchange in its most remunerative use, given the existing distribution of income. The most expensive imports are probably consumer durable goods, such as air conditioners, refrigerators, TV sets, and small cars, with customs charges at rates exceeding 100 percent. When such commodities are imported on full bonus, with a 160 percent premium, the buyer pays at least Rs. 17 per $1.00 of foreign exchange.[48]

Another way of assessing the value of foreign exchange is to estimate industrial production per unit of traded raw material inputs.[49] On the dual assumptions that availability of traded raw materials acts as the key bottleneck to greater output, and that domestic factor services, including nontraded inputs, are unlimited in supply, this figure indicates the value of industrial production made possible by an extra unit of imports. This value may be divided into three parts: the cost of traded inputs, indirect taxes collected on output and inputs, and factor payments within the country and to suppliers of nontraded inputs. In some contexts it may be useful to know the relationship between additional traded inputs and additional factor incomes. In evaluating the marginal worth of foreign exchange, however, the relevant figure is the total value of industrial output per extra unit of raw material inputs. The calculations are more realistic when depreciation charges on machinery and transport equipment are treated as current traded inputs.[50]

Table 3.7 sets forth estimated traded inputs, valued at world prices, per unit of West Pakistan industrial output, valued at domestic prices. These coefficients suggest a marginal foreign exchange value exceeding Rs. 15 per $1.00.

A second consideration in determining the shadow price of foreign exchange is the shadow price assigned to domestic factor payments. The calculations throughout this chapter contain no adjustment in the money cost of domestic labor, capital, or land services. Perhaps nonwage value added in industrial enterprises should be deflated, on the grounds that

48. Calculated as Rs : \$ $= (1 + z + t_i)4.75 : 1$, where $z = 160$ percent (bonus voucher premium) and $t_i = 100$ percent (ad valorem tariff rate).

49. This method was pioneered in Pakistan planning exercises by Wouter Tims, formerly of the Harvard Development Advisory Service.

50. In the short run, output may be expanded without additional capital equipment owing to excess capacity. Over a longer period of time, however, more capital equipment will be required.

various restrictions have given rise to large economic rents on industrial capital. Pakistan's brand of mercantilism could have had this effect. But at the margin the argument seems less plausible, especially since idle capacity characterizes most branches of manufacturing activity.

On the other hand, it can be argued that the market wage considerably exaggerates the opportunity cost of labor.[51] Thus, Pakistan's planners widely use a shadow price of common labor equal to 0.50 times the market wage. A "moderate" shadow price of foreign exchange (1.75) coupled with a "low" shadow price of labor (0.50) yields nearly the same conclusions in project and policy analysis as a "high" shadow price of foreign exchange coupled with market prices of labor. Nevertheless, even if the analysis in Table 3.6 of the resource cost of foreign exchange had evaluated common labor at a shadow price of 0.50, that table would still indicate a resource cost in excess of Rs. 8.3 per $1.00. This can be seen from the following example.

According to the 1965–66 West Pakistan Census of Manufacturing Industries, employment costs (including payments to skilled and professional labor) amount to about 25 percent of value added in large-scale industry.[52] The operation of large-scale industrial projects involves at least as much common labor as most big government projects (e.g., electric power stations, irrigation works, railway expansion, etc.). A 1.75 shadow price of foreign exchange (Rs. 8.3 per $1.00), coupled with an 0.50 shadow price on 25 percent of domestic factor payments, gives practically the same analytic results as a 2.00 shadow price of foreign exchange (Rs. 9.5 per $1.00), with no adjustment in domestic factor payments. But Rs. 9.5 per $1.00 is less than the cost or value of foreign exchange in industrial pursuits, as indicated by Tables 3.6 and 3.7. In other words, the currently used shadow prices of labor and foreign exchange may inadequately reflect the marginal premium value of foreign resources.

The third and most important consideration in determining the shadow exchange rate is the relevant alternative method of acquiring foreign exchange. If the alternative is larger industrial exports, then a shadow price higher than Rs. 8.3 per $1.00 is indicated. Similarly, if the alternative is greater industrial import substitution, then my impression—based on a limited examination of public sector projects—is that costs presently

51. Indeed, such a situation is implied by the assumption that traded raw materials constitute the only bottleneck to higher industrial output.

52. Government of West Pakistan, Bureau of Statistics, *Census of Manufacturing Industries: 1965–66* (preliminary release, February 1968). Much the same figure emerges from earlier censuses.

range in the vicinity of Rs. 15–20 per $1.00 of foreign exchange saved. But if the alternative is larger agricultural exports, the situation becomes more complicated. The answer then depends on the perceived role of agricultural rents. A closer examination of this issue follows.

Export promotion policies have been directed toward manufactured goods and minor primary commodities. (There was some shift of emphasis in the 1970 policy.) This helps explain why manufactured exports have grown so rapidly, and why exports of fish and miscellaneous primary goods have expanded faster than the major products (Table 3.1 and Figure 3.1). It also helps explain why the resource cost of foreign exchange earned by industrial exports so greatly exceeds that earned by agricultural exports (Table 3.6). The contrast, as of 1968, was between Rs. 5 per $1.00 and more than Rs. 18 per $1.00, even without making allowance for the forced procurement of rice at less than FOB export prices. Does the present situation therefore warrant a strategic shift towards agricultural exports?

The answer to this question depends largely on the treatment of windfall income changes. This is so whether larger marketable surpluses are stimulated by high prices or by subsidized inputs. Falcon's account of the post-1958 agricultural success story emphasizes tubewells, fertilizer, and improved seed, coupled with big doses of "new technology."[53] These ingredients were made possible by direct and indirect government programs, including large outright subsidies for fertilizer and disguised subsidies for tubewell construction and electrification. Subsidies may stimulate output more than the same volume of price increases, particularly when the subsidy program involves new techniques and requires no large bureaucracy. Nevertheless, subsidies, like higher prices, increase the agricultural rent on premarginal production. And subsidy gains are probably concentrated among large landlords, the ones most eager and able to implement new technology. Whether the stimulus is from subsidies or prices, the issue of windfall income gains must be squarely faced.

The issue cannot be dodged with a simple prescription to tax windfall gains directly. Land taxes in West Pakistan are fixed for long periods, 30 or 40 years, by statute and custom. Income taxes are unpopular and enormously difficult to administer. The most promising direct tax is higher irrigation rates on canal water. Presently these rates are only one-third to one-fourth the cost of public or private tubewell water. Irrigation rates can be increased, but probably not very fast. A mere 10 percent rise in crop prices, however, would expand agricultural money income by Rs.

53. W. P. Falcon, "Agricultural and Industrial Interrelationships in West Pakistan," *Journal of Farm Economics*, 49 (December 1967), 1139–1154.

900 million. Two-thirds of this price increase might be borne by the agricultural sector itself, through consumption of its own products.[54] But one-third or more, Rs. 300 million, would represent transfers from the urban-commercial-industrial classes to agriculture. Considering that present net irrigation receipts are less than Rs. 200 million, the government would find itself hard pressed to appropriate Rs. 300 million of windfall gains through higher water rates. Although much of the agricultural prosperity could be siphoned off by higher excise taxes on "luxury" consumer goods, bicycles, kerosene, fine cloth, this approach would penalize those not participating in the new prosperity, while barely touching the larger rental income of big landlords. To summarize: in the short run it seems unlikely that the government can achieve resource efficiency between industrial and agricultural exports without a significant transfer of income to the agriculture sector. What are the consequences of this dilemma?

If half the rental income accruing to the agricultural sector is viewed as a political cost, and if the elasticity of agricultural output with respect to changes in the agricultural-industrial terms of trade is as great as 0.5, then the marginal resource plus political cost of agricultural exports is approximately Rs. 11–13 per $1.00. This is shown in Case 2 of Table 3.6. If, under the same assumptions about rental income, the elasticity of agricultural output is only 0.2, then the marginal cost of agricultural exports rises to Rs. 21–23 per $1.00 (Case 3). This cost is about the same as the real resource cost of marginal manufactured exports. In terms of real resources, agricultural exports offer a cheaper way of earning foreign exchange than industrial exports. But if income transfers are given much adverse weight, then the marginal resource plus political cost of additional agriculture exports is possibly as great as the resource cost of additional industrial exports. Thus, in making any broad choice between West Pakistan industrial and agricultural products, two critical problems must be faced.[55]

54. Since some agriculturalists own more land than others, the statement that a large portion of any crop price increase is borne "by the agricultural sector" neglects the initial redistribution of income between landowners and agricultural labor. The initial redistribution, however, will be partly rectified as subsistence wages for agricultural work catch up with higher prices.

55. In addition, there is the problem of the relative position of raw jute vis-à-vis rice, wheat, and raw cotton. Considerations of resource efficiency dictate lower incentives for jute exports because foreign demand for jute is not particularly elastic. Table 3.6 assumes an elasticity of 2, but this could be too high. If efficiency considerations prevail, equity might require a compensating adjustment which would channel greater foreign exchange

First, what is the actual response of West Pakistan agricultural output to changes in the industrial-agricultural terms of trade, taking into account tubewells, fertilizer, and better seeds? This is an empirical question; preliminary answers might appear within the next few years.

Second, what are the political costs of larger agricultural rents? The answer to this question depends mainly on refined judgment. But economic analysis is also relevant. If the Ricardian model is accepted, it follows that agricultural rents can expand only at the expense of industrial and commercial profits. Higher commodity prices might initially fall on the common wage earner, but with a lag of one or two years the burden would descend on the profit shares of income. The economic question comes down to who uses property income more productively, the landlords or the industrial and commercial classes? At present, only loose and unreliable impressions can be brought to bear on this question. Any meaningful answer would need to include, among other things, consideration of the utlization of newly installed industrial and agricultural equipment, and the flow of funds between sectors.

Postscript

This chapter was written in the summer of 1968. In only a few instances have I updated the material to reflect events of 1969 and later. Since 1968, however, much new analysis has been done on the present and potential cost of foreign exchange.

In a sophisticated yet practical piece of research, MacEwan has employed linear programming techniques to estimate, among other parameters, the shadow price of export earnings. The shadow price is presently about 3 for the West Pakistan economy.[56] Although substantially qualified, this estimate broadly confirms the high economic cost of foreign earnings.

Meanwhile, the new technology in agriculture makes it possible to contemplate wheat, maize, and coarse rice exports. The policy consequences of this dramatic shift from foodgrain shortage to surplus have

earnings to East Pakistan. Higher bonus voucher rates might, for example, be set on West Pakistan than on East Pakistan *imports*. See the demand elasticity estimates suggested by R. F. Mallon, "Export Policy in Pakistan." For estimates of supply elasticities of jute production, see A. K. M. Ghulam Rabbani, "Economic Determinants of Jute Production in India and Pakistan," *Pakistan Development Review* 5 (Summer 1965), 191–228; and S. M. Hussain, "A Note on Farmer Response to Price in East Pakistan," *Pakistan Development Review,* 4 (Spring 1964), 93–106.

56. A. MacEwan, "Development Alternatives in Pakistan: A Multisectoral and Regional Analysis of Planning Problems" (Ph.D. thesis, Harvard University, August 1968), table 5.9, p. 271.

rightly attracted the attention of agricultural experts.[57] At the official exchange rate, the domestic price of coarse rice is perhaps 15 percent higher than the potential world price, though the strength of the coarse rice export market is subject to dispute. The 1969 prices of wheat and maize, however, apparently exceed international prices by between 70 and 100 percent. And the outlook for foodgrain prices is bearish for the next few years. Thus, if wheat and maize exports are to materialize, a painful downward adjustment in domestic prices, a substantial bonus voucher rate, or an adjustment in the exchange rate would be required. The same prescription could apply to coarse rice. The foodgrain situation thus differs markedly from the experience of raw cotton and basmati rice, which have traditionally sold at or below world prices at the official exchange rate.

Finally, the theoretical effective subsidy estimates have been broadly confirmed in a pilot study of cotton textile and leather firms, and a fuller-scale study of nine manufacturing industries.[58] These subsequent exercises indicate a high domestic cost of cotton textile, leather, and selected other manufactured exports, without, however, uncovering cases of negative value added.

57. A sampler of recent agricultural policy papers may be cited. Harvard Development Advisory Service, Pakistan, all mimeographed: J. N. Lewis, "Export Markets for West Pakistan Grains" (December 1968); "Export Prospects for West Pakistan Maize and Grain Sorghum" (December 1968); "Agricultural Price Policy in West Pakistan" (April 1969); "Procurement Prices for the 1969–70 Rice Crop" (May 1969); "The Cost-Price Squeeze on Agriculture" (July 1969); M. F. Long, "Key Problems of Agriculture in West Pakistan 1969–70" (April 1969). Ford Foundation, Pakistan, all mimeographed: O. Aresvik and G. W. McLean, "Comments on Rice Policy" (April 1969); J. N. Efferson, "Problems and Priorities of the Rice Industry in West Pakistan" (April 1969); J. W. Madill (with comments by O. Aresvik, I. M. Narvaez, and N. E. Borlaug), "Wheat Marketing in Pakistan: An Appraisal of Prospects and Requirements" (April 1969). Other organizations, all mimeographed: C. E. Finney, "Economic Aspects of Tractor Mechanization" (Lower Indus Project, Lahore, April 1969); "Returns to Private Tubewells, Fertilizers and Insecticides in the Irrigated Areas of West Pakistan" (Lower Indus Project, Lahore, July 1969); R. Lawrence, "Comparative Costs of Pakistan's Major Crops" (U.S. Agency for International Development, Pakistan, June 1969); W. C. F. Bussink, "Alternative Projections for Wheat Production and Consumption at the End of the Fourth Plan" (Harvard Development Advisory Service, Cambridge, June 1969); C. H. Gotsch and W. P. Falcon, "Eight Working Papers on Agricultural Policy" (Harvard Development Advisory Service, Cambridge, February 1969).

58. G. C. Hufbauer, Nayyara Aziz, and Asghar Ali, "Cotton Textile and Leather Exports: What Cost Foreign Exchange?" *Pakistan Development Review*, forthcoming; H. A. Syed, *Exports of Manufactured Goods: Costs and Policies* (Lahore: The Board of Economic Inquiry, Publication No. 144, 1970). Also see N. Islam, "Commodity Exports, Net Exchange Earnings and Investment Criteria," *Pakistan Development Review*, 8 (Spring 1968), 582–605.

Appendix A

Tables

Table 3.1. West Pakistan exports

Sector number[a]	Commodity	Value (millions of rupees) 1955[b]	1959	1964–65[c]	1967–68[c]	Annual compound growth rate 1955 to 1967–68[d] (percent)	Effective export tax (+) or subsidy (–) as percent of home value added[e] (percent)
1 to 10	Primary commodities[f]	575	303	683	855	3.2	–10
1	Rice	59	52	119	149	7.7	7
4	Raw and waste cotton	406	127	316	442	0.7	9
Part of 6	Raw wool and other animal hair	67	62	70	43	–3.5	10[g]
Part of 6	Fish, fresh, dried, processed	5	16	41	45	19.2	–32[h]
Rest of 1 to 10	Other primary goods	38	46	137	176	13.1	–67[j]
11 to 29	Manufactured commodities[k]	55	228	457	790	23.8	–114
11	Cotton textiles	8	146	271	422	37.3	–143
12 and 13	Other textiles	5	12	34	128	29.6	–110[m]
15	Tanned leather and leather goods	17	38	73	113	16.4	–75
20, 21, 22 23, part of 28	Metal goods	10	11	28	32	9.8	–90[j]
19	Cement and cement products	1	-	-	10	20.2	–102
Rest of 11 to 29	Other manufactured goods	14	21	51	85	15.5	–80[j]
1 to 29	Total West Pakistan exports	630	531	1,140	1,645	8.0	–58

Source: Government of Pakistan, Central Statistical Office, *Foreign Trade Statistics of Pakistan: 1955; Monthly Foreign Trade Statistics of Pakistan: June 1967; Monthly Statistical Bulletin* (various issues). Table 3.2 of this chapter.

[a] Based on the Rahman Khan-MacEwan input-output table. See Table 3.2.

[b] At the present official exchange rate, Rs. 4.75 = $1.00. In August 1955, the rupee was devalued from Rs. 3.33 = $1.00. No adjustment has been made for the devaluation; all figures are given in current prices.

[c] In 1960, the Pakistan government began presenting trade statistics on a fiscal year, July to June, basis.

[d] Compounded for a period of 12 years.

[e] Generally speaking, the effective tax rates are those in effect as of January 1, 1968, as estimated in Table 2.2. However, in certain instances where the Table 2.2 rates give a grossly misleading impression of the "average" relative level of taxation over the period 1955 to 1967–68, either because of the composition of exports contributed by the sector, or because of recent changes in the bonus system, an adjusted rate has been used. The adjustments are explained in the notes to specific rates. The tax rates for commodity groups (e.g. "primary commodities") are weighted averages based on the 1966–67 composition of exports.

[f] SITC sectors 0, 1, 2, and 3.

[g] In November 1967, raw wool was granted a 20 percent bonus for the first time. Previously it had not received any incentives. The figure here is a rough guess of the effective tax rate *prior* to the bonus voucher action.

[h] Fresh and frozen fish receive no bonus vouchers; fish dried in the sun receive 30 percent vouchers; fish otherwise preserved receive 40 percent vouchers. The rate here represents a rough average subsidy level, based on the 1966–67 composition of exports.

[j] Average rate derived from Table 2.2, based on the 1966–67 composition of exports.

[k] SITC sectors 4, 5, 6, 7, 8, and 9.

[m] The rate in Table 2.2 for "other textiles" refers to textiles based on synthetic fibers. The rate here takes into account jute textiles exported from West Pakistan, and woolen textiles. The resulting average is based on the 1966–67 composition of exports.

Table 3.2. Estimated potential and actual effective taxation or subsidization of West Pakistan exports

Sector number	Sector	Estimated parameters[a]				Minor export incentives[c]				Bonus vouchers[e]			
							Export performance licensing (EPL)						
		t_i	p_i	$_he_i$	Estimated tax or subsidy, as percentage of value added in absence of all incentives[b]	Rebate value as percentage of FOB export price	Rate as percentage of FOB export receipts	Value as percentage of FOB export price	Estimated tax (+) or subsidy (−), as percentage of value added, after minor export incentives have been applied[d]	Rate as percentage of FOB export receipts	Value as percentage of FOB export price	Estimated tax (+) or subsidy (−), as percentage of value added, after all incentives have been applied[d]	Estimated tax (+) or subsidy (−), as percentage of FOB export price, with all incentives[f]
(1)	(2)	(3)	(4)	(5)	(6)	(7)	(8)	(9)	(10)	(11)	(12)	(13)	(14)
1	Rice growing,[g,h] processing	–	–	–	–	–	–	–	1	–	–	7[j]	4
2	Wheat growing,[k] processing	–	–	–	−1	–	–	–	–	–	–	16[j]	9
4	Cotton growing,[g] processing	–	–	–	–	–	–	–	1	–	–	9[j]	6
5	Tea growing, processing	–	–	–	14	–	–	–	14	–	–	14	2
6	Other agriculture, forestry, fishery[g]	–	–	–	–	–	5	2.3	−3	30	48.0	−43	−45
7	Sugar refining, *gur* making	45	50	17	242	0.8	10	4.6	−35	30	48.0	−116[m]	−13
8	Edible oils	32	50	17	143	4.7	10	4.6	5	40	64.0	−125[m]	−38
9	Cigarettes, *bidi*, etc.	125	50	45	251	1.9	20	9.1	−32	40	64.0	−114[m]	−38

10 Other food and drink	25	50	9	24	5.9	25	11.4	−11	40	64.0	−75	−62
11 Cotton textiles[g]	21	-	11	109	11.0	8	3.6	−5	35	56.0	−143[m]	−35
13 Other textiles[n]	115	50	3	94	13.0	30	13.6	22	40	64.0	−55	−32
14 Paper and printing	32	20	-	29	8.5	30	13.6	−17	40	64.0	−85	−63
15 Leather, leather products[g,p]	24	-	1	7	8.8	20	9.1	−23	40	64.0	−75	−72
16 Rubber, rubber products	52	50	16	79	6.0	30	13.6	−24	40	64.0	−100[m]	−56
17 Fertilizer	−25[g]	-	−25[g]	4[g]	1.8	10	4.6	−6	-	-	−6	−4
18 Other chemicals	17	30	5	26	6.6	20	9.1	−8	40	64.0	−65	−63
19 Cement, concrete, bricks	15	-	30	106	11.7	10	4.6	−17	40	64.0	−102[m]	−66
20 Basic metals	23	30	3	166	15.7	30	13.6	−5	40	64.0	−175[m]	−51
21 Metal products	25	30	3	52	11.3	30	13.6	−11	40	64.0	−86	59
22 Machinery	20	30	6	59	12.7	30	13.6	−8	40	64.0	−73	−56
23 Transport equipment	28	30	8	108	17.5	30	13.6	−11	40	64.0	−105[m]	−54
24 Wood, cork, furniture	38	30	2	6	3.8	15	6.8	−16	40	64.0	−53	−45
28 Miscellaneous manufactures	64	30	4	54	11.6	30	13.6	−9	40	64.0	−79	−57
29 Coal, petroleum products	61	-	117	783	9.6	30	13.6	−30	40	64.0	−196[m]	−61

[a] t_i = customs duties and other import charges as percentage of CIF price. t_i values were estimated from the data on customs duties by commodity for 1966–67 in Government of Pakistan, Central Statistical Office, *Monthly Statistical Bulletin* (April 1968), and from sales tax rates implied by the data in Government of West Pakistan, Bureau of Statistics, *Census of Manufacturing Industries 1965–66* (preliminary release, February 1968).

p_i = scarcity premium over landed cost expressed as percentage of landed cost. Scarcity premiums are roughly but conservatively estimated using the work of Alamgir and the operation of the cash-cum-bonus system as background data. See M. Alamgir, "The Domestic Prices of Imported Commodities in Pakistan: A Further Study", *Pakistan Development Review*, 8 (Spring 1968), pp. 35–73. Alamgir found markups over landed cost of about 50–60 percent on licensed and free list imports, and about 10–20 percent on bonus imports. Presumably the markups on bonus imports represent normal trading margins; hence premiums of 30–50 percent are indicated. Scarcity premiums are, for present purposes, still scarcity premiums even though absorbed by the January 1968 cash-cum-bonus system.

${}_he_i$ = excise, sales, and other indirect taxes imposed on domestic production for the home market, expressed as a percentage of the ex-tax domestic selling price. The rates are estimated from Government of West Pakistan, Bureau of Statistics, *Census of Manufacturing Industries 1965–66* (preliminary release, February 1968). As a practical matter, only central excise and sales taxes are included in the calculations; provincial and local levies are ignored. Furthermore, taxes are expressed as ad valorem levels whereas in fact they largely consist of specific charges.

[b]Found by application of Equation (4). ${}_xW_i$ was estimated by using the subsidiary formulas to Equation (4), as given in Appendix B, assuming that subsidies on foreign sales are zero, and that foreign sales are subject to the same indirect taxes as domestic sales. ${}_xV_i$ was also estimated by using the subsidiary formulas to Equation (4). For these calculations it was assumed that indirect taxes are levied on production for export as well as production for the home market.

[c]"Minor incentives" include indirect tax exemption for exports. Tax and tariff rebates were measured originally as a percentage of the domestic selling price. Rebate rates on the domestic selling price were multiplied by $(1 + {}_he_i)(1 - {}_hs_i)(1 - {}_xe_i)(1 + {}_xs_i)$ in order to convert them to rebate rates on the FOB export price. This transformation is based on Equation (2). In the transformation ${}_xs_i$ includes export performance licenses and export bonus vouchers. For convenience, it was assumed that the rebate rate on domestic price equals 15 percent of inputs from sectors 7 to 29. The figure of 15 percent corresponds to domestic inputs equal to 60 percent of total inputs from the selected sectors, and taxed at 5 percent, and imported inputs equal to 40 percent of inputs from sectors 7 to 29, and subject to customs charges of 30 percent. The total amount of rebates indicated by this approach is Rs. 67 million, whereas for 1966–67 the actual rebates amounted to about Rs. 64 million, based on data in Government of Pakistan, Ministry of Finance, *The Budget: 1967–68* (1967), and figures given by Dr. Azhar, Central Board of Revenue. The export performance license rates are approximately those in force as of January 1968. The average premium value of imports brought in under export performance licenses is assumed to be 35 percent of landed cost and the average tariff on CIF value is assumed to be 30 percent.

[d]Found by application of Equation (4), with appropriate formulas for ${}_xW_i$ and ${}_xV_i$, taking into account tax exemption for exports. The tax rates with minor export incentives reflect the exemption of foreign sales from indirect taxes, the rebate of taxes and tariffs on inputs, and the value of export performance licenses. The tax rates with all incentives also reflect the bonus voucher awards.

[e]The rates are percentages of FOB export receipts paid in bonus vouchers as of January 1968. A premium of 160 percent on bonus vouchers is assumed in calculating their value.

[f]The relation between column (13) and column (14) reflects simply the relation between value added and FOB export prices.

[g]These goods are deemed exportable commodities, with the relationship between world and home prices for domestically used inputs determined by Equation (2). All other goods are deemed importable commodities, with the relationship controlled by Equation (1), so far as inputs are concerned, but by (2) for exports.

[h]The tax parameters for rice do not reflect the practice of procuring basmati (high quality) rice for export at lower than FOB prices. This practice was abandoned in 1968.

[j]Effective taxation of rice, wheat, and cotton increases with imposition of the bonus system, because inputs from the "exportable" sectors become more expensive.

[k]Even though wheat enjoys no formal tariff or license protection, the internal 1968 bumper crop price of Rs. 17 per maund (82 pounds) was about 100 percent above potential export prices and perhaps 50 percent above potential import prices. The central government, under the PL 480 program, was the sole importer, and during 1968 it supported prices by purchasing nearly 1 million tons of domestically produced grain. The support price was lowered to Rs. 15 per maund in 1969.

[m]Apparent subsidies greater than 100 percent (negative value added at world prices) may reflect aberrations in the input-output data, and erroneous parameters, or they may reflect uneconomic export production. The latter case would be similar to the Soligo-Stern analysis of uneconomic domestic production, but the results are not directly comparable because of different data and different assumptions about price formation. See R. Soligo and J. J. Stern, "Tariff Protection, Import Substitution and Investment Efficiency," *Pakistan Development Review*, 5 (Summer 1965), pp. 249–270. Also, S. R. Lewis and S. E. Guisinger, *Measuring Protection in a Developing Country: The Case of Pakistan* (Report No. 20, Harvard Development Advisory Service, Cambridge, December 1966). Also S. E. Guisinger, *Negative Value Added and the Theory of Effective Protection* (Report No. 95, Harvard Development Advisory Service, Cambridge, April 1968).

[n]The parameters for "other textiles" apply to synthetic textiles rather than woolen or jute goods. In Table 3.1, an attempt is made to estimate an average subsidy rate encompassing synthetic, wool, and jute textiles exported from West Pakistan.

[p]It is assumed that inputs to the leather industry from the leather industry in the RKM table are mainly hides and skins, the domestic prices of which are the same as the world prices.

Table 3.3. Approximate value of incentive measures applied to West Pakistan exports, circa **1966–67**

Scheme	Approximate CIF value of licensed imports or FOB value of bonus voucher exports (millions of rupees)	Approximate premium on licenses and bonus vouchers (percent)	Approximate value of incentive measure on 1966–67 exports (millions of rupees)
Exemption of foreign sales from central excise and sales taxes[a]	–	–	62
Rebate of customs duties, excise and sales taxes on inputs[b]	–	–	64
Export performance licenses[c]	90	50	59
Pay-as-you-earn[d]	10	40	4
Export bonus vouchers[e]	305	160	488
Total	405	–	677[f]

[a]Calculated on the basis of tax rates in Table 3.2 and the 1966–67 composition of exports.

[b]Rough estimate for West Pakistan during 1966–67 as given by Dr. Azhar, Central Board of Revenue, and estimated from Government of Pakistan, Ministry of Finance, *The Budget: 1967/68* (1967); *The Budget: 1968/69* (1968). A rough breakdown is: customs charge rebates, Rs. 43 million; sales tax rebates, Rs. 20 million; excise tax rebates, Rs. 1 million.

[c]Based on an assumed average premium value over landed cost of 50 percent, and an average tariff of 30 percent. The average premium may be exaggerated; see note (c) to Table 3.2. The figure on licensed imports represents the approximate issuance during 1966–67 for all Pakistan, but only a small proportion went to East Pakistan.

[d]Approximate value of approved PAYE applications actually implemented in a "representative" recent year; see Table 3.4.

[e]Value of bonus vouchers calculated by applying the January 1968 rates to the 1966–67 composition of exports.

[f]This total equaled 79 percent of 1966–67 West Pakistan exports of manufacturers and selected primary goods (bonus voucher exports, that is, since only such exports also benefit from the other incentive schemes), which were valued FOB at Rs. 857 million. In other words, incentive measures added 79 percent to FOB receipts from these selected exports. (The calculations exclude certain mini-benefits of unknown magnitude, such as income tax exemption, tax holidays of limited duration, export credit guarantees, and so forth.)

Table 3.4. Value of pay-as-you-earn applications sanctioned, 1963–1968[a] (in millions of rupees)

Category	West Pakistan	East Pakistan
By industry		
Cotton Textiles	163.7	0.7
Jute Textiles	–	53.1
Other Manufacturing	52.9	2.9
Total	216.6	57.7
By year		
1963	0.8	33.7
1964	4.4	5.1
1965	2.2	3.1
1966	34.3	9.0
1967	154.0	4.8

Source: Data supplied by Investment Promotion and Supplies Department, on a calendar-year basis (mimeo handout).

[a]Implementation has reached less than 20 percent of sanctions (15 or 20 small schemes implemented out of 110 approved plans).

Table 3.5. Average effective subsidy on selected manufactured exports[a] under different profit and value added assumptions

Prices	Base 1 Percent of export value added[b]	Base 2 Percent of export value added plus cost of nontraded inputs[b]
Prices as in 1962–63 input-output table		
Original results[c]	95	59
Original results modified for 1/3 lower profits on export sales than on home sales[d]	122	62
Original results modified for 1/3 higher profits on export sales than on home sales[d]	82	56

Table 3.5. Average effective subsidy on selected manufactured exports[a] under different profit and value added assumptions *(Cont.)*

Prices adjusted for 15 percent increase between 1962–63 and 1967–68, all of which accrues to value added[e]		
Original results[c]	76	55
Original results modified for 1/3 lower profits on export sales than on home sales[d]	86	58
Original results modified for 1/3 higher profits on export sales than on home sales[d]	69	53

Source: Tables 3.1 and 3.2, and data cited therein.

[a]Weighted average of cotton textiles, other textiles, tanned leather and leather goods, metal goods, and cement, using 1967–68 FOB exports as weights. See Table 3.1.

[b]The bases refer to export value added because, with assumed different profit rates on foreign and domestic sales, export value added differs from home value added. See Equation (4) and Appendix B.

[c]In these calculations, each element of the effective subsidy formula (Equation 4) was weighted separately, and the elements were recombined to obtain the weighted rate.

[d]Assuming an average gross profit equal to 25 percent of the sales price, a 1/3 change in the profit rate means an 8 1/3 percent changes in the sales price.

[e]A 15 percent increase in the price of manufactured goods cannot accrue *entirely* to value added, since some manufactured goods are used as inputs for other manufactured goods. However, the point of the calculations is to illustrate the impact of a big change in value added relationships, a change which could also be attributed to understated profits or overstated interindustry inputs.

Table 3.6. Marginal ratios between domestic resource plus political costs and foreign earnings[a]

Sector number	Sector	Assumed elasticity of foreign demand	Case 1: Marginal ratio when windfall gains to agriculture are not viewed as a political cost	Case 1: Implied marginal resource cost of foreign exchange (Rs. per $1.00)[b]	Case 2: Marginal ratio when ½ of windfall gains to agriculture are viewed as a political cost and elasticity of home supply is 0.5[c]	Case 2: Implied marginal resource plus political cost of foreign exchange (Rs. per $1.00)[b]	Case 3: Marginal ratio when ½ of windfall gains to agriculture are viewed as a political cost and elasticity of home supply is 0.2[c]	Case 3: Implied marginal resource plus political cost of foreign exchange (Rs. per $1.00)[b]
West Pakistan exports								
1	Rice[d] (basmati)	10	1.08	5.1	2.47	11.6	4.50	21.4
4	Cotton	10	1.07	5.1	2.57	12.2	4.81	22.8
11	Cotton textiles	5	e	e	-	-	-	-
15	Leather, leather products[f]	5	7.36	35.0	-	-	-	-
22	Machinery	5	4.41	20.9	-	-	-	-
28	Miscellaneous manufactures	5	3.80	18.1	-	-	-	-
East Pakistan exports								
3	Jute	2	2.09	9.9	4.37	20.8	7.77	36.9
12	Jute manufactures	3	5.83	27.7	-	-	-	-

[a]Based on Equation (5) (as further explained in Appendix B), parameters in Table 3.2, and parameters set forth in the chapter. If nontraded inputs had been excluded from costs and earnings, the net marginal costs per net unit of foreign exchange earnings from industrial exports would be very much higher.

[b]Found by multiplying the ratio by Rs. 4.75, the official exchange rate per $1.00.

[c]These calculations are relevant for primary goods only. For industrial goods it is assumed that windfall gains have no political cost.

[d]No allowance is made for the government procurement of basmati rice at less than FOB export prices, a practice abandoned in 1968.

[e]Data indicate negative net foreign exchange earnings; hence, indefinitely high resource costs per net marginal dollar of foreign exchange.

[f]In these calculations it is assumed that inputs of unfinished leather to the finished leather goods sector take largely the form of hides and skins, the internal prices of which are the same as the international prices.

Table 3.7. Estimated effects of an incremental dollar of imported raw materials on industrial production in selected sectors

Sector number	Sector	Value of traded inputs including depreciation on machinery and equipment, per unit of output[a] (1)	Implied value of extra industrial output per incremental dollar of imports[b] (Rs.) (2)	Indirect taxes per unit of output[c] (3)	Employment costs per unit of output[d] (4)	Gross profits per unit of output[d] (5)
8	Edible oils	0.450	10.6	0.195	0.128	0.227
10	Other food and drink	0.200	23.8	0.100	0.203	0.497
13	Other textiles	0.272	17.5	0.057	0.317	0.354
14	Paper and printing	0.291	16.3	0.029	0.207	0.473
16	Rubber, rubber products	0.303	15.7	0.167	0.120	0.410
18	Other chemicals	0.273	17.4	0.081	0.111	0.535
21	Metal products	0.311	15.3	0.061	0.245	0.383
22	Machinery	0.347	13.7	0.095	0.189	0.369
23	Transport equipment	0.530	9.0	0.123	0.110	0.237
28	Miscellaneous manufacturing	0.332	14.3	0.073	0.244	0.351
29	Coal, petroleum products	0.215	22.1	0.562	0.023	0.200

[a]The proportions per unit of output reflect the rupee cost of imports (at world prices) per rupee of output (valued at domestic prices). These coefficients are based on the RKM input-output table, adjusted to world price levels as explained in Appendix B.

[b]Reciprocal of column (1), times Rs. 4.75, the official exchange rate.

[c]Indirect taxes on output, expressed in terms of tax rate on gross sales price including taxes (as given in Table 3.2), plus 10 percent of the value of traded inputs for taxes paid on purchases from other sectors.

[d]Estimated from data in the Government of West Pakistan, Bureau of Statistics, *West Pakistan Census of Manufacturing Industries: 1964–65* (provisional, November 1967), on the assumption that the excess cost of traded inputs above world prices is divided between employment cost and gross profits in the same ratio as value added on output.

Table 3.8. Administration of export incentive schemes

Scheme	Policy agency	Approximate number of officers involved	Ad hoc or schedule	Executive agency
Tax and tariff rebates	Central Board of Revenue—customs sales, and excise tax divisions	20	Ad hoc[a]	Central Board of Revenue—customs, sales and excise tax divisions
Export performance licenses	Export Promotion Bureau and Chief Controller of Imports and Exports	20 20	Ad hoc and schedule[b]	Chief Controller of Imports and Exports
Pay-as-you-earn	Investment Promotion and Supplies Department and Central Investment Coordination Committee	10	Ad hoc	State Bank of Pakistan
Export bonus	Planning Commission and Ministry of Commerce	10	Schedule	State Bank of Pakistan

Source: Based on information from telephone conversations and correspondence.

[a]Upon application, a determination (requiring about six months per product) is made of the customs duties, sales, and excise taxes paid on the exporter's direct inputs. For certain very standard commodities, a uniform rebate rate is applied. For others, the ultimate determination may differ from exporter to exporter.

[b]The last export performance licensing list enumerated 143 commodities. These were not keyed to any standard classification, and many exporters had to negotiate their standing with the Export Promotion Bureau and the Chief Controller. (The scheme was abolished in early 1970.)

Appendix B

Effective Protection and Taxation Concepts and Domestic Cost of Foreign Exchange Savings and Earnings

General Notes

1. A unit of output, unless otherwise specified, is defined in terms of prices ruling on the domestic market, inclusive of indirect taxes and subsidies.
2. All prices are expressed in terms of the domestic currency unit.
3. Fixed coefficients are assumed to characterize the economic structure. If instead substitution prevails, then a distinction must be drawn between effective protection/taxation measured *before* and *after* resources move in response to policy. Furthermore, the effective protection and taxation concepts must be modified to reflect the substitution elasticities. See Naya and Anderson, "Substitution and Two Concepts of Effective Rate of Protection" American Economic Review, 59 (September 1969).
4. The value added expressions and their associated marginal cost, taxation, and protection concepts, may be defined in the following alternative ways (or combinations thereof): (a) to include the cost of nontraded inputs, on the argument that these have no foreign exchange potential; (b) to exclude depreciation charges on plant and equipment; (c) to include a factor multiplication correction for currency overvaluation.

Glossary of Parameters and Variables

${}_mP_{hi}$, ${}_xP_{hi}$ = home price of "importable" product i (${}_mP_{hi}$) or home price of "exportable" product i (${}_xP_{hi}$), inclusive of indirect taxes and subsidies.

${}_mP_{fi}$, ${}_xP_{fi}$ = foreign CIF price of "importable" product i, or foreign FOB price of "exportable" product i.

t_i = customs duties on product i (tariffs, sales taxes, and other charges levied against imports) expressed as a percentage of CIF price. In Pakistan, the sales tax is levied on both imported and domestically produced goods. Since the September 1965 war, both ordinary tariffs and the sales tax have been augmented by a 25 percent "defense surcharge." In 1968 a further surcharge of 10 percent was levied on imports of capital goods.

${}_he_i$, ${}_xe_i$ = excise, sales, and other indirect taxes imposed on domestic output of product i sold at home (${}_he_i$) or abroad (${}_xe_i$), expressed as a percentage of the domestic price net of taxes and subsidies (in the case of ${}_he_i$), or as a percentage of the FOB export price (in the case of ${}_xe_i$). If more than one tax is imposed, the taxes are added together to obtain ${}_he_i$ or ${}_xe_i$.

${}_hs_i$, ${}_xs_i$ = subsidies given on domestic output of product i sold at home (${}_hs_i$) or abroad (${}_xs_i$), expressed as a percentage of the domestic price net of taxes and subsidies (in the case of ${}_hs_i$) or as a percentage of the FOB export price (in the case of ${}_xs_i$). If more than one subsidy is awarded, the subsidies are added together to obtain ${}_hs_i$ or ${}_xs_i$.

p_i = scarcity premium on imports of product i, expressed as a percentage of landed cost (CIF price plus customs charges). Scarcity premiums will accrue to license holders, to the government through an auction system, or to exporters through a bonus voucher system. The premium will be negative in the case of redundant tariffs, that is, tariffs which afford less protection than their nominal level would indicate, owing either to domestic competition or to subsidies on domestic output.

c_i = freight and insurance charges as a percent of the FOB price of product i.

a_{im} = purchases by industry i from industry m, per unit of output by industry i, where the products of industry m are "importable" traded goods.

a_{ix} = purchases by industry i from industry x, per unit of output by industry i, where the products of industry x are "exportable" traded goods.

a_{in} = purchases by industry i from industry n, per unit of output by industry i, where the products of industry n are "nontraded" goods or services.

a'_{im}, a'_{ix}, a'_{in} = a_{im}, a_{ix}, and a_{in}, respectively, except that the coefficients are adjusted to reflect substitution induced by tariffs and subsidies.

da_{im}, da_{ix}, da_{in} = $(a'_{im} - a_{im})$, $(a'_{ix} - a_{ix})$, and $(a'_{in} - a_{in})$, respectively.

ϵ_{fi} = elasticity of foreign demand for commodity i.

δ_i = portion of windfall gains on premarginal output viewed as a political "cost," e.g., 0 percent, 50 percent, 100 percent.

η_{hi}, η_{fi} = elasticity of home supply (η_{hi}) or foreign supply (η_{fi}) of commodity i.

${}_hV_i, {}_xV_i$ = value added per unit of output sold at home (${}_hV_i$) or abroad (${}_xV_i$) by industry i.

${}_mW_i, {}_xW_i$ = value added, at world prices for inputs and output, per unit of output sold at home by "importable" industry i (${}_mW_i$), or sold abroad by "exportable" industry i (${}_xW_i$).

${}_mMR_i, {}_xMR_i$ = net marginal foreign exchange saved (${}_mMR_i$) or earned (${}_xMR_i$) by producing an extra unit of import substitute commodity i or export commodity i at home, after deducting the cost, at world prices, of inputs purchased from other sectors.

${}_mMC_i, {}_xMC_i$ = net marginal domestic resource plus political "cost" of producing an extra unit of import substitute commodity i (${}_mMC_i$) or export commodity i (${}_xMC_i$) at home after deducting the cost, at domestic prices, of inputs purchased from other sectors. ${}_mMC_i$ and ${}_xMC_i$ thus represent value added plus some portion of windfall gains on pre-marginal units. Value added is assumed here to represent resource cost, although some authors have corrected for the rental element in industrial profits (e.g., M. Bruno, "The Optimal Selection of Export-Promoting and Import-Substituting Projects," in United Nations, *Planning the External Sector: Techniques, Problems, and Policies,* Report on the First International Seminar on Development Planning [New York: 1967]).

${}_mR_i, {}_xR_i$ = ratio between marginal domestic resource plus political cost and marginal foreign exchange savings (${}_mR_i$) or marginal foreign exchange earnings (${}_xR_i$) on production of one additional unit, defined in terms of domestic prices, of import substitute or export commodity i, when costs are defined in terms of value added at home prices within industry i itself plus some portion of windfall gains, and savings/earnings are defined in terms of value added at world prices within industry i itself.

Assumed Price Relationships

$$ {}_mP_{hi} = {}_mP_{fi}(1 + t_i)(1 + p_i). $$

The left side represents the home price, and the right side represents the landed cost plus scarcity premium on competitive imports. ${}_mP_{hi}$, when divided by $(1 + {}_he_i)(1 - {}_hs_i)$ represents the resource cost of an extra unit of output, neglecting taxes and subsidies on inputs.

$${}_xP_{hi}/(1 + {}_he_i)(1 - {}_hs_i) = {}_xP_{fi}(1 - {}_xe_i)(1 + {}_xs_i).$$

The left side represents the producer's net receipts from home sales, and the right side represents the producer's net receipts from export sales ("net" means exclusive of taxes and inclusive of subsidies). The left side represents the resource cost of an extra unit of output, neglecting taxes and subsidies on inputs.

$${}_mP_{fi} = (1 + c_i)\,{}_xP_{fi}.$$

The CIF import price equals the FOB export price plus freight and insurance charges.

Definitional Relationships

1. Units of output are so defined that ${}_mP_{hi} = 1$, and ${}_xP_{hi} = 1$.
2. In the definitions of MR_i and MC_i it is assumed that all inputs are perfectly elastic in supply.
3. For convenience, the following shorthand notation is used:

$$(1 + \lambda_i) = (1 + t_i)(1 + p_i).$$

$$(1 + \phi_i) = (1 + {}_he_i)(1 - {}_hs_i).$$

$$(1 + \theta_i) = (1 + {}_he_i)(1 - {}_hs_i)(1 - {}_xe_i)(1 + {}_xs_i).$$

$${}_hV_i = {}_xV_i = \frac{1}{(1 + \phi_i)} - \sum_m a_{im} - \sum_x a_{ix} - \sum_n a_{in}.$$

$${}_mW_i = \frac{1}{(1 + \lambda_i)} - \sum_m \frac{a_{im}}{(1 + \lambda_m)} - \sum_x \frac{a_{ix}}{(1 + \theta_x)} - \sum_n a_{in}.$$

$${}_xW_i = \frac{1}{(1 + \theta_i)} - \sum_m \frac{a_{im}}{(1 + \lambda_m)} - \sum_x \frac{a_{ix}}{(1 + \theta_x)} - \sum_n a_{in}.$$

$${}_mMR_i = \frac{\left(1 + \frac{1}{\eta_{fi}}\right)}{(1 + \lambda_i)} - \sum_m \frac{a_{im}}{(1 + \lambda_m)} - \sum_x \frac{a_{ix}}{(1 + \theta_x)} - \sum_n a_{in}.$$

$$_xMR_i = \frac{\left(1 + \frac{1}{\epsilon_{fi}}\right)}{(1 + \theta_i)} - \sum_m \frac{a_{im}}{(1 + \lambda_m)} - \sum_x \frac{a_{ix}}{(1 + \theta_x)} - \sum_n a_{in}.$$

$$_mMC_i = {}_xMC_i = \frac{(1 + \delta_i/\eta_{hi})}{(1 + \theta_i)} - \sum_m a_{im} - \sum_x a_{ix} - \sum_n a_{in}.$$

Effective Protection and Taxation Formulas

Notes: Additional formulas may be found by combining the features of the enumerated concepts. Rates of protection or taxation may alternatively be expressed as percentages of value added at world prices, but when value added at world prices is negative, problems of interpretation arise. Rates here are expressed as a percentage of value added on home sales. By virtue of the assumed price relationships, this is the same as value added on export sales. If profits on exports are higher or lower than profits on home sales, then effective taxation should be expressed as a percentage of export value added.

Protection	*Taxation*
$U_i = \frac{{}_hV_i - {}_mW_i}{{}_hV_i}.$	$T_i = \frac{{}_xW_i - {}_xV_i}{{}_hV_i}.$

U_i and T_i show the percentage increase and decrease in domestic value added resulting from the operation of the tariff-licensing-tax-subsidy system.

Sample Calculation of Effective Taxation of Exports

Consider an imaginary manufactured good, widgets. The relevant parameters are given as follows.

Export performance license value is 7 percent of FOB export price of widgets.

Bonus voucher value is 48 percent of FOB export price of widgets.

No other export incentives are given and there are no indirect taxes on widget exports.

Therefore, for widget exports, $_xs_i = 7\% + 48\% = 55\%$.

The indirect tax on domestic widget sales, $_he_i$, is 5 percent.

The input coefficient for importable goods used in widget manufacture, a_{im}, expressed as a proportion of the domestic sales price of one widget, is 0.300.

The tariff, t_m, on importable inputs used in widget manufacture is 30 percent of the CIF price.

The scarcity premium, p_m, on importable inputs used in widget manufacture is 35 percent of the landed cost, that is, CIF price plus tariff.

The input coefficient for exportable goods used in widget manufacture, a_{ix}, expressed as a proportion of the domestic sales price of one widget is 0.200.

The domestic indirect tax, ${}_he_x$, on exportable goods used in widget manufacture is 15 percent.

The export subsidy, ${}_xs_x$, on exportable goods used in widget manufacture is 25 percent.

There are no other taxes or subsidies on the exportable inputs.

The input coefficient for nontraded goods used in widget manufacture, a_{in}, expressed as a proportion of the domestic sales price of one widget, is 0.100.

With these parameters, the following values result.

$$ {}_xW_i = \frac{1}{(1+0.05)(1+0.55)} - \frac{0.300}{(1+0.30)(1+0.35)} - \frac{0.200}{(1+0.15)(1+0.25)} - 0.100 = 0.204. $$

$$ {}_hV_i = {}_xV_i = \frac{1}{(1+0.05)} - 0.300 - 0.200 - 0.100 = 0.352. $$

$$ T_i = \frac{0.204 - 0.352}{0.352} = -42\%. $$

In other words, there is a subsidy of 42 percent on value added.

Domestic Resource and Political Cost of Foreign Exchange Savings and Earnings

Savings	*Earnings*
${}_mR_i = \frac{{}_mMC_i}{{}_mMR_i}$.	${}_xR_i = \frac{{}_xMC_i}{{}_xMR_i}$.

${}_mR_i$ and ${}_xR_i$ show the net marginal domestic resource plus political cost per net marginal unit of foreign exchange saved or earned. Costs and savings or earnings are both defined net of all purchased inputs; and purchased inputs are assumed to be perfectly elastic in supply.

Sample Calculation of Domestic Resource and Political Cost of Foreign Exchange Earned

Continue the widget example. In addition to the parameters already given, the following parameters also apply.

The elasticity of foreign demand, ϵ_{fi}, is 5.0.

The elasticity of home supply, η_{hi}, is 0.5.

The proportion of windfall income transfers to the widget manufacturers considered a political cost, δ_i, is 20 percent.

With these parameters, the following values result when nontraded inputs are treated as part of the net resource cost.

$$ {}_xMR_i = \frac{(1 - 1/5)}{(1 + 0.05)(1 + 0.55)} - \frac{0.300}{(1 + 0.30)(1 + 0.35)} - \frac{0.200}{(1 + 0.15)(1 + 0.25)} = 0.181. $$

$$ {}_xMC_i = \frac{(1 + 0.20/0.5)}{(1 + 0.05)} - 0.300 - 0.200 = 0.833. $$

$$ {}_xR_i = \frac{0.833}{0.181} = 4.6. $$

In other words, the net resource plus political cost of a marginal dollar of foreign exchange, counting nontraded inputs as part of the net resource cost, is 4.6 times the official exchange rate.

Equivalence of Effective Protection/Taxation and Domestic Resource Cost of Foreign Exchange Saved/Earned

When $\epsilon_{fi} = \infty$, $\eta_{fi} = \infty$, and either $\delta_i = 0$ or $\eta_{hi} = \infty$, then the following equivalences hold between the effective protection/taxation formulas and the domestic resource cost of foreign exchange saved/earned formulas cited above. The equivalences follow from the definitions of U, T, and R.

1. $U_i = 1 - \dfrac{1}{{}_mR_i}$.

2. $T_i = \dfrac{1}{{}_xR_i} - 1$.

Appendix C

Administrative Simplification

Pakistan's export incentive system is praised for its ingenuity and criticized for its complexity. Could a simpler system provide the same stimulus to export sales? This question has more relevance to countries just embarking on export promotion than to Pakistan. Once a complicated scheme, requiring constant administrative judgment, has been set in motion, its continuance is ensured by all the forces of bureaucratic self-preservation. This was as true of eighteenth-century England as it is of developing countries today. The early English excise schedule had as many as fourteen different levies applied to a single commodity, and each was computed separately![59] Simplification might eliminate precious "white collar" jobs; even worse, it might deprive agencies of their accustomed perquisites.

From the Pakistan exporters' viewpoint, perhaps the two most frustrating aspects are the number of agencies dispensing benefits and the ad hoc way those benfits are computed. Table 3.8, Appendix A, summarizes the administrative mechanism, apart from the mini-policies. Pay-as-you-earn is completely unsystematic. Export performance licenses and tax rebates are moving slowly toward a schedular approach.

The prevailing ad hoc administration of the minor schemes means that the exporter must visit at least five agencies to collect his full benefits. The impact of any subsidy program depends not only on its size but also on its direct and certain connection with performance. An ad hoc approach may in some cases achieve exquisite justice. In most instances it only dilutes the impact.

It would be better to put all schemes on a schedular basis, keyed to the commodity classification of exports, and to centralize their administration. In fact, the entire range of Pakistan's incentives could be disbursed against export shipping bills. The authorities need only cross-check shipping bills against actual export receipts and take pains to ensure an honest commodity classification of exports. The honest commodity classification is important because, as discrimination between exports becomes greater, the likelihood of bogus exports becomes more acute. During 1967, for example, "exports" of artificial silk enjoyed a minor boom: the cumulative force of different incentive schemes resulted in an export exchange rate higher than the black market rate.

Export performance licensing and pay-as-you-earn could be merged into the bonus voucher scheme. Indeed, in early 1970—some two years after this paper was written—the export performance licensing system

59. E. E. Noan, *The Organization of the English Customs Service, 1696–1786* (London: David and Charles, 1968).

was abolished and more liberal bonus voucher rates were awarded. The same type of consolidation could apply to the profit tax exemption, tax holidays, and other mini-policies.

These suggestions, however, should not obscure the genius in Pakistan's export promotion system. The bonus voucher scheme by itself represents a triumph of social engineering. In combination, bonus vouchers and minor incentives have kept continuous pace with changing internal and external circumstances. They achieve much the same goal as flexible exchange rates, without drawing the same opposition.

Moreover, all of Pakistan's measures are refreshingly indirect. They rely on the marketplace carrot, not the administrative stick. Any number of planners could be found who would gladly prescribe, in great detail, Pakistan's export composition for 1980. Instead of heeding such soothsayers, the government wisely allows scope and incentive for "improbable" exports such as cement and machinery. Broadly speaking, if a firm can develop export sales, it gains access to bank credit, capital equipment, and raw materials. Only moderate efforts are made to "push" export sales by allocating scarce resources to this or that "promising" industry ahead of performance. The indirect, post-performance approach is a cardinal virtue of the Pakistan system.

4 An Electric Power System Planning Model for West Pakistan

Henry D. Jacoby

One of the continuing problems in a growing economy is the selection, design, and scheduling of new sources of electricity supply. Those responsible for planning electric power are faced constantly with new choices among equipment of differing technologies and varying degrees of capital intensity—gas turbine, conventional steam, nuclear, and hydroelectric sources, for example—and with decisions regarding project scale and operating policy. The planning task becomes more complex as demand increases and markets expand and merge with one another. The operating characteristics of potential projects (and, therefore, their relative economic attractiveness) become more difficult to separate from the management of the network as a whole. In addition, the operation of the electric power system may be interrelated with the management of other parts of the economy. For example, a choice between hydro and thermal power may imply adjustments in the development of hydrocarbon fuel resources or in the rate of expansion of irrigated agriculture.

The planning of the electric power system of West Pakistan requires consideration of a wide range of these interdependencies. The planning model presented below was designed to assist with major investment and operating decisions in this situation. The model is a digital computer simulation of the long-run capacity expansion and short-run operation of the West Pakistan system: at its current stage of development it is used

NOTE: Early stages of research on this subject were conducted in connection with a Harvard Development Advisory Service team working with the Argentine National Development Council. Subsequent formulation of the planning model and development of computer programs took place under the auspices of the Harvard Water Program and with the assistance of Resources for the Future, Inc.

Special thanks are due to Robert Sadove and Christopher Willoughby of the World Bank staff. The model underwent considerable refinement in the course of the Pakistan application, and many of its better features are the result of their suggestions.

primarily to evaluate alternative investments in power generation and EHV (Extra-High Voltage) transmission.

The simulation analysis was undertaken as part of an overall study of the Indus Basin conducted by the World Bank in its capacity as administrator of the Indus Basin Special Fund.[1] The model was used as an aid to the evaluation of an agriculture and power development program prepared by the Bank's engineering consultants. This paper is concerned with the power problems of West Pakistan and with the choices that were faced in the Indus studies: the discussion begins with a description of the power system and closes with a sample of results from the analyses that were carried out. There is, however, another purpose of this presentation: to describe the way this type of simulation analysis is constructed and to argue the advantages of its use. The link between the problem and the results, then, is a summary of the technique of analysis that was applied.

The West Pakistan Power System

Some of the factors involved in planning the West Pakistan power network can be seen with reference to Figure 4.1. The largest power market is located in the agricultural region of the Punjab in the northern part of the province, the market being tied together by an EHV transmission loop. There are several major cities in the region, and there is a growing use of electric power for agricultural pumping. The hydroelectric power potential of the Province is also found in this zone, and at present the northern grid is fed by several hydro developments in addition to a number of thermal units. Most of the existing and potential hydro projects have two functions: provision of electric power, and surface storage of irrigation water. This power network is under the management of the West Pakistan Water and Power Development Authority (WPWAPDA).

The second power market of the province is located around the rapidly growing city of Karachi and nearby Hyderabad. Karachi is served by the Karachi Electric Service Company (KESC), a stock company in which the government holds a controlling interest. The supply system is composed of conventional thermal units at present, although a nuclear installation is anticipated in the early 1970's. Furthermore, if the two major markets were interconnected, the Karachi-Hyderabad system could utilize surplus hydro energy which is available in the north in months of high river flow.

1. Most of the World Bank's final report on this study as been published as P. Lieftinck, R. Sadove, and T. Creyke, *Water and Power Resources of West Pakistan: A Study in Sector Planning,* 3 vols. (Baltimore: Johns Hopkins Press, 1968).

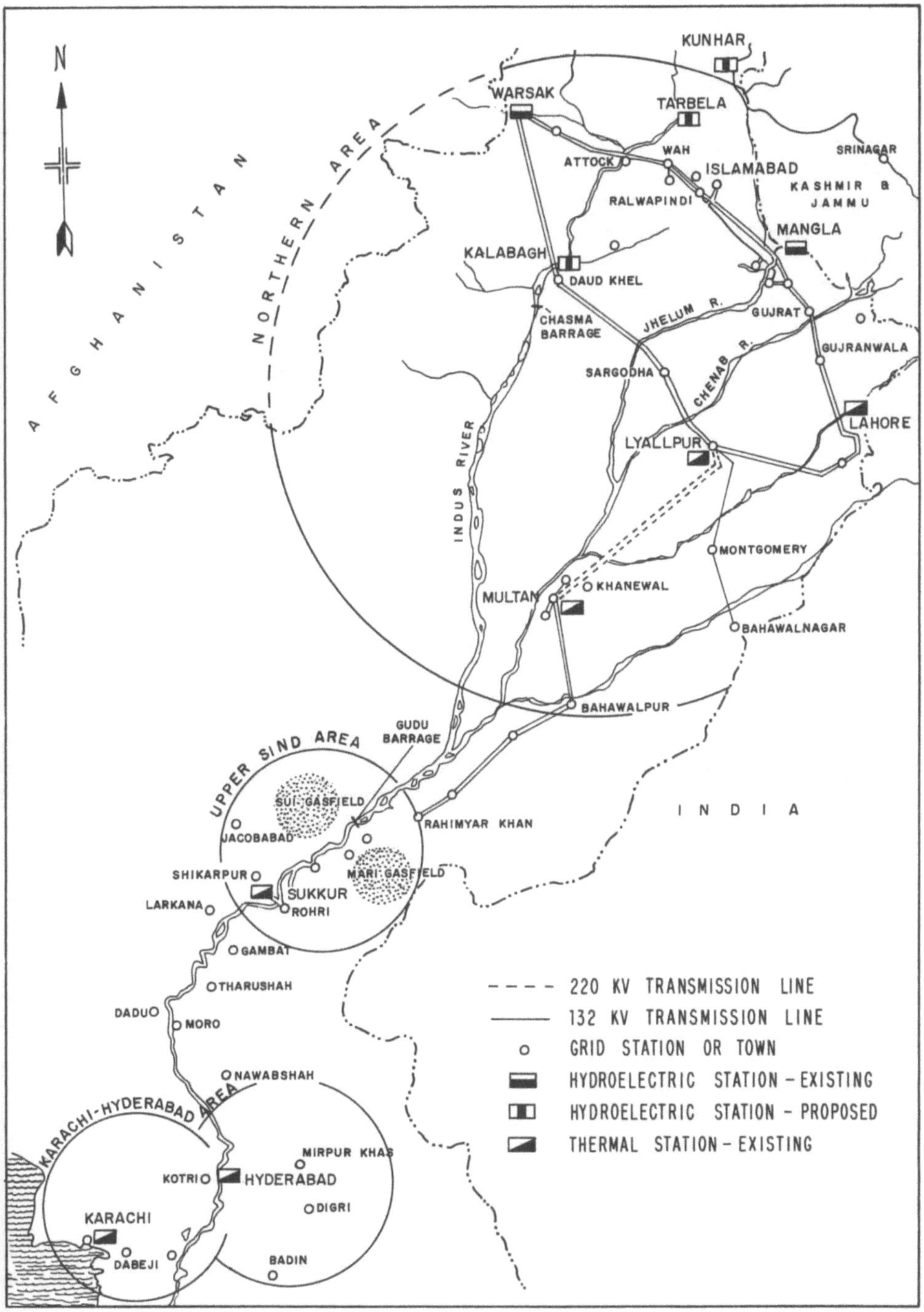

Figure 4.1. Major power stations and transmission lines in West Pakistan

A third area of interest is the Upper Sind, roughly halfway between the two major markets in the region. Pakistan's principal gas reserves lie in this area. There are two major fields, one on each side of the Indus River. On the western side is the Sui gas field. The gas in this region is of high quality, and is transported by pipeline both to Karachi and to the north. The Sui transmission to Karachi serves industrial and domestic demand, and the gas is burned in several of the newer thermal-electric power plants. Sui gas is also used in northern thermal plants. On the eastern side of the river lies the Mari gas reserve. Because the quality of this gas is low, to date it has been judged economically infeasible to transport it by pipeline to either of the major markets. It has been suggested, however, that thermal-electric generating stations might be constructed directly on top of the gas fields and the electric power itself transmitted to the south or north.

There are many different ways in which the future development of the power system can proceed; all of them, however, are closely interrelated with the management of irrigated agriculture. The most critical choice is among alternative multipurpose hydroelectric and irrigation developments in the north. There are a number of alternative sites for water control structures. For some the ultimate project scale has been fixed by previous design studies; for others the question of size remains open. Which projects should be built; and when? Each permutation of choices has an effect on the agricultural sector in that different amounts of irrigation water become available at different times. The purpose of the power analysis is to determine the effect of these various decisions upon the cost of the electric power supply of the province—the choice of sites and construction dates of big dams being the primary link between the agricultural and power aspects of the overall development program.

A second, related decision concerns the operating policy to be followed at several of the existing and potential hydro installations. In many analyses of these types of projects, irrigation is given first priority: operation studies of proposed new dams assure that water will be released in the manner most advantageous to the agricultural sector. This may mean that reservoir levels are drawn down to such an extent that power potential is severely curtailed. In addition, strict limits are often placed upon variation in the flow from dams over the course of a day, thus restricting the use of hydro energy for peak-load service. There are good reasons for such limits: surges in river flow can lead to problems with irrigation control structures and can cause scouring of canal bottoms. But what is the opportunity cost of such operating assumptions? One needs to know how the potential loss in agricultural output due to a revision in operating policy compares with the potential saving in electric power system cost.

Another decision concerns the long-distance transmission link between the northern and southern markets, or between either of these markets and the Mari generating site. When do the various stages of interconnection become economical, and how big should the transmission system be? It might be best, for example, to provide for the shipment of cheap Mari energy to either the north or the south, but not to invest in a complete north-south link. Alternatively, it might be preferable to build the full interconnection, so that excess hydro energy in months of high river flow could be transmitted to the south, and the low-cost Mari thermal power could be used not only to supply the south but also to firm up the northern market supply in dry months. The value of such an interconnection depends on the amount of excess hydro energy and on the ability of the southern market to utilize this energy. Looked at from another standpoint, the relative attractiveness of certain hydro developments depends on the availability of a link to the southern market for their output.

The proposed construction of a large thermal station at the Mari gas field presents another complex decision problem. The economics of the Mari development are inseparable from decisions about hydroelectric installation and operation and from plans for intermarket transmission. The relative prices chosen for Mari and Sui gas are also of critical importance to this problem. Finally—in addition to the major decisions regarding hydroelectric development, market interconnection, and utilization of natural gas resources—a number of choices must be made among alternative nuclear and conventional thermal installations in the two major centers of consumption. These choices, too, are influenced by developments elsewhere in the system: for example, the relative attractiveness of nuclear power for the southern market is greatly affected by the quantity of surplus hydro energy available from the north.

These various questions cannot be analyzed separately. The essence of this kind of problem is that interactions between different system elements weigh heavily in the evaluation of any individual subdivision of the whole. Well-developed conventional approaches to this type of planning problem do exist. An experienced engineer can, through a judicious combination of partial analyses, construct an accurate picture of the character of the overall system and of the relative attractiveness of individual investments. Partial analyses of this type can be quite satisfactory when the system is neither too large nor too tightly knit, and when critical economic parameters and system operating procedures are reasonably well fixed. But in a rapidly changing economy like that of Pakistan, critical input data—for example, market demand projections, design and operating policies of hydro developments, discount rates, and estimates of the opportunity costs of foreign exchange and domestic fuel reserves—are subject to change. In these circumstances the task of evaluating system investment by conventional partial methods becomes very difficult and time-consuming, and the engineering talent required for a thorough analysis of alternatives is often unavailable. It is at this point that a mathematical model of the power system can be useful.

The Power System Simulation Model

As noted above, the planning model developed for this study involves the use of digital computer simulation in analyzing potential investment in generation facilities in each of the three electric power markets and in evaluating EHV transmission connections among them. Instead of conducting a separate study of each new project, effort is directed toward an evaluation of alternative system investment plans or power development programs.

The analysis begins with a projection of electric power demand in each of the markets to be considered. Information is required on the output capacity, thermal efficiency, and fuel cost appropriate to each existing or potential nuclear- and thermal-electric facility, and also on the maintenance and operation (M & O) expense associated with the unit. For potential new plants, estimates of capital cost are required. Similarly, the capital and M & O costs of existing and potential hydroelectric developments and the monthly patterns of capacity and energy output are needed. Since the monthly availability of energy and capacility from a hydroelectric project depends on the size of the dam and on the reservoir operation policy followed, a separate project must be defined for each combination of physical design and water release schedule that is evaluated. In the Pakistan application these data are the result of separate simulation analyses of the operation of the dams themselves. For proposed intermarket connections, the analysis uses data on the carrying capacities of transmission lines and, again, appropriate cost information. Finally, the model requires ranges of values for economic parameters such as discount rates, foreign exchange rates, and opportunity costs of capital.

Alternative power programs are defined that are "equivalent" in that each will meet projected demand growth with an acceptable standard of service quality as evidenced by the maintenance of a certain quantity of "technical reserve." The evaluation of each plan is accomplished by a two-part procedure: (1) a detailed simulation of system expansion and operation over the planning period (twenty years in the West Pakistan study); and (2) an adjustment for the impact of different investment programs on system cost in the years beyond the planning horizon through the use of a "terminal correction."

As emphasized earlier, there is a strong interdependence among the various units that are part of the system at any point in time. In order to represent the essential operating characteristics of the system as they influence total fuel cost, the model simulates the monthly, daily, and hourly scheduling of production by different generating units and of power shipments over the intermarket transmission lines. This model of system energy scheduling is used to calculate the fuel costs incurred in each month of the planning period. These data are then combined with the capital and M & O expenditures implied by a particular investment schedule to produce a figure for the present value of total system supply cost over the period of analysis.

At the end of the plan period a collection of assets is passed on beyond the planning horizon. The form of the final asset structure differs according to the particular pattern of development followed, and this difference is reflected in a variation in the cost of meeting system power demand in the future. The second part of the analysis, therefore, involves the approximation of the economic effects of differing terminal conditions by a set of simple functions and the adjustment of the computer results to account for these effects.

Once the model has been formulated and programmed and the input data prepared, it is relatively easy to analyze a large number of alternative investment schemes. Each simulation analysis can provide a full range of information for sensitivity testing of critical assumptions, and the model can be updated to take account of new decisions and changing conditions so that it becomes a permanent part of the system planning procedure.

Defining Equivalent Alternative Systems

The projection of system power demand is exogenous to the model, and the alternative investment plans analyzed are "equivalent" in that each will meet projected demand growth in such a way as to maintain an acceptable standard of service quality. (All valid investment plans must provide sufficient generation and transmission capacity to serve expected market expansion.)[2] Alternative investment plans can be analyzed on the basis of a single projection, in which case it is assumed that investment to serve that particular rate of demand growth is always justified: the amount the consumer is willing to pay for the additional power he demands is assumed to be greater than the cost of supply within the relevant range of equipment, M & O, and fuel costs. Alternatively, it is possible to repeat the analysis using different projections in order to investigate the impact of projection errors or to study policy measures that might be used to restrict or promote demand growth.

In analyzing the West Pakistan system, it is necessary to develop demand projections for each of the three major markets and to design supply systems that can meet these demands. In order to facilitate the exposition of the way "equivalent" alternative plans are defined, however, the formulation of this part of the model is introduced in the context of a single isolated market rather than in terms of the more complex grid. Let the subscript i serve as an annual time index, $i = 1, \ldots, N$, where N is the length of the planning period. And let the subscript t be used as a monthly time index, $t = 1, \ldots, 12$. Because of seasonal variation in demand and in the capability and energy outputs of most hydroelectric projects, the analysis is conducted on a monthly basis. The main element in the demand forecast is a projection of peak loads, P_{it}, for each month of the planning period. Alternative system plans must satisfy this peak demand in every month and still maintain a certain minimum amount of technical reserve.

Suppose there are a number of generating units, $U_j, j = 1, \ldots, J$, that might be in service during some particular year where $j = 1, \ldots, \text{j}$ are the existing and potential thermal and nuclear units and $j = \text{j} + 1, \ldots, J$ are the hydro possibilities. Each thermal or nuclear unit is characterized by the amount of power that it can contribute to the system, Q_j, which is the rated or "nameplate" capacity of the generators less the consumption and losses within the plant itself. For purposes of defining alternative system expansion plans, thermal plant output capability is assumed to be constant over the year. The output characteristics of each hydro plant

2. Intramarket distribution networks are not included in the model as currently constituted. For justification of this emphasis on the suboptimization of investments in generating capacity and intermarket transmission, see H. D. Jacoby, *Analysis of Investment in Electric Power* (Economic Development Report No. 62, Center for International Affairs, Harvard University, Cambridge, January 1967). Another good source is R. Turvey, *Optimal Pricing and Investment in Electricity Supply* (Cambridge: M.I.T. Press, 1968). A useful sample of this type of analysis is provided by H. G. van der Tak, *The Economic Choice Between Hydroelectric and Thermal Power Developments*, World Bank Staff Occasional Paper No. 1 (Baltimore: Johns Hopkins Press, 1966).

are represented by its capacity, Q_{jit}, and the associated energy, H_{jit}, in each month of the planning period.

For each generating unit U_j there is a scale variable, x_{ji}, that is appropriate for each year. The variable x_{ji} is limited to the values zero and one. If plant U_j is in the system in a particular year, then $x_{ji} = 1$; if not, then $x_{ji} = 0$. During any year the system supply structure will be composed of a subset of U_j. Additions to and deletions from system generating capacity are planned under a set of 12N constraints of the following form.

$$(1) \qquad 0 \leqq \delta_{it} = \sum_{j=1}^{\mathrm{j}} \frac{Q_j x_{ji}}{1 + r_1} + \sum_{j=\mathrm{j}+1}^{J} \frac{Q_{jit} x_{ji}}{1 + r_2} - P_{it}.$$

The percentages of technical reserve selected for thermal and hydro units are represented by r_1 and r_2 respectively. The term δ_{it} indicates the system's excess reserve in month t of year i. If it is negative for any month the investment program will be ruled invalid.

All power development programs that meet the capacity constraints of Equation (1) in each month of the planning period are by definition "equivalent" alternatives. Such a program for the development of generating facilities is termed a generation plan, and each plan may be denoted by a matrix of zeros and ones, $X = \|x_{ji}\|; j = 1, \ldots, J; i = 1, \ldots, N$. The particular combination of plants in existence in any year, i, is indicated by the appropriate column vector, $\mathbf{x}_i = [x_{li}, \ldots, x_{Ji}]$.[3]

Total System Cost

Each power development plan that meets the constraints identified in Equation (1) has an associated time pattern of capital costs, M & O expenditures, and fuel consumption. The West Pakistan system has three markets, $k = 1, 2, 3$, and these are considered to be interconnected by one of several different transmission systems, T. The indicator used to compare the relative merits of alternative combinations of generation plan, X, and transmission scheme, T, is the present value of overall total system cost, $G(X, T)$, where

$$\begin{aligned} G(X, T) = &\sum_i \{[1 + \pi]^{-i} [K_i(X, T) + M(x_i, T) + \sum_t \sum_k F_k(x_i, T)]\} \\ (2) \qquad & - (1 + \pi)^{-N} \Gamma(x_N, T); \; i = 1, \ldots, N; \; t = 1, \ldots, 12; \; k = 1, 2, 3. \end{aligned}$$

3. In analyzing the three-market West Pakistan system, trial and error was required to identify a suitable set of alternative plans because of the difficulty of foreseeing how a particular combination of generation and transmission facilities located in different regions will perform when managed as a system.

The first term in $G(X, T)$ is the sum, over the years of the planning period, of the present value (at discount rate π) of the capital, M & O, and fuel costs associated with the particular generation plan. The last term in $G(X, T)$ is the present value of the terminal correction, $\Gamma(x_n, T)$.

The total cost of the power system, represented by Equation (2), is influenced by market demand patterns, plant characteristics, investment decisions, and system short-run operating rules. The computer model is used to simulate the long-run expansion and short-run operation of the power system, and essentially to provide an estimate of the first part of the equation. $K_i(X, T)$ represents the construction cost of new plants, and its value in any year depends on the particular investment plan. $M(x_i, T)$ represents the system maintenance and operation cost, which is a function of the type, size, and age of the facilities in place in any particular year.

The last element of system cost for each year of the planning period is the sum, over all months and over all markets, of the expenditure on fuel in each individual market, $F_k(x_i, T)$. The evaluation of $F_k(x_i, T)$ requires the simulation of system short-run operation. This is the most valuable aspect of the computer model as well as the source of most of its analytical complexity. Because of the interdependence among the generating units in existence at any point in time, estimation of the fuel cost incurred over any interval requires consideration of the particular system operating rules that determine how the different plants are used to meet the total system demand at each instant during the interval. Therefore, it is necessary to simulate the instantaneous, hourly, and daily scheduling or "dispatching" of the component units of the system supply structure.

In evaluating $F_k(x_i, T)$ for purposes of long-run planning, one desires a method of analysis that can represent, without excessive computation expense, system operating characteristics of economic significance. The model should represent system complexity, but only to the level of detail necessary to make wise use of available data and to draw out those characteristics of system short-run operation that have a significant effect on the particular decisions under study. In the model developed for West Pakistan, the system energy calculation is based on a monthly numerical approximation of the results of the optimal dispatching of system units. In effect, for each month the scheduling of production by all generating units within each of the three markets and the operation of intermarket transmission facilities are simulated in order to determine the power contribution of each individual plant and the shipments over each transmission line.[4]

The Terminal Correction

Under alternative development plans, the differential system supply cost during the years following the planning period may be significant. For example, a power program composed primarily of conventional thermal units imposes higher fuel costs on the system in future years than a program including heavy investment in hydroelectric facilities. The full impact of these differences among power programs during the planning period is reflected in the simulation analysis itself; the influence of different programs on succeeding years is represented by a set of simple functions that depend upon the structure of assets passed on beyond the N-year plan horizon into what might be called the "$N+$ period."

The composition of the system at the horizon is represented by x_N, the final column vector of the plan matrix. An attempt is made to isolate those differences in x_N (associated with different plans) that are likely to have significant influence on system cost in the $N+$ period. The differential impact on the more distant future of varying system structures at the plan horizon is then represented by a series of continuous functions that comprise the terminal correction, $\Gamma(x_N, T)$ of Equation (2). If an appropriate correction is not made, this fixed-horizon model biases selection against the introduction of long-lived and capital-intensive alternatives and in favor of the retention of old generating equipment.

In calculating this correction, there is no need to estimate the absolute value of post-horizon cost; what matters for the purpose of comparing alternative plans is the *relative* difference in their influence on future system cost. Therefore, the selection of a zero point for evaluating the terminal correction is arbitrary. Any final asset mix can be nominated as the zero point or "neutral" final system structure. Investment plans that yield a vector x_N which departs from the neutral structure are then rewarded or penalized in accordance with their influence on system expenses in the $N+$ period.

The functional form used to represent these terminal corrections may be described briefly. The symbol t is redefined as a continuous time signature for the $N+$ period, where $t = 0$ at the horizon or end of the planning period. Three elements of system cost may vary according to the

4. Full description of this procedure, which makes extensive use of market integrated load functions, is beyond the scope of this paper. It is presented in Lieftinck, Sadove, and Creyke, *Water and Power Resources of West Pakistan*, vol. III; and the complete derivation of the method is available in Jacoby, *Analysis of Investment in Electric Power*.

inheritance at time $t = 0$. First, system fuel cost, $C_1(t)$, will differ according to the particular combination of units that make up the final system structure. Similarly, system maintenance and operation cost, $C_2(t)$, will be influenced by the size, type, and age of each of the units that is in place at $t = 0$. In any case, the net difference in system M & O and fuel cost, as between two alternative final system structures, is considered to be significant only up to the point $t = \hat{t}$. Finally, a departure from the neutral structure may cause a net difference in capital expenditure to occur at time $t = t^*$, yielding a cost difference, $C_3(t^*)$. Thus the terminal correction associated with each significant deviation from the neutral x_N may be represented by a function[5] of the form

$$(3) \qquad \Gamma(x_N, T) = \int_0^{\hat{t}} [C_1(t) + C_2(t)]e^{-\pi t}\, dt + C_3(t^*)e^{-\pi t^*} .$$

The appropriate values of $C_1(t)$, $C_2(t)$, and $C_3(t^*)$ are determined by separate side calculations, sometimes requiring special runs of the simulation model itself.

No matter how the neutral final system structure is defined, the following differences in alternative power development plans generally require treatment by a function of the form of Equation (3):

1. The construction of different amounts of hydro capacity. Hydro generating equipment not only contributes a low-cost energy source to the future but also has a longer service life than other types of generating equipment.

2. The addition of different amounts of base-load thermal, peaking thermal, and nuclear capacity—resulting in differential patterns of future system energy cost.

3. The retirement of different combinations of old units, a difference that will affect all three of the component parts of Equation (3).

4. The existence of different amounts of excess reserve capacity at the end of the plan period—an inevitable result of planning the installation of generating units of discrete size.

5. The reader familiar with conventional methods of analysis of power projects (where the value of a hydro plant is defined in terms of an alternative thermal unit generating an equivalent amount of energy), will recognize that many project studies consist essentially of a function of this type defined at the *beginning* of the planning period. See, for example, U.S. Federal Power Commission, *Hydroelectric Power Evaluation* (Washington: U.S. Government Printing Office, March 1968). For further details of the procedure used in connection with this simulation approach, see Jacoby, *Analysis of Investment in Electric Power.*

Results for the West Pakistan System

In applying the model to the West Pakistan system many alternatives were studied. Approximately fifty system investment programs were considered. In evaluating them, about fifteen different intermarket transmission systems were analyzed, and over fifty existing and potential thermal units were considered. There were six hydro sites under consideration, but study of the various plant sizes, operating policies, and construction schedules involved the definition of over forty distinct hydro "plants" as described above. Most of the analysis was conducted under one basic demand projection, although, toward the end of the study, some of the major decisions were tested using variations in this forecast.

The application of the model to such a complex system required a multistage process. At the outset a wide variety of plans was defined and simulated. After analysis of the results presented by the model, it was possible to reject some plans and to drop certain major projects from further consideration. The early computations suggested refinements in the better development programs and indicated the potential attractiveness of completely different combinations of units. New plant and transmission systems were introduced, and new and revised plans were defined and evaluated. In the course of the study, this procedure was repeated several times.

As noted earlier, a number of planning problems were analyzed with the model. The results obtained from the application of the model to these problems are too extensive to be presented in detail here. Instead, three examples are given to demonstrate the application of the model and to indicate the type of useful information generated. First, the evaluation of the power benefits of a particular large dam is shown. Second, an application to the study of the timing of construction is discussed. And third, the use of the model to investigate alternative operating policies at a multipurpose dam is demonstrated. Results from the simulation of five different development plans are used in constructing these examples.[6]

Tarbela Dam Power Benefits

One of the major decisions studied concerned the Tarbela Dam on the Indus River. This is a very large multipurpose development providing irrigation water and electric power. The dam had received a great deal of

6. These examples represent the kinds of questions which were considered with the aid of the planning model: they should not be taken as a report of the conclusions of the Indus Study. The latter are presented in Lieftinck, Sadove, and Creyke, *Water and Power Resources of West Pakistan.*

attention from international lending authorities as well as from the Pakistanis themselves, and preparation of the project had progressed through preliminary design. Much of the planning of the agricultural sector of the province was dependent upon the decisions to be made about the existence, size, operation, and timing of this structure.

A key element needed for an economic evaluation of this project was a measure of the power benefits attributable to the Tarbela Dam itself. This measure was obtained by studying electric system expansion under two basic conditions. In the "without" condition, it was assumed that no Tarbela Dam was built. An attempt was made to find the investment plan that met system demand at least cost under this condition. In the "with" condition, the construction of the dam on a prescribed time schedule was assumed. All separable costs associated with power facilities were included within the power system simulation program, and a search was made for the investment plan that met system needs at least cost with the dam in place. The net difference in system supply cost under the best investment plans found for the "with" and "without" conditions was a measure of the power benefits attributable to the dam. This information was then combined with the results of analyses of the agricultural sector to form an overall evaluation of the project.

A number of different generation and transmission schemes was studied in the search for the best investment plans with and without the Tarbela Dam. Figure 4.2 presents results from a latter stage of the analysis and indicates the kind of information that it is possible to prepare. Once again, let X denote a particular generation plan and T refer to a specific transmission scheme. The plan (X_1, T_1) was the best program if the Tarbela Dam was to be built. It involved a particular pattern of construction of thermal and nuclear plants in the northern and southern markets as well as at Mari. During the planning period, a full transmission link was formed between the two markets. The plan (X_2, T_2) was the least expensive way of meeting system needs without Tarbela. It involved the construction of a purely hydroelectric project at a site other than Tarbela and a great deal more thermal generating capacity in both the northern and southern markets than plan (X_1, T_1) specified. There was a transmission link between Mari and the south, but the two major markets remained unconnected in this plan.

Figure 4.2 shows the results for these two power sector investment plans. The figure shows the power benefits (calculated at a discount rate of 0.08) attributable to the Tarbela Dam, $G(X_2, T_2) - G(X_1, T_1)$, under three foreign exchange rates and three sets of fuel prices. The alternative sets of fuel prices differ primarily in the value placed upon gas from the

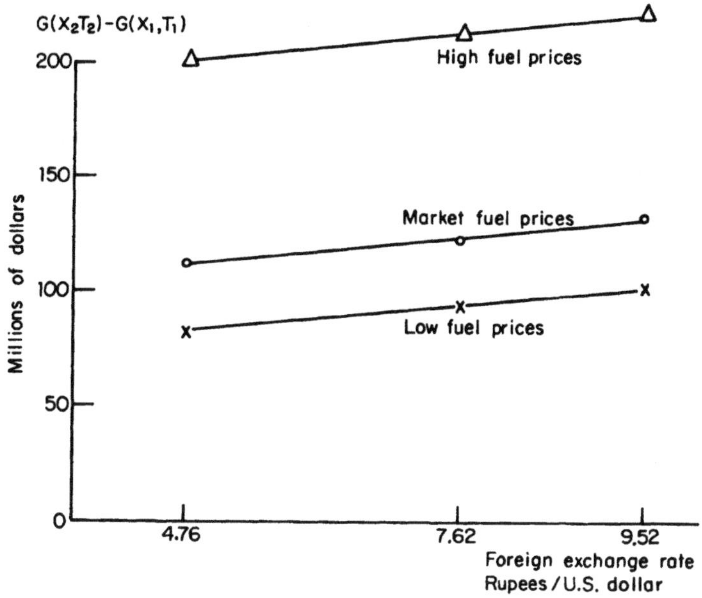

Figure 4.2. Power benefits of the Tarbela Dam

Mari and Sui fields. The "market" prices reflect current tariff schedules. The "low" and "high" prices reflect low and high estimates of the economic value of the output of the two gas sources.

The figure shows the net benefit attributable to the Tarbela Dam to be quite sensitive to variation in fuel prices.[7] At current fuel prices, for example, the net benefit attributable to the Tarbela Dam was approximately $110 to $130 million, depending upon the exchange rate. Using these data, it was possible to construct a rough estimate of net benefit at any fuel price between the high and low extremes by assuming the cost of each plan to be a linear function of the value attached to Mari and Sui gas. (A similar assumption must be made regarding the sensitivity of the net benefit estimate to the exchange rate in order to justify the connecting line segments shown in Figure 4.2.)

The power benefits from Tarbela are enhanced at higher exchange

7. It should be noted that the high and low fuel prices reflect rather extreme assumptions about the value of Mari and Sui gas. The high price is 3½ times the low. The economic value of the gas is uncertain because an analysis of this value depends upon an estimate of the total size of the gas reserves, and these quantities were subject to considerable dispute.

rates, as the figure indicates. This occurs because some of the thermal generation that would be displaced by Tarbela energy is based on imported fuel. The higher the exchange rate, the greater the value of the import saving. Since the import requirements for construction are nearly the same for the two alternative plans, variation in the exchange rate has only a small influence on the investment component of the costs presented in Figure 4.2.

Timing of Tarbela Construction

Another question raised in the study concerned the timing of construction of major projects. For example, an estimate of the effects of a long delay in the construction of the Tarbela Dam was desired. What would be the effect on the present value of overall electric system cost? Figure 4.3 shows a comparison of plan (X_1, T_1) with plan (X_3, T_3), which involved a four-year delay in the construction of Tarbela. In order to adjust to this delay, the overall pattern of investment had to be shifted. The construction of certain thermal plants was advanced, and the installation of the intermarket connection was delayed.

As Figure 4.3 shows, a delay in Tarbela construction would not have had a great effect on electric system cost. At the low and market fuel prices there was a saving of $1 to $3 million, but at high fuel prices there was a considerable increase in system cost. The savings in initial construction cost did not outweigh the increased fuel consumption that delay

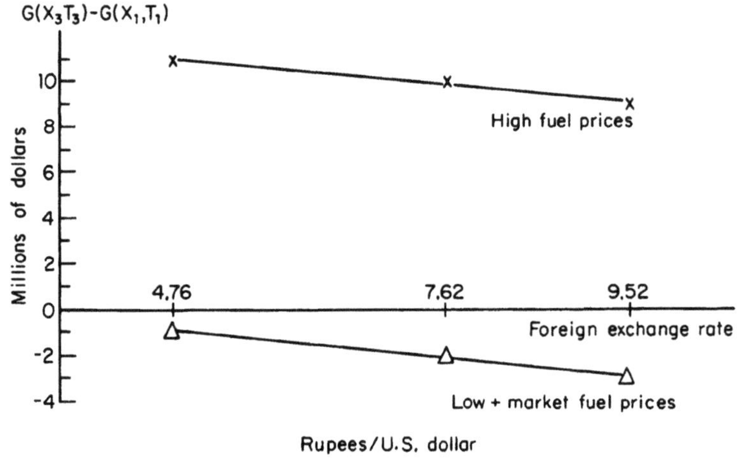

Figure 4.3. **Net change in system cost resulting from a four-year delay in the construction of the Tarbela Dam**

would involve. And the higher the price of fuel the greater the cost of waiting, so far as the electric power system was concerned.

Figure 4.3 also shows the influence of the foreign exchange rate on the system cost of a delay. The higher the rate the less it would cost to delay Tarbela, because the savings in postponing the high import component costs of the hydro station would be more than outweighed by the costs of increased imports for thermal plant construction and fuel. The results indicated, then, that if Tarbela was to be built at all, it was best from the standpoint of the electric power system to follow the earlier construction schedule. Full analysis of the effects of a delay, however, required integration of these results with a similar evaluation of the effect of the delay on the agricultural sector and on the present value of the construction cost of the dam.

Mangla Dam Operating Policy

A third type of decision studied with the use of the model concerned the selection of reservoir operating policies. West Pakistan is heavily dependent upon irrigated agriculture, and agricultural uses usually take first priority in any analysis of reservoir operation. Hydroelectric power is often considered to be a secondary use, and estimates of power potential are frequently based on reservoir release rules designed to maximize the quantity of irrigation water made available. In many instances, one would like to know the agricultural costs and the power system benefits resulting from the operation of a dam in a manner more favorable for power production.

A study was made of the power system benefits of different reservoir operating policies for the recently completed Mangla Dam. Operating plans anticipated drawing the reservoir level down to an elevation of 1,040 feet above sea level in the months of low river flow. At this low level, the capacity and efficiency of the power turbines would be reduced, and total energy production would be less than if the reservoir were maintained at a higher level. In order to investigate the effects of revising the operating policy, it was assumed that the reservoir was never drawn down below a level of 1,075 feet.

Analysis of the influence of such a change upon the electric power system is shown in Figure 4.4. The plan (X_4, T_4) assumed a 1,040-foot drawdown level at Mangla; (X_5, T_5) assumed a 1,075-foot minimum. With the higher drawdown level, the overall structure of the electric power system changed. Since the capacity of Mangla was increased, fewer thermal plants were needed, and the whole generation pattern was altered because of the availability of the additional energy.

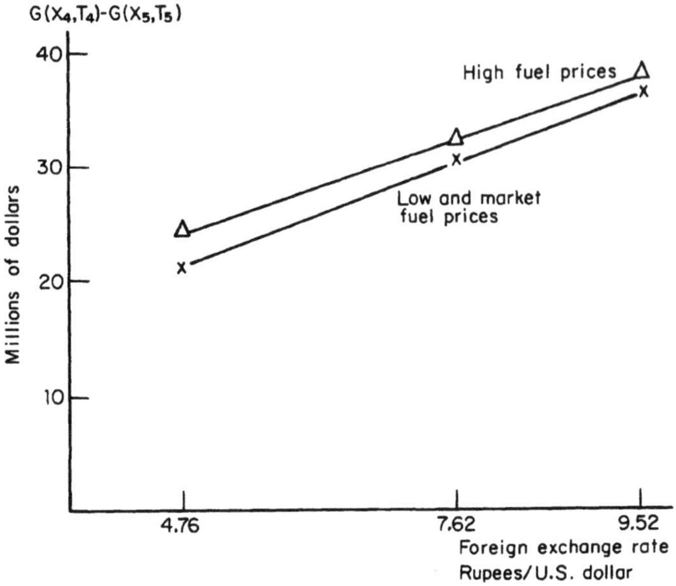

Figure 4.4. Net saving in system cost with revision in Mangla operation

The net reduction in system cost was not particularly sensitive to fuel prices, although it was affected by the exchange rate. The effect of different fuel prices was not great because the total amount of hydro energy generated varies only slightly between the two operating schemes. What did change was the total required investment in thermal capacity. Since the import component to thermal station construction is high, the value of the additional hydro capacity tends to rise at higher exchange rates.

On the basis of this analysis it was possible to argue that the present value of the contribution of the extra irrigation water (approximately one-half million acre-feet per year) to the agricultural sector needed to be in the neighborhood of $20 to $35 million in order to justify the operating policy currently planned. If the value of the additional irrigation were less than this, then serious consideration should be given to a revision in the Mangla releases.

Conclusions

The experience gained in this application of a digital simulation model to the West Pakistan electric power system shows that such models can be a powerful aid in the analysis of investment choice. The model can be tailored to the special economic conditions of a country like Pakistan and can be applied to complex choices about investment and plant operation. A disadvantage of the model is the lack of a feasible computation technique for this type of problem that would either converge upon an optimal investment mix or conduct a systematic search of the response of the objective function to the many possible permutations of the decision variables, x_{ji}. Under the simulation approach used here, the analyst must define each alternative plan to be investigated. But there is also considerable advantage in having the flexibility to consider fifty plans instead of just one, as is usually necessary, and by having the capacity to consider the electric power system as a whole rather than as a set of loosely knit subsystems.

In a discussion that advocates the use of large and complex computer models as an aid to investment planning, a warning should be given about the relative difficulty of system management under different development plans. The objective of the analysis was to model the system as it might *best* be operated in practice. And in attempting to do this, it was implicitly assumed that there was no failure of cooperation or communication among individual managers responsible for different parts of the system. It was assumed that they were capable of maintaining simultaneous coordination of the operation of many machines and transmission lines.

In West Pakistan, for example, it is easier to operate two separate markets than to coordinate the operation of an interconnected system where many layers of political organization and social structure and distances of many hundreds of miles separate the operator of a remote northern hydro station from the manager of a southern thermal plant. In most cases, these factors would not bias the selection among major alternatives. One should, however, always be aware of the possibility of system management difficulties, particularly in dealing with a large and complex country, and be prepared to adjust the analysis accordingly.

The conclusion to be drawn is that a model like the one developed for this particular problem cannot be successfully applied without a considerable input from engineering specialists, economists, and others familiar with the situation in the economy and the functioning of local institutions. With their cooperation the model can serve as a powerful tool to ease their individual analytical tasks and to aid the integration of their efforts.

5 Economic Aspects of Irrigation Project Design in East Pakistan

Robert Repetto

In East Pakistan as in most of the less developed countries there is a pressing need to reduce the capital intensity of development programs and projects, in irrigation and other fields. Two major approaches can reduce investment costs for each unit of benefits: first, acceptance of the occasional risk of smaller benefits in return for much lower capital costs; second, advancement of the time stream of benefits, with little change in capital costs. Adoption of these approaches in designing projects would result in considerable savings, even given the administrative problems of EPWAPDA (East Pakistan Water and Power Development Authority, the executive body), which are discussed in the concluding section.

Acceptable Levels of Risk in Irrigation System

Irrigation systems are usually designed after detailed surveys have identified the agricultural developments feasible in the project area following the development of available water resources, given soil, climatic, and market conditions. Typically, the result of such surveys is the proposal or forecast of a cropping pattern for the project area after development. From this proposed pattern an estimate is derived of total crop water requirements in the area in each period, usually in units of ten days to one month. Then, irrigation water requirements at the field in each time interval are calculated by subtracting the amount of usable rainfall considered reliable for the period, with perhaps an allowance for available stored soil moisture. The largest calculated irrigation water requirement for a time interval within the cropping year determines the size of the irrigation system required, with due consideration for water losses in distribution. For example, should the largest gap between total crop water requirements and reliable rainfall occur in the second half of

October, the irrigation system would be designed on the basis of these peak water requirements, with excess capacity in other time intervals. Although in a thorough study there may be several reconsiderations of the proposed cropping pattern in the light of the implied irrigation water requirements, the basic procedures remain the same.

The concept of "reliable" rainfall is related to the probability or statistical frequency of rainfall levels in each time interval, which can usually be established from rainfall records extending over many years. The choice of the amount of rainfall considered reliable for purposes of irrigation system design is basically a choice between lower and higher probabilities that that much or more rainfall will actually occur.

The probability or reliability factor chosen is important in calculating the size of the irrigation system needed to meet peak water demands. Should a very low probability factor be adopted, water shortages in critical periods would occur very frequently, and drought losses could become nearly as severe as in the absence of any project. Moreover, because cultivators would be deterred by the risk of severe drought from investing in fertilizers and pesticides, from leveling land and building field channels, and from adopting high-yielding but less drought-resistant seed varieties, little agricultural development would take place.

On the other hand, should a very high probability factor be adopted, the assumed rainfall level would be exceeded in most years, so that much of the installed irrigation capacity would be infrequently utilized. A large part of the total resources available for irrigation would be used in building extra irrigation capacity to meet improbable and infrequent contingencies in some project areas, rather than in extending basic facilities to additional areas. Because irrigation could be extended to a small area only, little agricultural development would be promoted with the available investment funds.

For optimal allocation of investment within the water sector, each project's supply capacity should be expanded to the point at which the expected marginal rate of return on investment is equal to the sectoral cutoff rate. The optimization process is quite complex, however. On the benefit side, one would assume each cultivator to be fully informed about the frequency distribution of rainfall, the production functions of all relevant crops, and the operating procedures of the project under all circumstances. For each level of irrigation capacity, there would be in each time period a probability distribution of total water availability at the field. Given these conditions, the cultivator would be presumed to maximize his objective function (which might or might not be his expected net income) with respect to the decision variables under his control. The relevant variables would include the cropping pattern in each season, the allotment of irrigation water to each crop in each time period, the degree of complementary investment in water control and conservancy field-works (e.g., for storage of water in off-peak periods), and the use of other agricultural inputs like fertilizer. The project designer would then decide, having estimated the cultivator's responses to each of his possible choices, what irrigation capacity in each project area would be economic.

This formulation highlights the need for a great deal of knowledge in order for this approach to be taken. This knowledge is unavailable in East Pakistan. Even for major crops, like rice and jute, little local research has been carried out on yield responses to water deficiencies at different points of the growing seasons or with various fertilization programs. Data on crop water "requirements" in the agronomist's sense are scanty. Knowledge about cultivators' cropping decisions is also fragmentary. In most project studies, cropping patterns are treated as if they were decision variables of the project designers, and adjusted "optimally" to the proposed water supply conditions. In fact, neither irrigation engineers nor extension specialists now have significant influence over farmers' cropping decisions. The little information available indicates that farmers adopt very slowly any radical departure from their traditional practices.

There are other areas of ambiguity and uncertainty. How much can society afford to pay to protect cultivators within a project area from the infrequent but ruinous drought which causes extraordinary hardship? What is the effect of greater or lesser risk on cultivators' willingness to invest in modern agricultural inputs and methods? For lack of answers to such questions, it was decided not to attempt to discover the optimal solution to the reliability problem, but instead to look for a good solution. In the pages which follow, the rule now used to decide irrigation system size is compared with another thought to be readily applicable, relatively simple, and more economic.

Cost-Benefit Analysis of the Dacca Southwest Project (DSW) with Alternative Degrees of Risk

At present, all irrigation projects in East Pakistan are designed on the basis of "90 percent dry year rainfall." This is the amount of rainfall which is equaled or exceeded, on the average, nine years out of ten. This rule had never been subjected to economic scrutiny but was rationalized as "common engineering practice," and by the general notion that a cultivator can afford to lose a crop only one year in ten. In practice, the required irrigation capacity under this criterion is calculated by (1) subtracting from total crop water requirements in each time period the amount of rainfall corresponding to the 10 percent frequency level for that time period, as estimated from historical rainfall records; and (2) adopting the maximum rainfall deficit for a time period as the peak irrigation requirement. This procedure leads to project designs featuring very low levels of average capacity utilization and low rates of return on investment at the margin.

To test the criterion of project design it is desirable to study first a particular project, drawing on data and analysis generated in a feasibility study. The project selected, the Dacca Southwest Project (DSW), is still in the planning stage. It calls for earthen dikes to protect a total area of almost 500,000 acres just north of the Ganges-Brahmaputra confluence against seasonal inundation. Large pumps are to lift water into the impoldered area from rivers in the dry season, and to pump rainfall run-off out during the monsoons. Natural drains and channels are to be used for both irrigation and drainage by providing secondary pumping capacity to lift water out of the main irrigation channels into the secondary distribution system.

The DSW scheme is thus a multipurpose project for irrigation, drainage of excess monsoon rainfall, and protection against seasonal overland flooding from the large adjacent rivers. The multipurpose character of the project would appear to change the fundamental nature of the problem: the size of the system is determined not solely by estimated irrigation needs, but jointly by irrigation, drainage, and flood control requirements. Similarly, benefits are attributable to the joint effects of irrigation, drainage and flood control. The choice among probability criteria depends on the frequency distribution of river stages and of rainstorms of given intensities over the project area, as well as on the distribution of rainfall levels within given time intervals.

These considerations, however, do not complicate the analysis unduly, for the following reasons. First, the criteria applied to the design of surrounding embankments are not questioned in this study. Losses from overtopments or breaches of these dikes behind which otherwise unprotected settlements will have been established might not be appropriately measured by narrow economic calculations. In more practical terms, the designers were forced to provide ample freeboard above design flood levels because of the possible future construction of other projects involving embankment upstream or downstream which would confine flood discharges and raise peak river levels. Therefore, the probability criterion adopted in dike construction matters little.

Second, careful studies by the project consultants generated convincing evidence that the benefits from pumping run-off from monsoon rains out of the polders cannot by themselves justify the capital and recurring costs of the pumping and distribution system. Drainage pumping within feasible limits cannot prevent the accumulation of water on low-lying ground after severe rainfalls, but can merely accelerate its removal. Because after a short time—say, a week at most—the length of time a crop is submerged has little further bearing on the extent of damage, there are rapidly diminishing returns for faster rates of drainage pumping. Over the relevant range the incremental benefits are small. For this reason, drainage requirements never determine the size of the system, but drainage pumping proceeds at the fastest possible rate, given the system capacity determined by irrigation requirements. The net drainage benefits can be treated as an addition to irrigation benefits. Drainage benefits encourage the adoption of higher irrigation reliability factors, since capacity established to meet peak irrigation requirements can always be used to remove water during the monsoons more rapidly than otherwise. Therefore, if peak irrigation capacity cannot be justified economically in such multipurpose schemes, where it can also generate supplementary drainage benefits at low marginal cost, then it certainly cannot be justified when intended for irrigation purposes alone.

In other respects, the DSW project area is a suitable subject for this pilot study. Cropping intensity is 148 percent, comparable to the provincial average of 135 percent. About 55 percent of gross cropped area is under paddy crop or paddy mixture, again comparable to the provincial average. Average annual rainfall is 74 inches, and 81 inches for East Pakistan as a whole. Average crop yields and size of agricultural holdings are also broadly comparable. Thus, the DSW area is not hydrologically or agronomically unusual. At the least, it is representative of the broad central belt bordering the major rivers. In this belt there are at least two million acres whose development can probably be analyzed in much the same way.

Examination of the rainfall frequencies in the DSW project area clarifies the choice of project design. The monthly frequencies plotted in Figure 5.1 reveal the distribution to be expected of natural phenomena constrained to be non-negative: with increasing values of the mean, as in the summer months, the distributions approach normality; with decreasing values of the mean, as in the winter months, the distributions become increasingly skewed and ultimately *J*-shaped. This is the overall pattern in East Pakistan, with interregional differences primarily in the mean monsoon rainfall: the monsoon is heavier in the south and east than in the north and west.

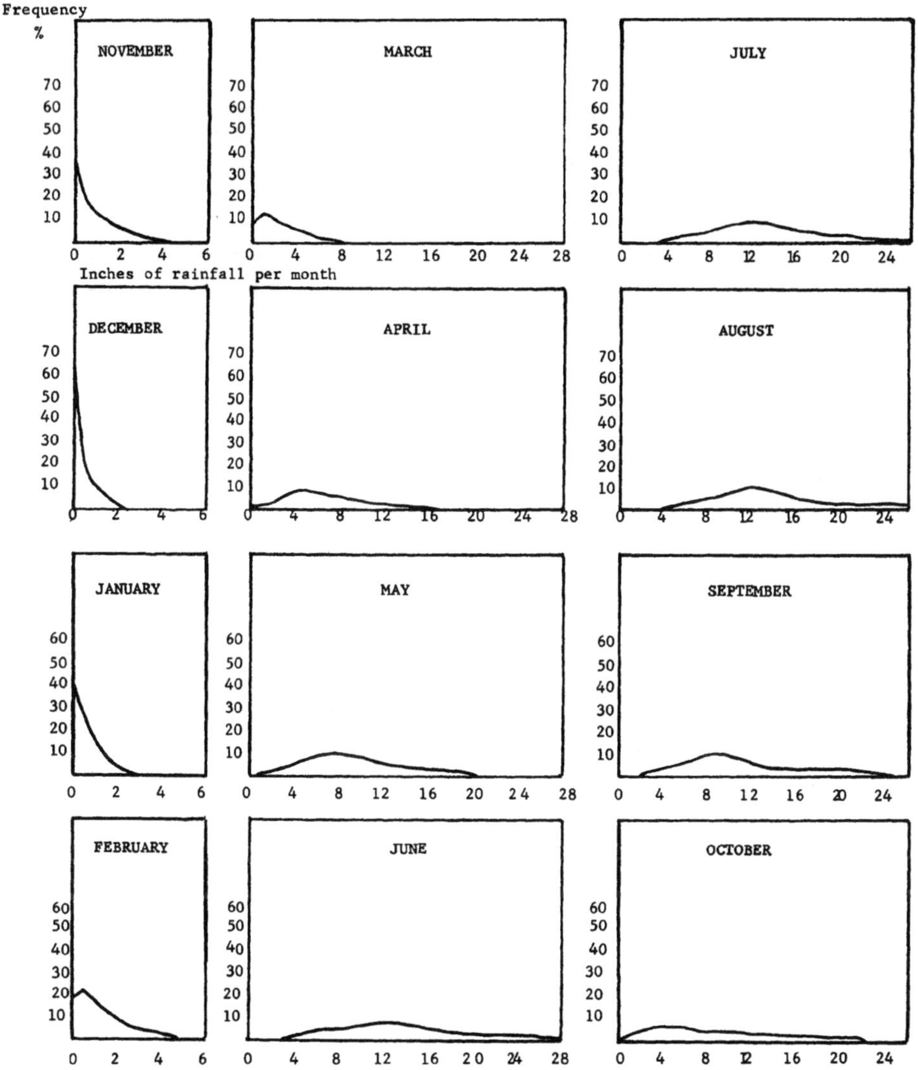

Figure 5.1. Monthly rainfall frequencies, Dacca Southwest Project area

The problem of choosing a rainfall reliability level is focused almost entirely on the spring and autumn months. In the winter months from November through February, it seldom rains. Therefore, whether the project is designed for the 90 percent dry year, the 80 percent dry year, or the 50 percent dry year, the estimated winter rainfall would be virtually nil. In the summer months from May or June to August or September, it almost always rains so much that irrigation is unnecessary or necessary only in small amounts. Therefore, the choice of reliability level makes a difference only in March, April, and October. The difference between the 90 percent and the 70 percent rainfall levels in these months might be two or three inches of water over the entire area, which would imply a major difference in irrigation supply capacity.

This preliminary consideration simplifies both the search for a less capital-intensive alternative to the 90 percent dry year criterion, and the treatment of project studies conducted under the 90 percent criterion. If the cropping patterns proposed for the project area are reasonable and likely to approximate those which cultivators will actually adopt, and if the peak water requirements determining the size of the system fall in the winter months, then it should be unnecessary to re-examine the design criterion. Any other criterion would lead to similar results because the estimated winter rainfall would remain virtually zero. Only those projects for which peak requirements occur in the spring and autumn months under the 90 percent dry year criterion need be re-examined. However, most projects are likely to fall in this latter category.

The alternative solution is to limit irrigation capacity to the peak requirements during the winter months when rainfall is nil, with this capacity used as intensively as possible in other seasons to provide supplementary irrigation.[1] It should be recognized that this alternative contradicts an influential body of opinion which holds that surface water for irrigation is the scarcest resource, particularly in winter, and that projects should consequently be designed to make maximum use of the larger supplies available in the other seasons.[2]

Comparison of the alternatives begins with the basic data presented in Table 5.1 on the monthly irrigation requirements over the entire project area if all cultivators use the irrigation supplies and adjust their crop-

1. This alternative begs the question of determining crop water requirements in the winter crops, which is primarily the question of forecasting the winter cropping pattern when irrigation is available. There is evidence, however, that cultivators will plant high-yielding rice varieties on much of their acreage under irrigation, unless deterred by permeable soils or market conditions especially favorable to the cultivation of vegetables, perennials, or other cash crops.

2. J. Th. Thijsse, *Report on Hydrology of East Pakistan* (Dacca, 1964), pp. 18 ff.

Table 5.1. Irrigation requirement by month

Item	January	February	March	April	May	June	July	August	September	October	November	December
Total acre—feet required	121,744	124,107	165,209	178,787	232,764	236,537	276,991	235,869	242,486	232,472	91,151	150,906
Total irrigable area—acres	292,157	300,169	362,239	360,426	386,954	401,639	392,039	306,685	363,805	370,194	304,413	313,775
Net irrigable area (less improvement)	287,780	295,670	356,800	355,020	381,150	395,620	386,160	302,080	356,350	364,640	299,850	309,060
Rainfall in inches —90% dry year	0	0	0	15	4.0	6.3	7.0	6.6	3.8	1.1	0	0
Rainfall in acre feet	0	0	0	44,360	127,200	207,500	225,400	166,000	113,400	33,420	0	0
Net acre feet required	121,744	124,107	165,209	134,407	105,564	29,037	51,591	69,869	129,086	199,052	91,151	150,906
Days per month	31	28	31	30	31	30	31	31	30	31	30	31
Discharge on field—cusecs	1,980	2,240	2,690	2,260	1,715	493	1,390	1,135	2,170	3,240	1,630	2,455
Discharge at farm outlet—cusecs	2,475	2,800	3,360	2,825	2,145	615	1,740	1,420	2,715	4,060	1,915	3,070
Discharge at secondary pumps—cusecs	2,745	3,110	3,730	3,135	2,380	680	1,930	1,575	3,015	4,470	2,125	3,410
Discharge at primary pumps—cusecs	3,020	3,420	4,100	3,450	2,620	750	2,120	1,730	3,320	4,920	2,340	3,750
Percentage of maximum discharge	55	63	75	63	48	14	39	32	61	90	43	69
Irrigation requirements—primary pumps—cusecs[a]	3,000	3,440	4,190	3,440	2,620	760	2,130	1,750	3,330	4,920	2,340	3,750

[a] Does not include 30 percent reserve at primary pumps.

ping patterns accordingly. Losses of water through seepage and evaporation between the primary and secondary pumps are estimated at 10 percent, losses between secondary pumps and farm outlets at 10 percent, and losses in the field channels at 25 percent. Because the soil is impermeable and evaporation rates are relatively low much of the year, these losses are perhaps exaggerated. Moreover, peak irrigation discharge is never more than 90 percent of peak irrigation capacity. Table 5.1 shows that maximum irrigation demands for the project as a whole occur in October (199,052 acre-feet at the field), with lesser demands in March (165,209 acre-feet), and in December (150,906 acre-feet).[3]

Thus the October peak irrigation demand is about 30 percent higher, and the March peak demand about 10 percent higher, than the demand in the rainless winter months. For reasons explained above, calculated winter irrigation requirements are invariant under different probability criteria. Also, it can be safely assumed that if it is worthwhile to irrigate at all it would be worthwhile to provide water to grow a crop during the winter season. Therefore, an alternative criterion is examined, one that reduces irrigation requirements in October and March to the level given by crop needs in December.[4]

Under this alternative criterion, peak irrigation requirements would be 3,750 cusecs at the primary pumps instead of 4,920 cusecs.[5] Therefore, drainage pumping capabilities would be lowered, and the risk of water shortage in exceptional drought years increased.

Despite the uncertainties surrounding the effects of flood waters on crop yields, it is necessary to consider the impact of the design change on drainage operations before considering its impact on irrigation, for the following reason. The rapidity with which monsoon run-off can be removed from the land determines where transplanted "aman" rice (the summer variety) can be grown instead of the lower-yielding, but flood-resistant, broadcast, aman. Because the seasonal crop water requirements of the former are higher than those of the latter, each change in the cropping pattern would change the crop water requirements in October and the value of the crop on the ground then.

3. For the cropping pattern forecast for one of the smaller polders, March appears as the peak month. For the area as a whole, the last fortnight of October has been identified as the ultimate peak period, because rainfall is then less and the predominant aman paddy crops are then in the flowering stage.

4. It would undoubtedly be economic to provide less than the full agronomic crop water requirements, but insufficient data on the response function are available to determine the margin.

5. The 30 percent reserve pumping capacity at primary pumps proposed by the consultants is ignored for the moment.

For this pilot study, it is useful to look at the consultants' analysis of design change impact on drainage operations. Because of the problems of equipment maintenance in East Pakistan, the consultants included a 30 percent reserve over peak irrigation capacity at the primary pumping plants. They considered the costs and benefits resulting from drainage rates of 1/2, 1/3, and 1/4 inch per day, and from no drainage pumping. The method employed in making these benefit comparisons involved estimation of the depth, duration, and area of flooding from the run-off of a design storm, at various rates of drainage pumping. (The design storm is a thirty-day storm of ten-year recurrence frequency, with a geometric rate of daily decay after the initial storm burst.) From these calculations it was possible to estimate the area in which transplanted aman, rather than lower-yielding broadcast aman, could be grown at each drainage pumping rate, and the consequent differences in benefits. Table 5.2 presents summary results from the DSW Feasibility Report.

These data are graphed in index form in Figure 5.2, which shows that pumping storm water from the land at faster rates would bring strongly diminishing returns. This is primarily because it makes no difference whether transplanted aman paddy is submerged for twelve weeks or for only two weeks; the crop is lost in either case.

The pump capacity determined by December's irrigation requirements would permit drainage of the project area at the rate of approximately 1/5 inch per day. It can be calculated from Figure 5.2 that the difference in benefits between pumping 1/5 inch per day and pumping 1/3 inch per day would be Rs. 6.8 million per year for the project area as a whole, or Rs. 17 per cultivated acre. The corresponding difference in operating costs would be Rs. 2.3 million per year. Therefore, the loss of annual net bene-

Table 5.2. Direct benefits and costs associated with several rates of drainage pumping with unchanged irrigation capacity

	Daily rate of drainage pumping			
Cost and benefits	None	1/4 inch	1/3 inch	1/2 inch
1. Net annual benefits (rupees per acre)	423	513	521	525
2. Capital costs (rupees per acre)	1,040	1,057	1,152	1,343
3. Operating costs (millions of rupees)	12.33	16.16	17.73	20.90

Source: Figure 5.2 and DSW Feasibility Report.

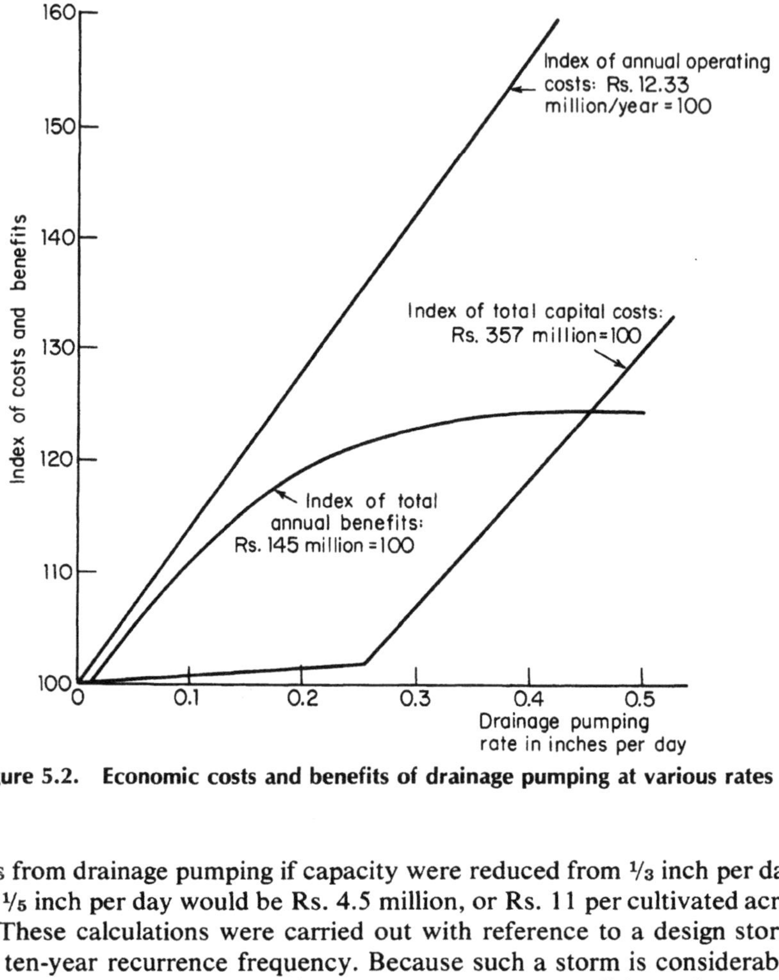

Figure 5.2. Economic costs and benefits of drainage pumping at various rates

its from drainage pumping if capacity were reduced from 1/3 inch per day to 1/5 inch per day would be Rs. 4.5 million, or Rs. 11 per cultivated acre.

These calculations were carried out with reference to a design storm of ten-year recurrence frequency. Because such a storm is considerably more severe than any experienced under average conditions, the extent of flooding in the average year and the consequent adjustment of the cropping pattern were significantly overestimated. The design storm rainfall (24.33 inches) is about twice that of the average thirty-day storm over the project area (12.54 inches). The maximum water losses from run-off through evaporation, infiltration, and entrapment in enclosed fields and other irregularities were estimated at a maximum of about 15 inches per month, which is greater than the rainfall which occurs during the average thirty-day period. Therefore, run-off from the storm of average size would depend critically on the distribution of the rainfall within the thirty-day period. From historical evidence the consultants concluded that this run-off would be about 45 percent of the design storm run-off. For the broad purposes of this study the same factor can be applied to the net agricultural benefit calculations. If this factor is used, the average yearly difference in net benefits between drainage at 1/3 inch per day and 1/5 inch per day would be Rs. 2 million over the whole cultivated area, or Rs. 5 per acre, because of a reduction of area under transplanted aman and an increase in area under broadcast aman.

Under full development the difference in net income per acre between these two crops is estimated from feasibility study survey data at Rs. 62, and the estimated total loss of direct benefits is only Rs. 5 per acre. Therefore, about 8 percent of the project area must be assumed to switch crops because of lower drainage capacity. In other words, if the entire project area switched from transplanted to broadcast aman cultivation, the loss would be Rs. 62 per acre. Because the estimated loss is only Rs. 5 per acre, an acreage shift of only 8 percent of the total is implied.

Similar reasoning results in a 3 percent reduction in peak October water requirements, owing to the increased acreage assumed under broadcast aman paddy, which requires less water in that month.

Under the design which reduces the capacity of the irrigation system to winter requirements, crop water requirements in October would be 226,272 acre-feet (7.44 inches) and irrigation capacity only 150,906 acre-feet (4.95 inches). Therefore design rainfall must be 75,366 acre-feet (2.49 inches) to make up the difference. Similarly, the design rainfall in March must increase from zero to 14,303 acre-feet (0.49 inches). The rainfall frequency data underlying Figure 5.1 indicate that this alternative implies a dry year reliability criterion for both October and March of approximately 75 percent. Changing from the 90 percent to the 75 percent level for two months only would reduce the system pumping capacity by 2,410 cusecs and designed channel capacity by 25 percent.

The implications of this choice can be made clear by concentrating first on the month of October, for which the larger absolute change is implied. With knowledge of the rainfall frequency function, it is possible to calculate the expected amount of water pumped, the expected amount of water available from irrigation and rainfall, and the expected water deficiency in years of shortfall, for each of the alternative designs. The statistical formulas are given in the Appendix. The main results are given in Table 5.3. The principle underlying the calculations is extremely simple: pumping will be at the maximum level so long as rainfall and pumped water together fall short of full requirements; otherwise, pumping will be just sufficient to make up any rainfall deficit (and zero if rainfall alone is greater than requirements).

Table 5.3. Comparison of October irrigation supply under two alternative designs

Irrigation supply	90 percent dry year criterion	Alternative criterion
1. Expected pump delivery		
a. in acre-feet	82,800	77,100
b. as percent of design capacity[a]	41	51
2. Expected water availability at the field		
a. in acre-feet	292,400	286,700
b. as percent of total crop water requirements	125	123
3. Maximum water shortage		
a. in inches	1.1	2.5
b. as percent of total requirements	14	33
4. Frequency of maximum shortfall	1 year in 80	1 year in 80
5. Frequency of any shortfall	1 year in 10	1 year in 4
6. Average shortfall in those years		
a. in inches of water	0.64	1.18
b. as percent of total requirements	8	16

Source: Calculated from Table 5.1 and rainfall frequencies by the method explained in the appendix.

[a]Excluding 30 percent reserve capacity at the primary pumps.

Under the 90 percent dry year criterion proposed by the general consultants, average utilization of design capacity in the month of peak irrigation demands would be only 41 percent, even after irrigation has been fully extended to the entire project area. In other months of the year, as Table 5.1 indicates, irrigation demands would be substantially less. Under the alternative (75 percent dry year) criterion, the average level of utilization after full development would still be only 51 percent.

On the average, the provision of an additional 50,000 acre-feet of irrigation supply capability at the field would result in the delivery to the field of an additional 5,700 acre-feet of water. This implies an average rate of utilization of the additional capacity of only 12 percent.

The maximum water shortfall, expected only once every eighty years, would be 14 percent of total consumption requirements in one case and 33 percent in the alternative. In those years in which some shortfalls occur, the average shortage under the original criterion would be 8 percent of crop needs; under the alternative criterion, the average shortfall would be 16 percent of crop needs. These shortages would occur one year in ten, and one year in four, respectively.

The next question concerns the impact of these differences on agricultural yields and project benefits. Although empirical evidence on the effect of marginal water shortages on crop yields in East Pakistan is scarce, it is clear that the general consultants are mistaken in their planning assumption that to prevent the loss of more than one crop in ten years, it is necessary to adopt the 90 percent dry year design criterion. Although *some* water shortage occurs one year in ten under this criterion, it averages only 8 percent of crop requirements and is at most 14 percent of crop requirements (assuming full development of the project area). There would be *no* significant drought damage, let alone loss of a crop, under this criterion.

Although the shape of the response curve depends on crop, soil, climate, growth stage, fertilization program, and other factors, one strongly suspects diminishing returns as water application approaches full consumption requirements.[6] Nevertheless, because of lack of data a much more pessimistic assumption is adopted: that the loss of income is proportional to the shortage of water (below full consumption requirements). This represents the maximum loss. The cultivator can always give full water requirements to a fraction of his acreage. Then even if the unirrigated part of his crop is lost, the overall loss would only be proportional to the relative water shortfall. On this basis, Table 5.4 indicates the expected reduction in direct agricultural income under the alternative design criterion. Under the alternative criterion, the value of the crop on the ground in October would be Rs. 146 per acre after the shift in cropping patterns. Water shortage would average 16 percent one year in four, or 4 percent overall. Therefore, under the pessimistic assumption, the expected loss in agricultural income would be Rs. 6 per acre, or Rs. 2.4 million over the whole cultivatable area.

The maximum loss the farmer would face, one year in eighty, would be Rs. 39 per acre or 28 percent of the net value of the crop. This risk would arise only after irrigation had been fully developed in the whole area. This level of risk should not be a serious deterrent to the use of modern inputs which return three or four rupees for each rupee invested.

6. A functional relationship exhibiting strongly diminishing returns was suggested by R. Dorfman, *Report on Land and Water Development in the Indus Plain* U.S. Department of Interior Panel on Water Logging and Salinity in West Pakistan (Washington: The White House, January 1964), appendix 5, p. 419.

Table 5.4. Agricultural costs and benefits in the aman season under alternative criteria

Costs and benefits	90 percent dry year criterion	Alternative criterion
	Rs. per acre	
1. Average agricultural incomes from the aman crops	151	140
2. Average annual loss of income from smaller irrigation supply	–	6
3. Maximum loss of income under total drought, one year in 80	12	39

Source: Table 5.3 and the assumption that income loss is proportional to water shortfall.

A similar analysis of changes in irrigation performance during the *aus* (spring) cropping season, and the associated changes in benefit levels, can be carried out. Without extended discussion, the results are presented in Table 5.5.

Average utilization of pump capacity in March would actually be greater than that in October because there is less variation in the March level of rainfall. More importantly, even under the 75 percent dry year criterion, there would be only a nominal shortage of water: 0.18 inch on the average, once every four years. Because crop water requirements cannot be calculated within a range of error of 3 percent in either direction, this shortfall can be considered negligible. Therefore, it is unnecessary to consider the loss of agricultural benefits during the spring season from restricted irrigation operations.

In summary, total losses associated with the smaller size of the system under the alternative criterion would not be more than Rs. 4.3 million in the average year, or Rs. 11 per acre (Rs. 5 per acre from flooding, and Rs. 6 per acre from additional drought damage). This amounts to about 2 percent of the total annual benefits expected to flow from the project under full development, despite the reduction of irrigation and drainage system size by about 25 percent.

Before deciding to base the DSW project largely on a system of secondary irrigation pumping from natural channels and drains, the project consultants considered an alternative distribution system based on gravity canals branching from appropriately located primary pumping stations. The latter system is the most common solution to the distribution problem in East Pakistan. By using the preliminary cost information generated by comparison of the two systems, it is possible to calculate the order of magnitude of cost savings not only for the actual project design, but also for the rejected design based on gravity flow distribution.

As actually designed according to the 90 percent dry year criterion, with secondary pumping from natural drains and with 30 percent excess reserve at the primary pumps, estimated project costs are Rs. 395 million, or Rs. 1150 per cultivated acre. Of this amount, the field costs associated with flood embankments and proportionate share of the overhead costs total Rs. 141 million. The costs attributable to irrigation and drainage are therefore estimated at Rs. 254 million.

The cost reductions which would be realized if capacity were reduced by 20 percent were estimated directly by the design engineer from the project consultants' organization. Savings were estimated under the most conservative assumption: that *no* field costs would change except the costs of the pumps themselves. That is, it was assumed that earthwork and field structures and pumphouse facilities would be entirely unaffected by a 25 percent reduction in design capacity. This assumption is justified by the special nature of the distribution system, which minimizes the need for gravity canals. On this basis, the estimated reduction in capital costs is Rs. 30 million, of which Rs. 23 million represents field costs and the

Table 5.5. Comparison of March irrigation supply under two alternative designs

Irrigation supply	90 percent dry year	75 percent dry year
1. Expected pump delivery		
a. in acre-feet	107,600	106,450
b. as percent of design capacity	54	70
2. Maximum water shortage		
a. in inches	0.00	0.48
b. as percent of total requirement	0.00	8.7
3. Frequency of maximum shortfall	-	1 year in 12
4. Frequency of any shortage	-	1 year in 4
5. Average shortfall in those years		
a. in inches	-	0.18
b. as percent of total requirement	-	3.2

Source: Calculated from rainfall frequencies and data in Table 5.1, by the method explained in the appendix.

remainder overhead, interest during construction, and the like.[7] This amounts to about 12 percent of the costs attributable to irrigation and drainage.

From the calculation in the previous section, the most pessimistic estimate of the expected annual loss after full development is Rs. 4.3 million. For comparison, estimated total annual benefits from the project after full development are Rs. 447 per acre or Rs. 175 million overall.

The undiscounted benefit-cost ratio on the whole project would thus be about 2.3 times that on the final 50,000 acre-feet of capacity, even under the most unfavorable assumptions. These last additions to capacity bring a greatly reduced return on the extra investment, while contributing little meaningful extra reduction of cultivators' risks. It would seem much more profitable to use that last 3,940 cusecs of pump capacity (7,010 less 4,170 at the primary pumps: 4,950 less 3,850 at the secondary pumps) to provide a basic level of winter irrigation and supplementary summer irrigation to an additional 100,000 net acres, and generate several times greater benefits.[8]

In order to estimate the cost savings under the hypothetical alternative distribution system based on gravity canals, it is necessary to employ some rather crude costing methods. In accordance with an empirical generalization contained in an IBRD report on water economics,[9] an exponential scaling factor of 0.75 is applied to the costs of pumps, irrigation channels, and land acquisition for the irrigation system. Again, no cost reductions are assumed for flood embankments, drainage channels, or transmission lines and facilities. The capital cost savings under the alternative distribution system are estimated at about Rs. 65 million, or 25 percent of the project costs attributable to irrigation and drainage.[10]

7. The cost of pumps is in foreign exchange. At a more realistic exchange rate, total capital cost savings might be Rs. 50 million, not Rs. 30 million.

8. In the particular case of the DSW project, the argument is even stronger than stated so far. The project consultants recently discovered an error in their initial calculation of the lift, or "head" required at the primary pumps to bring water into the polders from the river. On revision, since the discharge of a given pump is inversely related to the "head" at which it operates relative to the design lift, it seems that October peak irrigation requirements appear only at the secondary pumps. Consequently, the peak capacity at the primary pumps can be justified only by drainage benefits, which are half the total benefits estimated earlier. Therefore, the benefit-cost ratio in the whole project would be closer to five times that on the final 50,000 feet of capacity. In the more general case, under single-lift pumping into gravity canals for example, the analysis and results presented above continue to apply without modification.

9. H. G. van der Tak, *Economic Aspects of Water Utilisation in Irrigation Projects* (IBRD, Washington, D.C., January 22, 1965), p. 28.

10. The savings would be greater with a higher foreign exchange price.

The undiscounted benefit-cost ratio on the project as a whole would thus be 6.5 times that on the last 50,000 acre-feet, which indicates an even steeper descent on the marginal productivity curve. Since organized irrigation, including both large- and small-scale irrigation, extends to only 400,000 acres out of 21,000,000 net cultivated acres, it would undoubtedly be mistaken to pursue such diminishing returns in limited project areas.

This conclusion is strengthened by the fact that irrigation demands in East Pakistan will never materialize on 100 percent of the theoretical command area. Small average farm size, extreme fragmentation of holdings, and minor topographical irregularities mean that labyrinthine field channels—difficult to construct—are required for irrigation. Therefore, many cultivators will find it impossible or unprofitable to convey water to all their theoretically irrigable plots. Indeed, the pace of development of water use within a command area must be expected to be relatively slow in East Pakistan, despite the striking innovations that have been evolved in the organization of small cultivators for cooperative irrigation. Under such circumstances, it is preferable to underdesign the system initially, especially since it is easy to expand capacity later by adding more pumps. By phasing construction and installation to keep pace with organizational development and the growth of effective demand for irrigation, major capital savings can be realized.

Although the foregoing analysis pertains to an area of 500,000 acres in the center of the province, the conclusion would probably be the same elsewhere in East Pakistan. In the north and the west, where summer rainfall is lighter and summer water requirements more dependent on irrigation, the case for a winter-oriented design might be somewhat weaker. In those same areas, however, the need for drainage pumping would also be less in the summer months, and the scope for more intensive utilization by this means diminished. Furthermore, seed research has so far favored the winter season with dwarf wheats and IRRI rice varieties, which will become increasingly popular over the coming years and increase the relative value of *rabi* (winter) season crops.

Capital Cost and Construction Periods

The DSW project illuminates another critical design choice in irrigation projects in East Pakistan—the choice between single-lift and two-stage pumping systems. This choice has considerable bearing on the gestation period of projects and thus on the capital intensity. Two-stage pumping was chosen for the project, appropriately, but the weight of practice and opinion remains on the side of the alternative.

Two-stage pumping works as follows: during dry periods, water is first pumped into the natural drains, depressions, and low-lying channels, then lifted by a system of smaller pumps out of these low channels into the laterals and ditches of the distribution network. The conventional method pumps water only once, into major canals running along the high ground within the project area, so that water will flow by gravity into smaller canals and ultimately down to the farmers' fields.

This conventional method has several disadvantages in East Pakistan. The land is so flat that water flows slowly under the force of gravity; therefore the major canals need a large cross-section to transport the necessary water. This increases the land required. The local topography is quite irregular; therefore extensive filling of low spots with earthwork is required along the path of canals. Also the process of siltation has concentrated the sandier and more permeable soils along the high ground; therefore seepage losses and the danger of waterlogging adjoining areas are high.

The major disadvantage to the conventional solution is that it involves acquisition of a great deal of land with which the local inhabitants are very reluctant to part. In order to command the great expanse of the project area, major canals must occupy the high ground. However, in order to keep out of the floods, people also occupy the high ground. Consequently, a network of canals almost inevitably runs afoul of every densely populated patch of ground in the region, impinging on roadways, gardens, orchards, and sometimes even houses and schoolyards.

The alternative solution, by contrast, minimizes land acquisition: drains and natural channels abound in most areas because of the tremendous wash of water over the terrain each year, and these are used for distribution. The slope of the land is so gradual that a moderate improvement permits reversal of the natural flow. Fields can then be irrigated by pumping water into the lower end of natural drains. Because these channels are lower than the surrounding land and at the level of the groundwater table much of the year, there is little problem of seepage or waterlogging. Little valuable arable land has to be acquired.

This is a tremendous practical advantage. Land acquisition is difficult everywhere in the subcontinent, but especially so in East Pakistan, where the average farm consists of three acres split up into five or six distinct plots. The identification of plots and the establishment of titles are difficult and time-consuming. Conflicting or contested titles are a serious problem when land is to change hands. The work of assessment is also difficult. Dispossession of unauthorized occupants is a problem: mosques, graveyards, and other holy places spring up overnight so that land cannot be condemned. The Deputy Commissioner, responsible for acquisition, is overburdened with other work and is reluctant to antagonize local interests on behalf of a distant authority. Owners consider the government's assessments inadequate, and experience has taught that recalcitrance has its reward. It is almost impossible for the government to avoid appeals to the court by those who would try to show cause why their holdings should be exempted. And once on the court calendar, which is a long one, proceedings can be dragged on and on. Reform of land acquisition legislation and procedure has been a matter of considerable discussion and study, but no satisfactory solution to this complex problem has been devised as yet.

In other EPWAPDA undertakings, land acquisition problems have been an important source of delay in project completion. These schedule overruns have been substantial, as Table 5.6 indicates.

Long gestation periods such as these are largely responsible for the high capital intensity of major irrigation projects, in other areas as well as in East Pakistan, because over the critical early years there is no output or benefit at all.

Analysis of the relative costs of single-lift and two-stage pumping, while considerably better than no analysis, largely misses the point. The differences in capital costs are minor: two-stage pumping saves money on land acquisition and the canal system, but involves more spending on pumps and transmission lines. However, by minimizing delays from land acquisition problems, this system shortens the gestation period and advances the time-stream of benefits. Because the water authority is not a revenue-receiving body, one might expect it to be somewhat sensitive to variations in project costs, but much less sensitive to variations in the time stream of benefits. Fortunately, because cost considerations proved insufficient

Table 5.6. Initial and actual gestation periods for major water schemes

Name of project	Commencement date: date of sanction	Completion target	Actual date of completion
Ganges-Kobadak: Kushtia Unit	1954	1962–63	1970–71
Faridpur Drainage	1956	1965–66	1968
Feni Flood Prevention	1957	1960	1968
Coastal Embankments	1960	1965	1971
Groundwater Pump Irrigation Project	1959	1965	1968
Dacca-Demra Project (revised)	1962	1967–68	1967–68

for a decision, the project consultants were swayed by the land acquisition problem to adopt double pumping.

The advantage of double-pumping is pronounced. If it prevents a delay of a single year in project completion the overall present value of the savings from two-stage pumping will be approximately 30 percent of the total capital costs attributable to irrigation and drainage. This is indicated by Table 5.7, in which annual capital costs and net agricultural benefits are discounted at 8 percent.

The advantages of two-stage pumping, Rs. 91 million, are all in the form of faster realization of benefits. In the face of a severe shortage of development funds, measures such as this to shorten the pay-out period are very important.

Moreover, the flexibility introduced by a double-pumping distribution system is conducive to faster development of irrigation and better discipline among the water users. A gravity flow system gives little scope for

Table 5.7. Comparison of phased costs and benefits under single-lift and two-stage pumping[a] (millions of rupees)

	Single-lift pumping			Two-stage pumping		
Year	Capital cost	Net benefit	Discounted difference	Capital cost	Net benefit	Discounted difference
1	8.9	0	−8.2	10.8	0	−10.2
2	32.0	0	−27.4	32.7	0	−28.0
3	60.5	0	−48.2	62.2	1.8	−47.9
4	81.8	1.8	−58.8	87.6	6.8	−59.5
5	64.0	6.8	−38.9	71.2	16.7	−37.0
6	58.6	16.7	−26.4	63.3	26.5	−23.2
7	28.4	26.5	−1.1	25.6	61.7	+21.0
8	21.5	61.7	+21.7	-	95.0	+51.4
9	-	95.0	+47.5	-	125.1	+62.5
10	-	125.1	+56.6	-	150.4	+69.5
11	-	150.4	+64.5	-	175.8	827.0
12–30	-	175.8	753.0	- .	-	-
			734.3			825.6

[a]The phasing of capital costs and agricultural net benefits under two-stage pumping was adjusted from polder-by-polder, item-by-item data given in the project feasibility report. In essence, because the estimated schedule seemed optimistic in the light of past experience, a year was added to the construction schedule of all polders and internal works. The phasing of agricultural benefits was correspondingly retarded. The figure of Rs. 825.6 million also includes an adjustment for replacement of all secondary pumps in year 15, which is not shown in Table 5.6.

selective distribution of water: either a branch operates or it doesn't; either a branch is constructed or it isn't. In the past, this has exacerbated problems of revenue collection, since cultivators see capacity irrevocably installed whether any money is paid or not. With small pumps, installation can proceed in step with effective demand, and pumps can be removed, if necessary, for non-payment of charges. This flexibility is valuable in East Pakistan, where organization is a critical constraint on water resource development.

Conclusion: Project Design and the Planning Process

The problems dealt with in the foregoing analyses fit a common pattern that is a subject of great concern and frustration to most planning agencies. Although capital is recognized as scarce, ministries and agencies continue to propose schemes which are needlessly capital intensive, and to follow practices which prolong gestation periods. Planning bodies continually face the unpleasant choice between poor projects and no projects at all. However, planning bodies bear a large share of the responsibility for the inappropriate design criteria that is so often implicit in development projects. They fail to realize that project design is too important to be left to design engineers. Because most officials in the planning agencies are either civil servants and generalists, or economists, they are apt to defer to the engineers on technical matters (and have an exaggerated idea of what constitutes a technical matter). This deference is seldom discouraged by the engineers and technicians.

It is too seldom realized that, although all investment projects necessarily have a technical or engineering aspect because of the physical tasks involved, the integration of the bits of technical knowledge is overwhelmingly an economic function. Such integration can be done only by engineers who understand economics, or vice versa. Since this understanding is hard to locate in either camp in the developing countries, a wide gap evolves between project design and project evaluation. First the technical people design the project, then the economists and planners evaluate it. The technical agencies formulate the scheme according to their lights, and it returns to the planning authority as a finished project report. Then the planners set about the work of evaluation. At this stage, they are faced with a virtual *fait accompli.* Few planning agencies are so well supplied with project studies that they can send back all the unsatisfactory ones and wait six or eight months for revision. Consequently, evaluation by the planning authority comes to be regarded by the technical people as one more minor obstacle between them and the money.

Confronted with a summary of a lengthy project study in which they have not participated, economists in the planning agency find it difficult to assess the evidence, pinpoint the critical assumptions and areas of weakness, or identify the key issues. Nobody knows this better than the engineer in the agency, who knows exactly where the weaknesses are. Within the planning body, a tendency emerges to view with suspicion the schemes submitted by the agencies. The spirit of collaboration tends to decay into one of rather lopsided contest.

Left largely to their own devices in project design, the technical agencies respond to the real forces apparent to them. Organizational considerations are strong. Within each agency, there are drives toward greater employment, prestige, and bounty that are an inducement to propose more and bigger projects. The more projects the agency can get approved or included in the plan, the larger its claim on resources. The emphasis within the agency tends to be on establishing feasibility for as many schemes as possible, rather than on evolving an optimal investment program. This emphasis quickly communicates itself to the agency's consultants. Although at the center development funds may appear very sharply limited, to the agency the supply seems quite elastic at the actual cost of capital to them. At the center, the need to reduce capital-output and capital-labor ratios may be obvious, but to the agency it seems safest to adhere to conventional designs and conventional engineering practice, although these conventions probably developed in labor-scarce and capital-abundant economies. There is little incentive to depart from "common engineering practice," and incur personal risk of technical difficulty.

Two major conclusions emerge, neither one particularly novel. First, the planning authority can best contribute to project formulation at the beginning of the process, not at the end. Planners operating in the project field need to put more faith in early studies of basic issues, relying even on very preliminary data, and less faith in lengthy and glossy feasibility reports which settle in the second chapter for one line of development, sweeping all the basic issues under the rug, and fill the rest of two volumes with peripheral data and engineering details that are completely irrelevant if the basic approach is wrong. One major function of early studies would be the identification of crucial questions or areas of uncertainty which need more study, more data collection, or a larger input of technical knowledge. Since consultants' terms of references could be sharpened and focused on the really important aspects of the projects, better feasibility and project reports would result.

Second, the planning authority cannot maintain direct and continuing presence in the project design process. It is impossible to station a senior planning official in every design meeting to uphold the scarcity of capital against the claims of safety, convenience, ambition, and the sanctity of established procedure. Therefore, project design can be integrated into the planning process only if priorities and scarcities are made manifest in policy measures that cause actual discomfort to a sufficient number of important people. The limitations of a fixed budget could cause such discomfort, even to those whose subjective time preference is conditioned by the fact that they expect a new posting after a few years. However, the practice of applying shadow prices in project evaluation work by the planning authority, which is currently the procedure in a number of countries including Pakistan, is doubly unworkable. Not only are shadow prices applied at the wrong end of the project planning process and by the wrong people, but they are also being applied to projects designed under an entirely different set of prices, the observed ones. By then it is too late to do much about the misallocation of resources. Even if directives are issued to the various agencies instructing them to use shadow prices in project design, there will be little improvement. Scarcities still do not impinge on the agencies' proclivities. Only an actual increase in the cost of capital to the investing agencies will have an appreciable impact.

The scarcity of investment capital for development in East Pakistan, as in most developing areas, dictates a determined effort to lower capital-intensities. As this study illustrates, the reduction of gestation periods, by whatever means, can be an important source of savings. Moreover, the cost of insurance against small risks encountered in project design can easily be excessive. Should some communities be completely insured, there might be no funds left to provide other communities with any insurance whatever.

Appendix

Calculation of Expected Operation of the Irrigation Systems

The computations yielding estimates of expected levels of pumping, water availability, and water shortage were based on the following statistical relationships.

U = total crop water requirements in the peak month.
K = design capacity of the system.
p = the designed system plant factor for that month: the designed supply of water to the field per unit of capacity.
R = the design rainfall level for the month.
$f(r)$ = the rainfall frequency function for the month.
b = a pre-set probability level expressing the choice of the reliability factor,

where $$\int_0^R f(r)dr = b.$$

(1) $$R + pK = U.$$

This simply defines the system capacity which corresponds to the predetermined probability factor. Then if

w = the amount of irrigation water pumped during the month,

(2) $$w = \min(pk;\ U - r); \qquad w \geqq 0.$$

That is, in the peak month enough water is pumped to make good the rainfall deficit or to fully use available capacity, whichever is the smaller.

(3) $$P(w = pK) = P(r\ s U - pK) = \int_0^{U-pK} f(r)dr.$$

That is, pumping will be at the maximum so long as rainfall is not greater than the gap between full consumptive use requirements and full irrigation supply.

(4) $$E(w) = pK \int_0^{U-pK} f(r)dr + \int_{U-pK}^{U} [(U - r)]f(r)dr.$$

If rainfall is less than this gap, pumping will be at the maximum; if rainfall is greater than total crop requirements, pumping will naturally be nil; and for intermediate rainfall levels, pumping will make good the deficit. Expected total water availability is thus no more than the sum of expected pumping and expected rainfall.
If

x = total water availability during the month,

(5) $$E(x) = E(w) + E(r).$$

The maximum water shortage which can occur is the difference $(U - pK)$ between full crop water requirements and the full irrigation supply level, and this would be experienced only if no rain fell during the month. The expected shortage in years of shortfall is much less than this, since some rain is likely to occur. Considering just those years in which shortages occur, the average shortfall is

$$E(s) = \frac{\int_0^{U-pK} [(U - pK) - r]f(r)dr}{\int_0^{U-pK} f(r)dr}. \tag{6}$$

Application of these statistical concepts to the particular problem at hand yields the results indicated in the text.

6 Relative Price Response, Economic Efficiency, and Technological Change: A Study of Punjab Agriculture

Walter P. Falcon and Carl H. Gotsch

Since World War II, agricultural economists throughout the world have given increased attention to the factors that influence the production decisions of farmers. This interest has come about for two widely different reasons: the desire of several developed countries to *limit* agricultural production, and the desire of most underdeveloped nations to *expand* agriculture as part of their development effort.

Analyses of farmer decision-making in the United States have produced many important theoretical and empirical results.[1] In recent years, the techniques developed in the United States have also been used successfully in less developed countries, often with surprisingly similar results. Because of such studies, the discussion of peasant response to economic incentives has moved from the realm of speculation, based largely on a priori assumptions of peasant behavior, into the realm of "positive" economics. In both the developed and less developed worlds, however, only a nominal amount of work has been done on the differential effects of technological change on various agricultural activities. Although it is generally agreed that agricultural development hinges on an ability to infuse rural areas with new inputs such as fertilizer, improved seeds, and tubewells, little quantitative evidence has been presented regarding the way these radically new inputs are likely to affect the overall composition of the cropping pattern. As a result, price policies carried over from earlier periods may produce a socially undesirable mix of commodities.

1. See, for example, W. W. Cochrane, "Conceptualizing the Supply Relation in Agriculture," *Journal of Farm Economics,* 37 (December 1955), 1161–1176; G. L. Johnston, "Supply Functions—Some Facts and Notions," in E. O. Heady, ed., *Agricultural Adjustment Problems in a Growing Economy* (Ames, Iowa: Iowa State University Press, 1958); Marc Nerlove, *Dynamics of Supply* (Baltimore: Johns Hopkins Press, 1958); and E. O. Heady, ed., *Agricultural Supply Functions* (Ames, Iowa: Iowa State University Press, 1961).

Before many predictions can be made about the interaction of technological change and supply elasticities, historical experience must show convincingly that farmers do, in fact, exhibit a significant amount of economic rationality. In Pakistan, researchers have concluded that farmer decision-making is, in general, economically rational.[2] However, all of the previous studies have assumed simpler farmer-decisions rules than is probably warranted. Hence, even though there is little question that West Pakistan farmers *do* respond to price, the magnitude of such response is still in question.

The discussion of farmer decision-making in West Pakistan is divided into two parts. The first part examines the historical experience in some detail. The Punjab, the major agricultural region of West Pakistan is described and the distributed-lag models are then used to extend some of the earlier work on historical price responsiveness. A programming model which permits a normative examination of the relationship between water supplies, agricultural output, and prices is then introduced. In the second part of the chapter, technological change is introduced into the programming model via activities that produce additional water supplies. Normative supply curves are then generated and compared with the long-run historical elasticities.

The major conclusion reached from the econometric analyses is that farmer sensitivity to economic variables is high even in the low-income agriculture of West Pakistan. The relative price relationships appear to be of the same magnitude as those found in the United States; moreover, the water analyses suggest that the supply curves will both shift and increase in elasticity as a result of the technological change embodied in the water development program now being undertaken in West Pakistan. Both these observations have a significant bearing on agricultural issues, including input subsidies, export taxes, price supports, rural taxation, and food imports.

Decision-Making in the Traditional Agriculture of Punjab

To appreciate the amazingly complex nature of rational decision-making in Punjab agriculture, it is necessary to understand several im-

2. See W. P. Falcon, "Farmer Response to Price in a Subsistence Economy: The Case of West Pakistan," *American Economic Review*, 54 (May 1964), 580–591; Ghulam Mohammed, "Some Physical and Economic Determinants of Cotton Production in West Pakistan," *Pakistan Development Review*, 3 (Winter 1963), 491–526; S. M. Hussain, "A Note on Farmer Response to Price in East Pakistan," *Pakistan Development Review*, 4 (Spring 1964), 93–106; and S. K. Qureshi, "Rainfall, Acreage and Wheat Production in West Pakistan: A Statistical Analysis," *Pakistan Development Review*, 3 (Winter 1963), 566–593.

portant details of the rural environment.[3] Of particular significance is the irrigation system, which serves some 13 million cropped acres of the northern zone of the Indus Basin. This vast system of perennial and nonperennial canals is one of the world's largest irrigation networks, with approximately 30 million acre-feet of water per year presently diverted from the five rivers that flow into the area. Most parts of the northern canal network were installed between 1880 and 1920 and have one important element in common: the areas commanded by these canals are large relative to the water they deliver. Thus in both the *kharif* (spring) and *rabi* (fall) seasons, over 50 percent of the cultivable land usually lies fallow. Moreover, that area which is cropped receives only a relatively small water application.[4] In addition, because canal supplies vary greatly throughout the year and between years, canal water supplies are both a critical and an uncertain input in large agricultural areas of West Pakistan. Water, not land, is the most binding constraint for the majority of farmers in West Pakistan.

A second feature of West Pakistan agriculture is the complicated crop calendar (see Figure 6.1). Unlike cultivation in most parts of the United States, which occurs in one season with rather clearly defined planting and harvesting dates, cultivation in Punjab can be carried on throughout the year. Because of the large number of crops commonly grown and because of the overlapping of seasons, the Punjabi farmer is faced with an extraordinarily large number of decisions concerning his cropping alternatives.

A third significant characteristic of West Pakistan is its *average* scale and level of technology. To a considerable extent, agriculture in the Indus Basin is poor and traditional. Average farm size is approximately eight cultivated acres, and rural per capita income is only about Rs. 350 ($74) per year. Farming is generally nonmechanized, and although cultivators are now beginning to use commercial fertilizers, improved seeds, and pesticides, many farming practices are as they have been for centuries.

On the other hand, the averages presented above are misleading. Although 60 percent of the West Pakistan farmers have "subsistence" farms that are less than 7.5 acres, approximately 20 percent of the land

3. For a fuller discussion of agriculture in West Pakistan, see Sir William Roberts and S. B. S. Kartar Singh, *A Textbook of Punjab Agriculture* (Lahore: Civil and Military Gazette, 1951); Government of Pakistan, Ministry of Food and Agriculture, *Report of the Food and Agriculture Commission* (Karachi, November 1960); and Government of the United States, *Report on Land and Water Development in the Indus Plain*, (Washington: The White House, January 1964).

4. Water applications per acre in West Pakistan are only 1/3 to 1/2 of those found in comparable areas of California.

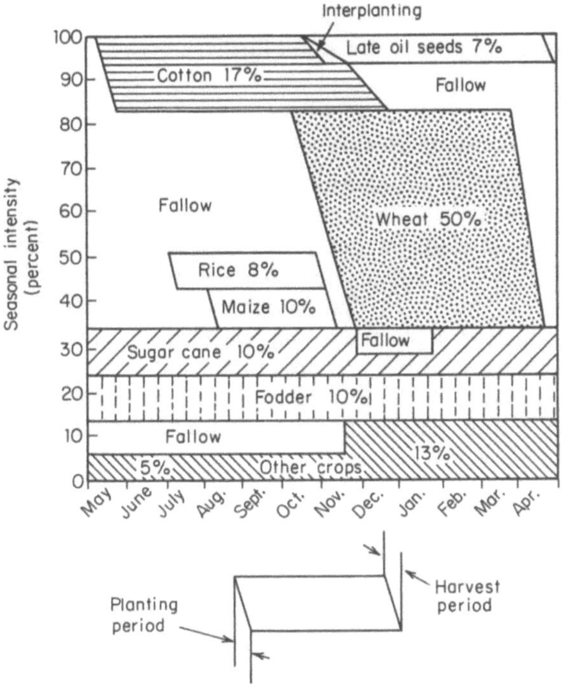

Figure 6.1. Typical cropping pattern, Punjab, West Pakistan
Source: Harza Engineering Co., *A Program for Water and Power Development in West Pakistan, 1963–1975–Supporting Studies* (for the West Pakistan Water and Power Development Authority, Lahore, September 1963).

is in "economic" units of more than 25 acres.[5] Although smaller than in many other countries, the commercial segment composed of larger farms is dynamic. This group, for example, has been mainly responsible for the recent annual installation of more than 10,000 private tubewells for irrigation.

A final characteristic of the irrigated agriculture of West Pakistan is due to the nature of the industries and institutions that serve it. Marketing, processing, storage, extension, and credit services are rather rudimentary, and rural prices exhibit great seasonal and inter-year variation. As a result of these and other factors, foodgrain self-sufficiency has been

5. Government of Pakistan, Ministry of Agriculture and Works, *1960 Pakistan Census of Agriculture*, vol. II (Karachi, October 1963), p. 13.

historically important for survival, and is still a major consideration in farm planning for many of the small farmers.[6]

Price Response in West Pakistan—The Historical Experience

Given the type of agriculture described above, it is not surprising that early opinions varied on the decision-making behavior of farmers—particularly on whether or not they responded to changes in relative prices.[7] In part, the different viewpoints arose because various agricultural economists failed to distinguish between cash and food crops, between production and marketing elasticities, and between acreage and yield responses. However, several recent commodity studies have concluded that West Pakistan's farmers are price and income conscious. In large part, the discussion has now shifted from "if" to "how much."

The Relative-Price Estimation Model[8]

The extent to which farmers react to changes in relative prices between crops has an important bearing on public policy toward agriculture. The government, through such instruments as export bonuses, taxes, and import of agricultural products, can (and does) significantly alter relative prices between the major crops of West Pakistan. The first empirical question dealt with in this study is how much these changes have affected the level and the composition of output.

A number of econometric models for estimating historical supply responses at the farm level have been proposed in the literature. Because crops are planted months before they are harvested and sold, such models nearly always introduce prices in a lagged form. In the simplest version, the independent variable consists of the appropriate relative prices lagged one year. More sophisticated studies, seeking to avoid the unnecessarily restrictive assumption that farmers are influenced only by the prices of the preceeding year, include in the estimation model the prices of a

6. This point is developed at length in W. P. Falcon, "Farmer Response to Price in an Underdeveloped Area: A Case Study of West Pakistan," (Ph.D. thesis, Harvard University, 1963), chapter 1.

7. In this chapter, the concern is with the relative profitability among crops. How farmers have responded to changes in factor prices (i.e., the terms of trade for agriculture), though important, is outside the scope of this essay.

8. See Falcon, "Farmer Response to Price in a Subsistence Economy"; Ghulam Mohammed, "Some Physical and Economic Determinants of Cotton Production"; Qureshi, "Rainfall, Acreage and Wheat Production in West Pakistan"; and Hussain, "A Note on Farmer Response to Price."

number of preceding periods, each weighted according to its chronological relationship to the present.

By specifying that the relationship between price and cropping decisions be one of exponentially declining influence, a simple estimation equation in only two easily observable variables can be obtained.[9] Assume, for example, that the decision to plant cotton in year t is a function of expected prices in year t, the latter being defined as follows:[10]

1. $$O_{c.t} = \propto + \beta P_{t-1} + \beta\lambda P_{t-2} + \ldots + \beta\lambda^{n-1}P_{t-n}$$

where

$O_{c.t}$ = acreage devoted to cotton in year t
$\propto$ = constant
β = coefficient of price response
λ = coefficient of "expectation" ($0 \leq \lambda \leq 1$) describing the influence of a particular past price on the formation of farmer price expectations.

If $\lambda = 0$, the expected price in year t is established solely on the basis of price in year $t - 1$, the simplest lagged supply response model. However, if λ equals 0.5, then prices of preceding years also have an effect on expected prices. This influence is greatest for the years neartest t, because $(\lambda)^{n-1}$ approaches zero as $t - n$ decreases.

The above form of the distributed lag is not completely general because of the restrictive assumption about λ. The advantage of Equation (1) lies in the fact that with the above assumption about the relationship between the betas (that is, λ), a simple estimating equation (2) can be derived that provides estimates of both long- and short-run responses to price.[11]

2. $$O_t = a + b.P_{t-1} + d.O_{t-1}$$

where:

b = the short-run price response

9. See Nerlove, "Estimates of Elasticity of Supply," *Journal of Farm Economics*, 38 (May 1956), and *Dynamics of Supply;* L. M. Koyck, *Distributed Lags and Investment Analysis* (Amsterdam: North Holland Publishing Co., 1954); and Raj Krishna, "Farm Supply Response in India-Pakistan: A Case Study of the Punjab Region," *Economic Journal*, 73 (September 1963), 477–487, for a fuller discussion of the assumptions and technicalities of the distributed-lag approach.

10. In this formulation, the prices can be thought of as the ratio of cotton prices to cotton-substitute prices. By making this ratio, it is possible to keep the idea of relative profitability and yet remove one dimension from the equation.

11. For the algebra involved, see Nerlove, *Dynamics of Supply*.

$\frac{b}{1-d}$ = the long-run price response

O_t = the output of cotton, year t

P_{t-1} = actual cotton price, year $t - 1$.

It is thus possible to estimate a rather complicated formulation of expected prices with only two directly observable historical variables. Because of this advantage, Equation (2) is the basic model used for the empirical work of the next section.

The Estimates

In analyzing the effects of relative price on the production of different crops, there are two reasons for disaggregating output into its yield and acreage components. First, it cannot be assumed that farmers react with their land input in the same manner as with their labor, fertilizer, water, and other nonland resources. Although it might be expected a priori that an increased relative price would result in both a large acreage and a higher yield, the two types of responses may be of entirely different magnitudes. As discussed in the section on irrigation water allocation, this is especially likely when there is fallow land and a general shortage of irrigation water. Second, weather effects are likely to create more variation in yields per acre than in acreage planted. Therefore, by eliminating the yield component, and by using acreage rather than output as the dependent variable, many of the estimation problems involving weather can be avoided. These acreage responses can be thought of as a lower bound of the supply elasticity, because any price-induced changes in yields from nonland inputs would be in addition to the acreage effect.

Acreage Effects. The acreage supply functions for the various crops of the former Punjab are shown in Table 6.1. The equations, all of which were fitted in logarithmic (constant elasticity) form, are of the distributed-lag variety described previously. In addition, a water variable has been added to each equation to take into account the critical nature of that input in the region.[12] (Availability of relevant water data was also the determinant of the particular years that were included in each equation.)

12. Additional empirical work by the authors has shown that the irrigation-water variable should also be treated as a distributed lag; that is, farmers must prepare land in response to expected water supplies throughout the growing season. A simplifying assumption was made that the lag pattern was the same for water as for price. Thus the structural equation was:

$$O_t = \alpha + \beta P_{t-1} + \beta\lambda P_{t-2} + \beta\lambda^2 P_{t-3} + \ldots + \gamma W_t + \gamma\lambda W_{t-1} + \gamma\lambda^2 W_{t-2} + \ldots + \epsilon.$$

Table 6.1. Acreage elasticities, former Punjab

Crop	Equation number	Lagged relative price	Lagged relative price	Lagged acreage	Water supply[a]	Constant term	Corrected R^2	Durbin-Watson statistic	Years included
A		P_{t-1}	P_{t-2}	A_{t-1}	W_t	a	R^2	$D.W.$	
Rainfed wheat	3	−0.09[b] (.08)[d]		0.51 (.11)	0.07[c] (.01)	6.99	0.64	2.70	1932–61
Irrigated wheat	4	0.06[e] (.03)		0.81 (.09)	0.12[f] (.06)	1.59	0.90	1.80	1932–64[g]
Rice	5	0.16[h] (.09)		0.61 (.14)	0.63[j] (.26)	−1.10	0.91	2.40	1932–64[g]
Cotton	6	0.29[k] (.08)		0.92 (.14)	0.29[m] (.15)	−1.50	0.67	2.20	1932–56
Sugarcane	7	0.14[n] (.08)	0.30[n] (.08)	0.88 (.06)	0.89[q] (.37)	−8.4	0.98	1.60	1940–64[g]

[a]The formulations in Table 6.1 assume that the expectations coefficient for the water variable is also equal to λ. This is a restrictive, though simplifying, assumption that seems justified on the basis of work in progress by the authors.

[b]Wheat price divided by *gram* (chick-pea) price.

[c]September plus October rainfall.

[d]Standard error of the regression coefficients.

[e]Wheat price divided by weighted average cotton and sugarcane prices.

[f]Rabi water supplies, 8 major canals.

[g]Excludes 1950–51, 1951–52, and 1952–53. Data unavailable because of the Indus Basin dispute.

[h]Rice price divided by weighted average cotton and sugarcane prices.

[j]Rabi water supplies preceding year, 8 major canals.

[k]Cotton price divided by weighted average rice and sugarcane prices.

[m]May plus June water supplies, 8 major canals.

[n]Sugarcane (*gur*) price and weighted average cotton and oilseed prices.

[q]Rabi plus Kharif water supplies, 8 major canals.

The results are strikingly consistent. They indicate supply elasticities at least as large as those found for the United States.

Each of the commodity equations has special features worth noting briefly. For wheat, the main foodstuff of West Pakistan, the difference in price responsiveness between the rainfed and the irrigated areas indicates an interrelationship of historical price response and water supplies. In the rainfed areas of the former Punjab, climatic conditions virtually determine acreage. Relative prices play almost no role because the other crops that are feasible under the moisture conditions are extremely limited. (Although it would seem from acreage statistics that *gram* (chick-pea) is a large potential competitor, these figures are misleading because gram and wheat are often sown together as a contingency against low rainfall—gram being an even more drought-resistant crop.)

These characteristics of wheat production are summarized in Equation (3). A crude estimate of September-October rainfall is an extremely significant variable, whereas the price variable is insignificant and even of the wrong sign.

The contrast between rainfed and irrigated wheat (Equations [3] and [4]) indicates an increased price responsiveness when the water constraint is partially relaxed. Although irrigation supplies in the fall season remain an important determinant, relative price now enters the equation in a significant way. Although the short-run price elasticity is low (0.06), it is still important given the absolute magnitude of wheat acreage. With some 6 million acres of irrigated wheat in West Pakistan, a 10 percent variation in relative wheat prices has a short-run effect of approximately 200,000 tons.[13] Because annual price changes to farmers of 10 and even 20 percent are common, the price responsiveness in wheat has important implications for food policy.[14]

The equation for rice (5) indicates the intermediate character of that commodity in the former Punjab. Although rice is an important foodstuff, many of the finer varieties are grown as a cash crop for eventual export. It is encouraging on grounds of consistency that irrigation water supplies again are a significant determinant, and that the price elasticity of 0.16 falls about halfway between wheat and a "pure" cash crop such as cotton.[15]

For cotton and sugarcane (Equations 6 and 7), the two major cash crops of the area, price elasticities are both higher and more significant in a statistical sense.

The 0.3 price elasticity for cotton is slightly lower than was found in two earlier studies, although it is still of the same order of magnitude.[16] The water variable for cotton created some difficulties in estimation since

13. Average wheat yields are about 0.5 ton per acre; thus .06 × 6,000,000 acres × 0.5 tons per acre is approximately 200,000 tons.

14. The average absolute change in annual wheat prices at Lyallpur was 11.2 percent for the 10 years ending in 1964–65. Seasonal fluctuations were even larger.

15. The price elasticity of 0.16 is similar in magnitude to the 0.12 estimate of Hussain, "A Note on Farmer Response to Price," for *aus* (summer) rice in East Pakistan. It is significantly lower, however, then the 0.3 estimate of Krishna, "Farm Supply Response in India-Pakistan," for an earlier period in undivided Punjab.

16. See Falcon, "Farmer Response to Price in a Subsistence Economy," and Ghulam Mohammed, "Some Physical and Economic Determinants of Cotton Production," whose estimates, using different types of equations, were 0.4 and 0.5, respectively.

acreage was uncorrelated with total canal flows over the season. However, canal flows for the "planting months" of May and June proved significant. Regrettably, these data were available only through 1956 and thus it was not possible to examine how well the equation "explained" the recent years, which are most relevant for policy purposes.

The sugarcane equation adds a final point to the questions of magnitude and methodology. Sugarcane is, at minimum, a year-long crop. In West Pakistan it is usually *ratooned* (cut back) and allowed to produce a second crop as well. Thus, "short-run" for cane is usually two years. These technological observations are reflected in Equation (7), where lagged prices for years $t - 1$ and $t - 2$ have both been included. The sum of these price coefficients (0.44) can be regarded as the short-run price response. The size of this elasticity, the largest of all those computed, underscores the potential importance of price and import policies for sugar.

The conclusion that emerges for the former Punjab is that when climatic and technological conditions permit, farmers allocate acreage in response to changed relative prices. Although all of these short-run elasticities are less than 1.0, and therefore inelastic by the usual definition, they are sufficiently large to be important in agricultural planning. The specific policy implications of these estimates, as well as an interpretation of the long-run elasticities implied by the equations, is deferred to the section on the effect of supplementary water supplies.

Yield Effects. Just as a farmer might react to price by allocating his land input, so *might* he respond with nonland inputs to alter yields per acre. By substituting yield for acreage variables in the previous equations, it was possible to obtain estimates of these effects.

The yield response equations proved just as consistent as the previous acreage estimates—but in a startlingly different way. *None* of the yield equations contained statistically significant price variables, nor did several variations in the form and structure of the yield formulation provide results that were any more significant. An explanation of these yield results rests on an examination of theoretical, empirical, and statistical factors.

First, climatic factors probably affect yields more than they affect acreage. Therefore, the price effects on yields may have been "swamped" by other factors—thus making it impossible to estimate the price reactions.

Second, during most of the three decades under study there were few technical possibilities for altering yields, which were virtually stagnant.

Inputs such as fertilizers and pesticides, which might have been altered in response to changed prices, were virtually unknown.[17] The possibility did exist of altering the relative amounts of labor used in different cultivation processes. However, as a number of writers have noted, the cultivation practices for particular crops in different regions remained the same.[18] Thus, without an extensive discussion of whether the marginal product of labor was zero or near zero for different crops, whether labor was a free good as seen by the farmer, or whether there were some minimal shifts in the allocation of labor among crops, the conclusion is clear. The reallocation of labor and the use of inputs such as fertilizer and pesticides, in response to changed relative prices were not important variables in explaining yield variations in the former Punjab during the three decades, 1930–1960.[19]

Finally, there remains the puzzling case of irrigation water. One might expect that as relative prices of a particular crop increased, two reactions would have occurred: (a) more acres of the crop would have been grown, and (b) a larger volume of water *per acre* would have been applied, thus giving a yield response. However, the empirical evidence suggests that only the area response was significant. As the discussion in the next section will indicate, this asymmetric response represented optimizing behavior on the part of the farmers. Therefore, in spite of the limited number of estimates presented above, the historical evidence on the effect of relative prices in the former Punjab seems fairly conclusive. Although relative prices were an important determinant of acreage, especially for crops grown primarily for sale, they were unimportant as a determinant of variations in yields.

17. The general features of Punjab agricultural technology during this period are discussed at length in C. H. Gotsch, "Technological Change and Private Investment in Agriculture: A Case Study of Pakistan Punjab" (Ph.D. thesis, Harvard University, 1966).

18. See Falcon, "Farmer Response to Price in an Underdeveloped Area," for more details.

19. In all probability, the effects of prices on the use of fertilizer and other inputs changed during the late 1960's as the result of new seed varieties for wheat and rice. This question is dealt with at length in Carl H. Gotsch and Walter P. Falcon, *Agricultural Price Policy and the Development of West Pakistan*, vol. I (Cambridge: Organization for Social and Technological Innovation, 1970). This volume, written after this chapter was completed, incorporates a series of new production technologies into a linear programing framework and addresses the question of optimal resource use given the new varieties. It is therefore analogous to and complementary with this chapter, which focuses almost exclusively on the water-allocation issue. In both analyses, a series of linear approximations has been used to relax the restrictive assumptions of fixed production coefficients for water, fertilizer, and other inputs.

Allocation of Irrigation Water

In the preceding section, it was argued that land allocation in response to relative prices indicated that West Pakistan farmers behave as if they are profit motivated. It was also pointed out that land is generally not the limiting factor in West Pakistan. In this respect, the region is similar to other arid zones of the world where the decision to grow a certain amount of a crop is usually a decision about the allocation of limited amounts of irrigation water. In this section, the water allocation problem is developed at some length because it permits a fuller explanation of the significance of the area models and the insignificance of the yield models attempted in the preceding section.

Water Allocation under Certainty of Water Deliveries

Water allocation decisions, important in examining the relationship between price response and water availability, can be studied with the aid of a conventional linear programing tableau. The typical cropping pattern shown in Figure 6.1 can be translated easily into a matrix of land and water requirements, such as the one for a typical Gujranwala farm shown in Table 6.2. The water coefficients, given in acre-inches, refer to the monthly water requirements per acre under crop; the land coefficients, given in acres, refer to the area occupied by a crop during a given time period. The constraints in the right-hand column refer to water and land availability, while the net revenue figures of the last row indicate the income per acre from each crop.

The matrix presented in Table 6.2 indicates that a rational response to changes in relative prices requires a fairly complex set of calculations. The farmer, in attempting to maximize profits, must bear in mind the changed price relationship among crops, as well as their relative water requirements and the time distribution of the available water supplies. For example, a small increase in the price of cotton might be expected to cause an increase in cotton production relative to rice, the other major kharif crop. However, there is some overlap in the growing periods of cotton and wheat. If water is in short supply during the month of October, it may not pay the farmer to grow more cotton. To do so would mean a reduction, not only in rice, but also in wheat. Indeed, for sufficient price changes, profit maximization would lead to an entirely new set of critical water periods. As some of the solutions to the programing problem presented will indicate, this result serves to link closely the magnitudes of price response with irrigation water availability.

Although the model presented in Table 6.2 provides considerable insight into the trade-offs involved in distributing water efficiently among

Table 6.2. Linear programing matrix[a] (Gujranwala rice tract, typical 12.5-acre farm)

Activity constraint	Fine rice	Coarse rice	Kharif fodder	Kharif vege-tables	Cotton	Wheat after fallow	Wheat after rice	Gram	Oil seeds	*Berseem* (clover)	Rabi vege-tables	Sugar-cane	Fruit	Resource availa-bility
Water (acre-inches per acre)														
April	–	–	1.7	1.7	1.7	0.8	–	–	–	6.3	–	8.0	7.0	32.7
May	–	8.5	3.8	3.8	5.5	–	–	–	–	–	–	13.9	9.4	39.0
June	8.0	14.9	6.9	6.9	3.7	–	–	–	–	–	–	15.4	8.5	43.2
July	11.4	11.6	4.3	4.3	2.7	–	–	–	–	–	–	9.3	4.5	42.4
August	9.5	4.7	1.8	1.8	6.3	–	–	–	0.8	1.3	–	7.3	4.2	42.0
September	13.2	2.4	0.8	0.8	11.7	1.3	–	3.4	2.5	3.4	–	10.7	9.3	43.2
October	3.5	–	–	–	7.7	4.2	–	2.4	3.6	3.8	6.9	10.0	7.7	35.7
November	0.5	–	–	–	–	1.6	2.1	2.5	3.5	4.2	4.2	3.6	3.8	24.4
December	–	–	–	–	–	1.9	2.0	2.7	3.3	3.1	3.1	3.1	2.0	21.8
January	–	–	–	–	–	2.2	2.3	2.1	2.1	2.7	2.2	1.6	1.3	22.7
February	–	–	–	–	–	4.8	4.3	–	0.1	5.0	3.6	8.7	2.4	29.0
March	–	–	1.3	–	–	7.1	7.3	–	–	8.5	5.6	3.5	3.9	35.2
Land (acres)														
April	–	–	1.0	1.0	1.0	1.0	1.0	–	–	1.0	–	1.0	1.0	12.5
May	–	1.0	1.0	1.0	1.0	–	–	–	–	1.0	–	1.0	1.0	12.5
June	1.0	1.0	1.0	1.0	1.0	–	–	–	–	–	–	1.0	1.0	12.5
July	1.0	1.0	1.0	1.0	1.0	–	–	–	–	–	–	1.0	1.0	12.5
August	1.0	1.0	1.0	1.0	1.0	–	–	–	0.5	–	–	1.0	1.0	12.5
September	1.0	1.0	1.0	1.0	1.0	0.5	–	0.5	1.0	1.0	–	1.0	1.0	12.5
October	1.0	0.5	1.0	–	1.0	1.0	–	1.0	1.0	1.0	1.0	1.0	1.0	12.5
November	0.5	–	1.0	–	0.5	1.0	0.8	1.0	1.0	1.0	1.0	1.0	1.0	12.5
December	–	–	–	–	–	1.0	1.0	1.0	1.0	1.0	1.0	1.0	1.0	12.5
January	–	–	–	–	–	1.0	1.0	1.0	1.0	1.0	1.0	0.5	1.0	12.6
February	–	–	–	–	–	1.0	1.0	1.0	1.0	1.0	1.0	0.5	1.0	12.7
March	–	–	–	–	–	1.0	1.0	0.5	–	1.0	1.0	1.0	1.0	12.8
Net revenue (Rs./acre)	161.6	122.6	219.6	320.0	79.6	159.1	85.6	86.1	88.3	321.0	420.0	550.0	520.0	–

[a]For a full description of the data underlying the derivation of these coefficients, see Carl H. Gotsch, *Technological Change and Private Investment in Agriculture: A Case Study of the Pakistan Punjab* (Ph.D. thesis, Harvard University, 1966).

crops, it still does not reflect fully the difficult water allocation problem. The choice between using water to increase yields and using it to extend acreage has been sidestepped entirely thus far. In the linear programing context, the crop-water activities used were chosen under the assumption that a particular yield would be obtained from a crop if, and only if, the monthly water requirement indicated by the matrix was applied. Numerous researchers have reported, however, that such an assumption is a gross oversimplification of the relationship between water applications and yield. Irrigation water-yield ratios can vary widely and some thought must be given to the most likely shape of the yield function of crops with respect to water.

Water-Yield Relationships. In recent years, agriculturists have shown increasing interest in crop-water relationships. Unfortunately, their intention has nearly always been to ascertain the amount of water required by plants. Often called "consumptive use," this parameter is generally measured under conditions that ensure very limited moisture stress on the plant during the growing season; therefore it is more or less synonymous with the amount of water needed to maximize plant yields.

No attempt will be made here to examine in detail the literature on the characteristics of crop production with respect to water. However, a substantial amount of evidence, both theoretical and empirical, is accumulating which suggests that a function of the general form shown in Figure 6.2 is most appropriate for relating yield to successive increments of water.[20]

Rational Irrigation Practices and Diminishing Returns to Water

The foregoing discussion has indicated that farmers can respond in terms of either acreage or yield (or both) to changes in the relative price structure. How is it, then, that only the acreage models in the section on price response in West Pakistan were statistically significant? With the

20. The interested reader is referred to I. U. Ifegwu Eke, "Economic Models for Determining the Productivity of Water in Agriculture" (Ph.D. thesis, Harvard University, 1963), and ILACO (International Land Development Consultants), "Desk Study on the Relation between Crop Yields and Water Consumption" (unpublished monograph, Arnhem, 1965), for comprehensive reviews of the work that has been done in this area. These data suggest that $2/3$ of the field capacity for water will produce about 90 percent of maximum yield and that about $1/2$ of the full requirement will produce approximately $2/3$ of the maximum yield. In West Pakistan, work done by Ch. M. S. Gill, *Fifty Years of Agricultural Education and Research*, vol. II (Lahore, 1960), chapter XIV, also indicates strongly diminishing returns to wheat, cotton, sugarcane, and gram.

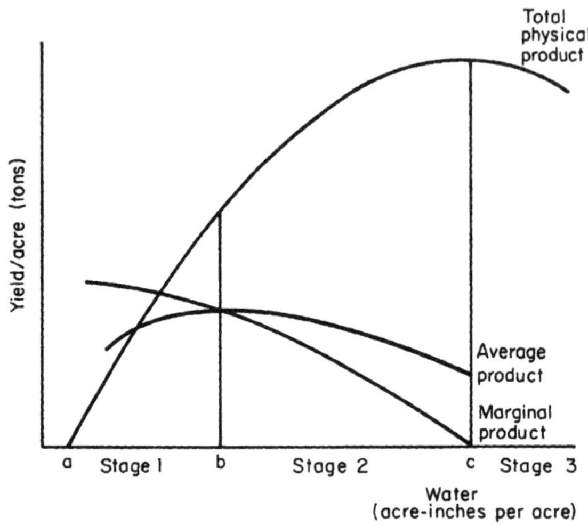

Figure 6.2. Diminishing-returns water-response curve

a = Wilting point
b = Optimal allocation when land is a free good
c = Field capacity

comments on the shape of the crop-water relationship as background, it is possible to offer a partial explanation for this result and, at the same time, to provide some insight into the causes of the serious soil-salinity problem in the Indus Basin.

Assuming that the input-output relationship between crop yield and water exhibits diminishing returns as indicated in Figure 6.2, what would the optimum allocation of water per acre be?

Production functions which include ranges of increasing, decreasing, and negative marginal returns can be divided into three segments.[21] The function in Figure 6.2 has been truncated approximately at its inflection point but it still exhibits the three so-called stages: *ab, bc,* and >*c*. Production at any stage other than *bc* is economically irrational. In the special case where the economic value of an input is zero, rational resource use requires that production take place at the appropriate border of Stage 2. For example, if the variable resource were "free" (its opportunity cost were zero), profit maximization would require that it be added to the fixed resource until its marginal product is also equal to zero. A similar argu-

21. See E. O. Heady, *Economics of Agricultural Production and Resource Use* (Englewood Cliffs, N.J.: Prentice-Hall, Inc., 1952), chapter 4.

ment holds for the fixed resource and the edge of Stage 2 marked by the point of maximum average production. Therefore in Figure 6.2, if land is a "free resource," production would be carried out at point "*b*." Alternatively, this point may be thought of as maximizing the productivity of the variable resource, water.

Many studies of the Indus Basin confirm that farmers are indeed applying deltas substantially below those associated with maximum yields. Harza Engineering estimates, for example, that of the average full crop requirement of 2.7 acre-feet per acre required during the kharif season, only about 80 percent, or 2.2 acre-feet per acre, are supplied by the canal system. They also report that even more extensive "underwatering" occurs during the rabi season.[22]

Tipton and Kalmbach, in preliminary studies for the Feasibility Report on Salinity and Reclamation Project No. 5, have also noted that application of less than the consumptive use requirement is a standard agricultural practice. Present cropping intensities in the project area, according to their estimates, are in the neighborhood of 125 percent. If the full consumptive use requirements of the crops were to be met, irrigation supplies would be available for only about 100 percent intensity.[23]

Given the profit maximizing nature of underwatering, which is evident from the nature of the crop-water production function, one can expect little increase in the amount of water applied per acre, particularly in situations where large acreages are left fallow each season for want of water, and where land is virtually a free input to the farmer.

The failure of the earlier yield models to give significant results is consistent with the foregoing conclusion. As farmers increase or decrease acreages they tend to hold deltas—and hence yields—constant. It is only when the land constraint, or what might be called a "feasible intensity" constraint, becomes binding that increased yields can be expected as a result of increased water application per acre.

The short-run rationality embodied in spreading scarce water thinly has had, however, serious side effects for the Indus Basic in the long run. The failure to supply enough water per acre to ensure a continual downward movement of the salts in the soil profile has resulted in a salinity

22. Harza Engineering Co., *A Program of Water and Power Development in West Pakistan, 1963–1975—Supporting Studies* (for the West Pakistan Water and Power Development Authority, Lahore, September 1963).

23. Tipton and Kalmbach, Inc., *Salinity Control and Reclamation Project V* (for the West Pakistan Water and Power Development Authority, Lahore, 1966).

problem that each year reduces yields and forces abandonment of thousands of irrigated acres.[24]

It is thus ironic that "rational" economic actions by farmers have led to the severe salinity problem of West Pakistan. Although cultivators have been roundly criticized for underwatering, few critics have appreciated the time horizon or the extent of knowledge required to act otherwise. Soil salinity takes years, even decades, to develop and the decreases in yields resulting from the buildup in salts are almost imperceptible in the short run. Moreover, given the low level of consumption and income of the average farmer, and hence his preference for present over future production, it is unlikely that he would have acted differently even if he had understood the relationship between underwatering and salinity. Even from a social or national point of view, it would have taken a very low social discount rate to have justified a behavior other than that employed.

A Linear Programing Model Incorporating Diminishing Returns

Although there is a growing recognition that water response curves are nonlinear, very little empirical work exists which permits or includes nonlinear functions. As the previous discussion indicated, however, nonlinear relationships between yields and the per acre application of water are fundamental to a quantitative understanding of the water allocation problem in Pakistan. Therefore, an attempt must be made to incorporate this concept into the programing model.

Convex functions can be approximated to any desired degree of accuracy by a series of straight-line segments. When applied to the production function for a particular crop, these linear segments may be interpreted as activities which produce the same commodity but with different input-output coefficients. For example, if the water response curve for wheat has the form shown in Figure 6.3, activities can be constructed at representative points *a, b, c,* and *d.* Choice of any one of these segments corresponds to the choice of a point on the production function.

Table 6.3 presents solutions to the linear programing models both with and without the assumption of nonlinear water response curves. The

24. Soil salinity can arise in two ways. Except in extreme cases, it can be treated by consistent downward percolation of water through the soil profile. Soil salinity occurs when salts have been left in the root zone by many years of under irrigation, but the groundwater level is still 10 feet or more below the surface. This is the easiest type of salinity to treat. Salinity also occurs when groundwater tables rise to the point that capillary action causes the water to move upward into the root zone, to be evaporated there. The latter problem is the more difficult to treat because, in addition to higher deltas per acre, drainage is also required.

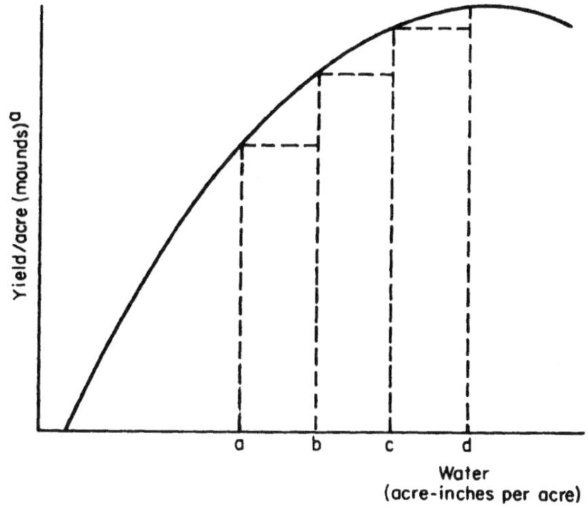

Figure 6.3. Approximated water response curve for wheat
[a]Maund, the standard unit of weight in Pakistan, is equal to 82 2/7 pounds.

comparison emphasizes the quantitative importance of incorporating nonlinear functions into any examination of decisions regarding water allocation in West Pakistan. Use of input-output coefficients which imply that consumptive use requirements are met (Model 1) produces a cropping intensity well below that observed historically. Incorporation of nonlinear functions, on the other hand, results in a significant decrease in yields and an increase in acreage under crop, both of which are consistent with available empirical material. In addition, net revenue increases by Rs. 240 (13 percent), indicating that the farmer may be wiser than those who accuse him of underwatering and those who insist on full consumptive-use coefficients for planning.

Effect of Supplementary Water Supplies on Farmer Price Response

There is a strong relationship between the ability of West Pakistan farmers to alter their cropping patterns in response to a change in relative prices and the availability of irrigation water supplies. In view of the magnitude of the proposed water development program planned for the Indus Basin,[25] one can question whether the elasticity calculations based

25. This irrigation program is remarkable for its size and complexity. The Third Five Year Plan calls for an increase in irrigation water utilization from 68 to 90 million acre feet between 1965 and 1970.

Table 6.3. Cropping patterns, cropping intensities, and yields under linear and nonlinear water response curves (Gujranwala rice tract, 12.5-acre farm)

Crops	Model I Linear response curves (consumptive use)		Model II Nonlinear response curves	
	Acreage	Maunds per acre	Acreage	Maunds per acre
Fine rice	1.14	18.0	1.23	17.1
Coarse rice	0.63	23.0	1.07	21.8
Kharif fodder	0.80	250.0	0.80	250.0
Kharif vegetables	0.10	–	0.10	–
Wheat after fallow	1.36	12.5	2.99	9.2
Wheat after rice	0.68	6.8	0.98	5.2
Gram	0.52	7.0	2.43	6.2
Oilseeds	1.24	6.0	1.56	5.6
Berseem	1.60	450.0	1.60	450.0
Rabi vegetables	0.20	–	0.20	–
Sugarcane	1.00	500.0	1.00	429.0
Fruit	0.30	–	0.30	–
Total acreage	9.57	–	14.26	–
Cropping intensity (based on cultivated acreage)[a]	79%	–	116%	–
Net Revenue	Rs. 1857	–	Rs. 2097	–

[a] Fruit is counted twice because it is a year-long crop overlapping both seasons. No yields are given for fruits and vegetables because these are an aggregation of very different commodities.

on the earlier time-series data will be appropriate guides for future agricultural price policy. In the following section, the linear programing model developed earlier is used to explore this question from a normative point of view.

As a first step, the new technology (tubewells) for producing water must be incorporated into the model. This is done by adding a series of activities that delivers water to the water-using rows; that is, additional water is made available for crop use. The operation of such activities incurs a cost (the variable cost of running a tubewell) and the objective of the program now becomes the maximization of net crop revenues minus the cost of pumping.

Table 6.4 indicates that the introduction of tubewells into the linear programing tableau radically alters the agricultural picture presented by the optimal solution of the model. Cropping intensities increase to the extent that land is now binding, yields are higher, and the composition of the cropping pattern changes substantially. The total net revenue for the representative farm grows by nearly 40 percent, indicating the strong incentive for farmers to invest in the new technology.

Of primary interest for the present study, however, is the effect of an increased, highly flexible water source on the supply curve of various crops. Such curves are defined as the amount of a particular crop farmers *should* be willing to supply at varying prices when other technology, the prices of other crops, and weather are held constant. The curves can easily be derived from the programing model by varying the price for a given crop, computing the net revenue associated with each price, and then re-solving the model for each variation. The linear programing model is an optimizing model, and therefore, the supply curves derived by parametrically varying prices are normative in nature. That is, they describe what farmers should do at varying prices in order to maximize profits, and thus they differ conceptually from the supply estimates presented in the section on price response in West Pakistan, which show what farmers have done. Nevertheless, one can expect the new tubewell technology to exert a profound influence on (1) the optimal *level* of output at current prices (shifts in the supply curve), and (2) the elasticity of farmer price responses.

The two effects described above are readily discernible in Figure 6.4. The equilibrium level of sugarcane output at current prices more than doubles as a result of a flexible supply of supplementary water. Moreover, over the relevant range, Curve II is much more elastic than Curve I. This comparative increase in price elasticity is significant in that Curve I is in some sense analogous to the long-run supply elasticities derived in the section on price response in West Pakistan.[26] The link is that the latter estimates assume a time lapse sufficient for farmers to have made all the adjustments implied in the normative curve.

The choice of sugarcane as an example is not arbitrary. Throughout the 1960's cane prices to growers have been substantially above world market prices and are held there by factory price guarantees and a restric-

26. Indeed, for sugarcane, the relationship is remarkable. A crude calculation of the elasticity of Curve I gives a value of approximately 2.7. The estimate based on time-series data is slightly greater than 3. The normative and long-run historical elasticities for cotton and rice are also of similar magnitudes. Wheat, however, presents an anomaly since the normative elasticity is much greater than the long-run response indicated by Table 6.1.

Table 6.4. Cropping patterns with and without supplementary water from tubewells (Gujranwala rice tract, 12.5-acre farm)

Crops	Without tubewell		With tubewell	
	Acreage	Maunds per acre	Acreage	Maunds per acre
Fine rice	1.23	17.1	5.53	18.0
Coarse rice	1.07	21.8	2.01	23.0
Kharif fodder	0.80	250.0	0.80	250.0
Kharif vegetables	0.10	-	0.10	-
Wheat after fallow	2.99	9.2	2.21	12.5
Wheat after rice	0.98	5.2	5.76	6.8
Gram	2.43	6.2	-	-
Oilseeds	1.56	5.6	-	-
Berseem	1.60	450.0	1.60	450.0
Rabi vegetables	0.20	-	0.20	-
Sugarcane	1.00	429.0	1.00	500.0
Fruit	0.30	-	0.30	-
Total acreage	14.26	-	19.51	-
Cropping intensity (based on cultivated acreage)[a]	116%	-	158%	-
Net revenue	Rs. 2097	-	Rs. 2877	-

[a] Fruit is counted twice because it is a year-long crop overlapping both seasons. No yields are given for fruits and vegetables because these are an aggregation of very different commodities.

tive government import policy.[27] Historically, the distortion of cane prices has been minimized by the extremely high water requirements of sugarcane. In fact, many areas served by nonperennial canals grow virtually no cane at all. As Figure 6.4 indicates, however, and as evidence from other tubewell areas corroborates, large-scale groundwater development has substantially altered the relative profitability of the sugar crop. Therefore, if the government does not want further inroads into land which might be devoted to export crops such as rice and cotton, or food crops, some adjustment will be required in its present sugar policy. A failure to make these alterations may prove quite costly, in terms of both budget expenditure and national income forgone. Quantitatively, it

27. For a fuller discussion, see Government of Pakistan, Ministry of Food and Agriculture, *Report of the Pakistan Sugar Commission* (Karachi, July 1959).

appears that maintenance of the status quo in sugarcane output in the face of a widespread increase in water availability will require a decrease in the guaranteed mill price (Rs. 2.0 per maund) of 25 to 30 percent—at least in the Multan-Montgomery area.

Other examples of the effects of additional water supplies on the cropping pattern are given in Figures 6.5, 6.6, and 6.7. Figure 6.5 indicates that at the wheat price prevailing in the late 1960's (approximately Rs. 15 per maund), farmers who install tubewells but who use traditional seed varieties are likely to *reduce* wheat production substantially.[28] This result is due to the profitability of growing cotton, which competes with wheat for land. Figure 6.5 also indicates that only a small price (or yield) increase is required for wheat to overcome the comparative advantage of cotton production. On the basis of the derived curves, one can expect wheat output under tubewells to be substantially greater at Rs. 17.5 per maund than when only canal water is available. Such a possibility would be of special importance if the substantial imports of wheat supplied under concessional terms (through the United States Public Law 480) were to be cut off.

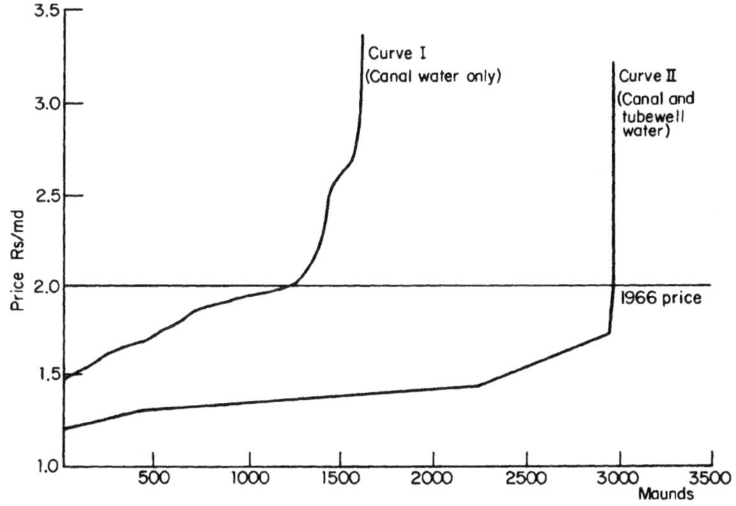

Figure 6.4. Normative supply curves for sugarcane

28. With the introduction of new wheat and rice varieties after 1967, the profitability situation for food grains relative to sugarcane and cotton changed rather dramatically. This point, and its implications, are discussed in C. H. Gotsch and W. P. Falcon, *Agricultural Price Policy and the Development of West Pakistan*, chapter 4.

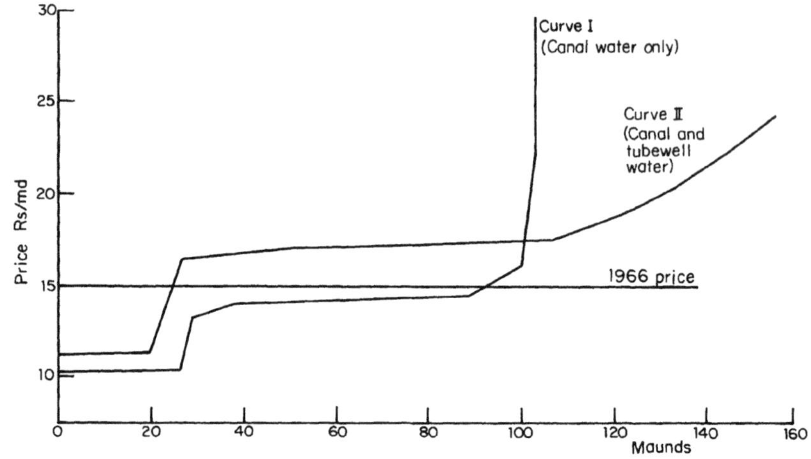

Figure 6.5. Normative supply curves for wheat

The effect of additional water supplies on the historical wheat-cotton relationship may be even more significant as a result of the introduction of the new "dwarf" wheats. Yields of the new varieties are two to three times that normally achieved with indigenous varieties.[29] Such yield increases depend in part, however, on several additional irrigations during the growing season—irrigations which could easily be supplied with tubewells.

Figures 6.6 and 6.7 illustrate other major cash crops for which substantial increases in supply at current prices can be expected once supplementary water becomes available. Surveys of farmers who have already installed tubewells strongly support the conclusions obtained from the normative analysis. For example, based on a relatively large sample of tubewell and nontubewell farmers, Ghulam Mohammed[30] shows that in Gujranwala District, tubewell farmers in the early 1960's increased the percentage of area under rice from 36 percent to 62 percent; he also reports that in the Multan-Montgomery area cotton acreage was increased from 27 to 38 percent. At the same time, wheat acreage remained essentially stagnant in both areas.

29. Norman Borlaug, "Progress Report on the Accelerated Wheat Improvement Program in West Pakistan" (mimeo, Ford Foundation, Karachi, November 1965); and A. A. Qureshi and Ignacio Narvaez, "Annual Technical Report, Accelerated Wheat Improvement Program, West Pakistan, 1965–66" (mimeo, Ford Foundation, Lahore, August 1966).

30. Ghulam Mohammed, "Private Tubewell Development and Cropping Patterns in West Pakistan," *Pakistan Development Review*, 5 (Spring 1965), 1–53.

It is a major shortcoming that the curves in Figures 6.4 to 6.7 are static. Large increases in the supply of wheat, for example, might be expected to reduce prices, which in turn would affect relative net revenue. Further exploration of the model requires: (1) the introduction of demand schedules for various crops; and (2) dynamic macro variables, especially the growth in consumer incomes. Even without these considerations, however, the conclusion that large-scale water development programs can be expected to change radically the supplies and the price elasticities for most agricultural commodities appears to be well substantiated.

Conclusions and Warnings

Many of the conclusions of this study have been noted in passing. However, three points seem worthy of emphasis, as do some words of caution.

The first point is that historical responses of Punjabi farmers to changes in relative prices have been large by world standards. The short-run supply elasticities, mostly within the 0.1 to 0.5 range, indicate the potential power of price policy as an instrumental variable in Pakistan. This is particularly true for cash crops whose elasticities are clustered at the upper portion of the scale. As an example, the series of reductions in export duties for cotton during the early 1960's might be cited; these tax

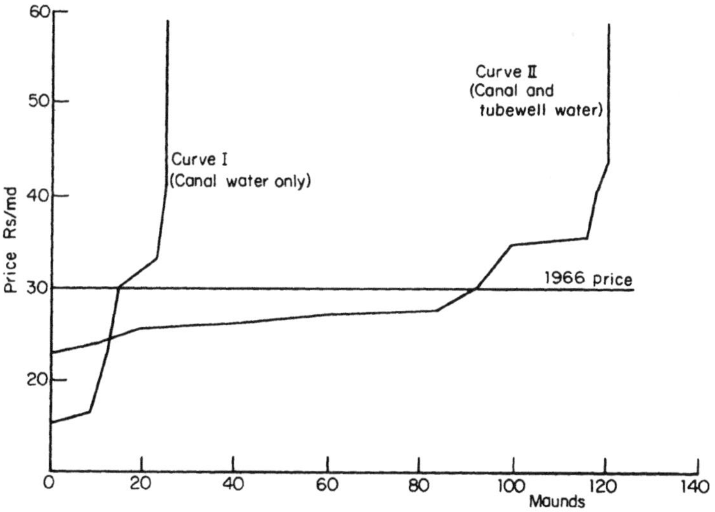

Figure 6.6. Normative supply curves for cotton

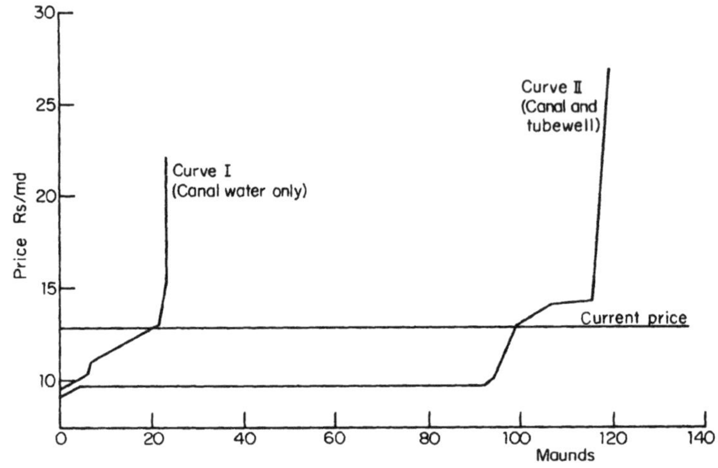

Figure 6.7. Normative supply curve for fine rice

changes have probably increased the relative price received by cotton farmers by about 20 percent.[31] This reduction, and the long-run acreage response it induced, were undoubtedly factors in the rapid growth of cotton production and exports.

The second point, demonstrated by the empirical estimates of supply response as well as by the models on water use, is that Punjabi farmers have allocated inputs efficiently. These general conclusions add to the growing literature that farmers, although poor, allocate their resources in an efficient manner.[32] Methodologically, the programing approach appears to offer a useful method for verifying the efficiency of farmer actions, for assessing the differential effects of changing technology, and for examining the interaction between technical change and price policy.

The third point, indicated by the specific calculations for the normative supply functions, is that supply elasticities are sensitive to changes in technology. Although the specific calculations presented here should be regarded only as suggestive because of their static and regional character, they do offer a partial explanation for certain recent commodity developments in West Pakistan. For example, the general rightward shifts

31. For a fuller discussion, see W. P. Falcon and C. H. Gotsch, "Agricultural Development in Pakistan: Lessons from the Second Plan Period," in G. F. Papanek, ed., *Development Policy——Theory and Practice* (Cambridge: Harvard University Press, 1968).

32. This idea is most succinctly stated in T. W. Schultz, *Transforming Traditional Agriculture* (New Haven: Yale University Press, 1964).

in the curves for cotton, rice, and sugarcane, a result of breaking the water constraints by the use of tubewells, are consistent with recent growth rates of 7.1, 7.8, and 10.6 percent per annum respectively. These shifts are in marked contrast to the leftward movement indicated by the models for wheat output between 1960 and 1966. The normative wheat curves indicate, however, that with higher relative net revenues per acre (through higher prices and/or yields) wheat production is likely to expand significantly, although at the expense of the other crops. Most importantly however, this set of curves indicates the necessity of constant review of agriculture price policy under conditions of rapidly changing technology.

With regard to the changes in slope (as opposed to shifts in the curves), the normative supply curves indicate that the price elasticities of supply for most crops will probably increase in West Pakistan as a result of the water development program. To be sure, this is a statement of what farmers "should do" to maximize incomes; however, the historical models have shown that farmers have generally behaved in a rational manner. These changes in elasticities indicate the increased potential for altering future cropping patterns through price and technology policies that affect the profitability of agricultural commodities.

7 The Rural Public Works Program in East Pakistan

John Woodward Thomas

Even a tourist, unconcerned with the problems of economic development, quickly becomes aware that human labor is in plentiful supply on the Indo-Pakistan subcontinent. The ubiquitous guides who point out the splendors of the Taj Mahal, who follow the visitor through the forts and tombs of Lahore and Delhi, or who direct him along the Grand Trunk Road from the Khyber Pass to Calcutta never fail to point out that it took thousands of men, without the benefit of modern technology, to build these monuments and public facilities.

After British rule replaced the Hindu, Sikh, and Moghul dynasties of the area, the practice of intensive utilization of human labor declined. In the early days of independence, both India and Pakistan tended to eschew labor-intensive forms of development in favor of more capital-intensive programs. As the strategy of industrialization failed to make an impact on the problem of unemployment, both nations were forced to seek new ways to accelerate their development efforts.

In East Pakistan, particularly, the need for more rapid development was acute. There are few poorer areas of the world. If East Pakistan had been considered separately on the basis of gross national product per capita in 1960, it would have ranked ninety-third among the world's ninety-six then independent nations.[1]

NOTE: I must acknowledge an important intellectual debt to Richard V. Gilbert, whose ideas have been central in shaping the Works Program and this analysis. The only publicly available statement of his views is contained in his "The Works Program in East Pakistan," *International Labor Review*, 89 (March 1964), 213–220. I am grateful also for the comments and assistance of Richard M. Hook and Richard Patten.

1. Norton Ginsburg, *Atlas of Economic Development* (Chicago: University of Chicago Press, 1961), p. 18; Taufiq M. Khan and Asbjørn Bergan, "Measurement of Structural Change in the Pakistan Economy: A Review of the National Income Estimates," *Pakistan Development Review*, 6 (Summer 1966), 199–200.

The East Pakistan Rural Public Works Program was part of a renewed attempt to break this pattern of stagnation by converting idle labor into capital, raising the level of nutrition of the landless and unemployed, providing basic rural facilities that would promote the growth of agricultural production, and stimulating the economy by providing new demands for domestically produced goods. Between 1962, when the Rural Works Program was initiated on a province-wide basis, and 1969, the Government of East Pakistan invested $168 million in the program; between 1963 and 1968 expenditures on the program averaged about 8 percent of the annual Provincial development program. The Program's decentralized implementation with planning and administration through local councils was an innovation in the conduct of Pakistan's development programs.

Many foreign economic analysts have judged the Rural Works Program a success. Edward S. Mason has described it as "probably the most successful attempt to use effectively the services of underemployed agricultural workers that has been undertaken in any less developed country."[2] A United Nations economic survey has reported that the program "has given new confidence to the rural masses, provided a powerful stimulus to the growth of rural leadership and strengthened the institutions of local government."[3]

These views are far from universal. Other observers, including many Pakistanis, view the program as politically corrupt and of little economic value. In the only study of the Program published so far, a Pakistani economist states that "the programme to date is [nothing] more than a slightly more elaborate welfare or relief measure introduced into the rural areas, along with the slightly more sordid motive of winning the allegiance of the narrow class of Basic Democrats."[4]

Clearly, the Rural Public Works Program, better known as the Works Program, is a controversial subject. The purpose of this study is to examine some of the aspects of this controversy and to analyze the economic contribution of the Program to rural East Pakistan with the use of original data.

2. Edward S. Mason, *Economic Development in India and Pakistan* (Occasional Paper No. 13, Harvard Center for International Affairs, Cambridge, September 1966), p. 56.

3. United Nations, *Economic Survey of Asia and the Far East for 1965* (Bangkok, 1966), p. 126.

4. Rehman Sobhan, *Basic Democracies Works Programme and Rural Development in East Pakistan* (Dacca: Bureau of Economic Research, University of Dacca, 1968), p. 238.

The Rural Economy of East Pakistan

To comprehend the necessity for a labor-intensive works program in rural East Pakistan, it is essential to have an understanding of conditions in that area. The census of 1960 reported a population of 53.9 million, of whom 94.6 percent lived in the rural areas. With an average of 1,037 persons per square mile, East Pakistan's population density was more than double that of the Netherlands, Japan, or Taiwan, the most densely populated nations of the world, and twice as much as that of Kerala, the most densely populated state of India. In 1970 the population of the province was estimated at 70.2 million, after an annual growth for a decade of approximately 3.2 percent.[5]

East Pakistan has few natural resources. Its plentiful population and rich agricultural land constitute its only substantial endowment. Yet wastage of manpower resources is high. In the 1960's voluntary and involuntary unemployment was estimated at 33 percent of total available labor man-days.[6]

In spite of East Pakistan's rich agricultural potential, its vast rural population was, by 1960, living in wretched circumstances, devoid of hope and resigned to a world in which change came only with the frequent natural disasters that made life even more difficult. The poorest third of the population existed on an average daily intake of 1,600 calories, which is far below the minimum necessary for the maintenance of good health. In 1959, output of rice, the principal food crop of East Pakistan, was lower than the annual average during the period 1947–50.[7] By 1960 the rice surplus of the first half of the century had been replaced by a deficit that required the import of over half a million tons of foodgrains

5. These population and land area statistics are derived from Government of Pakistan, Central Statistical Office, *Monthly Statistical Bulletin,* quoted in USAID Mission to Pakistan, *The Statistical Fact Book* (Lahore, 1968), table i-1; Government of Pakistan, *1961 Population Census of Pakistan* (Karachi, November 1961); United Nations, *Demographic Yearbook, 1964,* Special Topic Population Census Statistics III, 16th ed. (New York, 1965); Government of India, *The Statistical Abstract of the Indian Union, 1961* (Delhi, 1966).

6. These figures are derived from the Pakistan Advisory Group, *Long Term Perspectives for the Pakistan Economy* (mimeo, Harvard Development Advisory Service, Karachi, April 1964), appendix 4, p. 3, table 1, and also from Wouter Tims, "Employment by Regions and Sectors, 1950–1985" (mimeo, Harvard Development Advisory Group, Karachi, June 11, 1965), p. 2.

7. Government of Pakistan, Ministry of Food and Agriculture, *Report of the Food and Agriculture Commission* (Karachi, November 1960), p. 21.

annually throughout the 1960's. Even this was far too little to provide adequate levels of nutrition at reasonable prices.[8]

Given the stagnation in agriculture, any growth that occurred in the 1950's took place in the industrial sector, and the benefits of this growth were concentrated in urban areas, thus contributing to a rapidly growing inequity in the distribution of wealth. With priority given to industrial development, less than 20 percent of the province's development expenditures were going directly into agricultural development programs, despite the fact that 77 percent of the labor force was employed in agriculture.

The difficulties of utilizing the human and land resources in East Pakistan are numerous. Water is the critical factor. Most of the province's 55,000 square miles are in the deltaic plain of the Ganges and Brahmaputra Rivers. The annual monsoon brings an average of 80 inches of rainfall, concentrated in the months of June and July, and produces an annual flood that normally covers one-third of the land area of the province. But from November to June there is almost no rainfall, and agriculture is possible only if water for irrigation can be obtained from the rivers that traverse the area or from the supply of groundwater. Water management facilities are essential for successful agriculture in East Pakistan.

In the days before Independence, some facilities for water control were developed and maintained by the landholders, the wealthy Hindu "zamindars." By tradition, they conscripted peasants to maintain the rural facilities: drainage and irrigation channels, flood protection embankments, and farm-to-market roads. The zamindars provided the planning, organization, and capital needed; the peasants provided the labor which represented the largest portion of the cost. Partition in 1947 and the exodus of the zamindars deprived the rural areas of their sources of leadership and the capital for maintaining existing facilities.[9]

At the same time the departure of the zamindars precipitated a social revolution in East Pakistan. The zamindars' lands became available to

8. Government of East Pakistan, East Pakistan Bureau of Statistics, *Statistical Digest of East Pakistan*, No. 3 (Dacca, 1965), p. 243.

9. Although there is no way to document adequately the magnitude of the flow of capital out of East Pakistan after Independence, some indication of it may be obtained from A. Sadeque's estimate that in the five years following Partition, the net outflow of Hindu capital from East to West Bengal amounted to Rs. 285.9 crores ($599.4 million). This movement occurred when there was almost total prohibition on the flow of capital out of Pakistan, and when the most mobile capital had already been transferred. A. Sadeque, *The Economic Emergence of Pakistan* (Dacca: Government of East Bengal Press, 1954), p. 25.

the peasants who had actually been farming them, and land tenancy declined sharply. Statistics for 1960 reveal that only 2 percent of East Pakistan's agricultural land was cultivated by farmers who owned no land of their own.[10] However, the problem of tenancy was quickly replaced by another problem, land fragmentation. Muslim inheritance laws dictate that property must be equally divided among heirs. As the population grew, land was divided and subdivided until by 1960 the cultivated area per farm had dwindled to an average of 3.1 acres, with most farms fragmented into several noncontiguous plots.[11] By that time also, one and a half million rural inhabitants were classified as landless laborers.[12]

During the same years, most rural facilities, which had been developed in pre-partition years, deteriorated. Means of controlling water declined, leaving the rural inhabitants subject to drought and flood. The adverse effects of natural calamities became so widespread that 70.7 percent of the East Pakistani villagers responding to the government's Sample Survey of 1961 reported that they had sustained loss due to natural disaster during the preceding year.[13]

Such a situation created a descending spiral. Each year the government spent increasing amounts on relief, including work relief, which maintained life but contributed nothing to the development of rural facilities. As agricultural production stagnated, real government revenue declined. The cost of importing food for the growing rural population increased at an alarming rate. Because most rural people lived in subsistence agriculture, the rural economy provided little effective market to encourage the development of industry. Yet the greater the drain on the economy, the less the government was inclined to invest in rural areas.

General Mohammed Ayub Khan's regime, which attached high priority to political stability and economic development, perceived the East Pakistan situation as a threat to its objectives. The stagnation of East Pakistan's economy and the resentment that this caused required that programs to improve East Pakistan's economic situation be created and implemented.

10. Government of Pakistan, Agricultural Census Organization, Ministry of Food and Agriculture, *Pakistan Census of Agriculture, a Summary of East Pakistan Data* (Lahore, 1960), p. 11.

11. *Ibid.*, p. 4.

12. Government of Pakistan, Ministry of Food and Agriculture, *Report of the Food and Agriculture Commission* (Karachi, November 1960), p. 37.

13. Government of Pakistan, Central Statistical Office, *National Sample Survey (Third Round), 1961* (Karachi, 1963), p. 27.

The Formulation of the Works Program

The administration of the Works Program was based on the existing but little utilized structure of local government, and the Basic Democracies system that was built into that structure in late 1959 (and abolished in 1969). The two central purposes of the Basic Democracies system were: to activate local government so that the people could participate in the solution of their problems by planning and implementing development programs for their own areas; and to legitimatize the existing government through the indirect election of the president and legislators, with members of local government bodies serving as the electors. A four-tiered governmental structure was instituted. At its base were 4,053 Union Councils (a "union" is an administrative area of approximately 12,000 people living in wards or villages), with one Union Council member representing each ward. Above these were 413 Thana Councils (a "thana" is an administrative area averaging 125 square miles and a population of approximately 150,000). At the next level were seventeen District Councils, followed by four Divisional Councils. Except for the Union Councils, each council was composed of members elected from the council immediately subordinate and of government officials serving ex officio. The Union Council was given taxing powers and development responsibility; coordinating and supporting activities were assigned to the Thana and to the higher councils. By intermingling government officers and elected representatives, the government hoped to blend their viewpoints and experience and to reorient them, as a functioning unit, toward development.

Much was expected of the Basic Democracies system, but development efforts sponsored by local councils moved very slowly. The poverty of the rural community left little room for the exercise of new taxing powers. The government, although requesting Basic Democracies to foster economic development, provided only small grants to the councils. In 1961–62, only $360,000 out of East Pakistan's total development budget of $151 million, went to the Basic Democracies.[14]

The Second Five Year Plan, scheduled to begin in mid-1960, provided the government of Ayub Khan with the opportunity to set forth its own goals and strategies of economic development. But available resources fell far short of what was needed. A strategy to close the resource gap was suggested by Dr. Richard V. Gilbert, Director of the economic

14. Government of East Pakistan, Finance Department, *Approved Development Program of East Pakistan Government for the Year 1961–62* (Dacca: East Pakistan Government Press, 1961), pp. 28–29.

advisory group working with the Pakistan Planning Commission. This strategy, developed within the Planning Commission, basically called for an expanded program of United States Public Law 480 assistance.[15]

The Planning Commission's proposed program contained the following elements.

1. *Expanded External Resources* were to be obtained under P.L. 480 for specified types of programs.

2. *A Works Program* in East Pakistan, financed from rupees generated by the sale of P.L. 480 commodities in Pakistan, was to receive high priority. The works program was seen as a double-edged instrument for development: (a) it would build the facilities desperately needed for the development of rural East Pakistan, create employment in the agricultural slack season, and raise rural incomes; and (b) it would create the purchasing power in the rural economy that would result in adequate demand for the commodities provided by foreign aid. The additional demand pumped into the rural areas by the works program would also avoid a sharp drop in agricultural prices, which otherwise would certainly affect incentives for domestic production unfavorably.

3. *Programs directly promoting agricultural development* were to receive high priority. The Planning Commission felt that food aid would eliminate the necessity for crash programs to attain food self-sufficiency. Food aid could therefore buy time in which to put together a soundly conceived and carefully implemented agricultural program that would improve agricultural technology and develop agricultural supply systems. In addition, stabilization of basic foodgrain prices would reduce farmers' risk and encourage a production mix which would result in an output of higher value.

4. *Price stabilization* was also a major Planning Commission objective in expanding the P.L. 480 program. Production of basic crops had increased very little since 1947 while development expenditures, as well as population growth, had increased demand for food and clothing. Inflationary pressures had been the consequence. Food and fiber available under the expanded P.L. 480 program would meet some of this demand directly.

15. Government of Pakistan, Planning Commission, *Memorandum on the United States Surplus Agricultural Commodities Aid to Pakistan* (Karachi, January 1961); Government of Pakistan, Planning Commission, *Use of Resources Provided by Expanded P.L. 480 Aid* (Karachi, April 1961; Government of Pakistan, Planning Commission, *Price, Income, Fiscal and Foreign Exchange Aspects of Expanded P.L. 480 Programme* (Karachi, April 1961).

Reactions to the Proposed Program

The proposal for a greatly expanded P.L. 480 program ran counter to much of the thinking of development planners of the time. A foreign economist who worked in Pakistan has provided a colorful statement of opposition to P.L. 480 aid. "The delivery of P.L. 480 wheat . . . has very often resembled a forced feeding operation of a singularly unnegotiated character. . . . The central point is that this spuriously 'easy' form of aid insidiously handicaps the nation's own efforts to feed itself . . . it has placed in mortal jeopardy the very national pride that has sustained Pakistan."[16] The fear most commonly voiced was that P.L. 480 aid would serve as a disincentive to local agriculture.

Five principal objections to a works program were also raised: (1) that the program would be unproductive and "make-work" in nature, as had been the case with work relief programs in the subcontinent during periods of famine or other calamities; (2) that there would be insufficient administrative talent in the rural areas to manage the program or that it would divert already overcommitted administrative, management, and technical personnel from the existing development program, and therefore sacrifice growth for employment; (3) that a decentralized program would lead to waste, corruption, and misuse of funds, and particularly that works program funds would be used for political handouts; (4) that facilities constructed in this manner would not be maintained; and (5) that East Pakistanis, who are traditionally rice eaters, could not be induced to eat P.L. 480 wheat, and that therefore the P.L. 480 commodities could not meet the demand created by increased incomes, causing further inflation.

In spite of these concerns, the prospect of additional aid through P.L. 480 was attractive, and the government moved toward obtaining it without committing itself to a works program for East Pakistan. This situation provoked Richard Gilbert to state that "Failure to develop such a [works] program is the principal irrationality of the Plan. . . . A works program, in the context of the labor surplus which in the East Wing, as in India, is probably of the order of 25%, is so obvious a necessity that I find myself getting furious at the array of argument, pseudoanalytical or practical, that is thrown up."[17] In October 1961, an agreement under

16. Joe R. Motheral, "The Effect of Government Policy and Programs on Agricultural Production in Pakistan" (mimeo, paper presented to a seminar at the Harvard Center for International Affairs, Cambridge, December 1960), pp. 7–8.

17. Richard V. Gilbert, letters to David E. Bell, December 4, 1960, p. 4, and Gustav F. Papanek, December 29, 1960, p. 4.

which the United States would, over a four-year period, supply Pakistan with $621 million of agricultural surplus commodities was signed.

The Pilot and Province-Wide Works Programs

A step toward the evolution of the Works Program also took place in 1961, when Akhtar Hameed Khan, Director of the East Pakistan Academy for Rural Development in Comilla, agreed to undertake a pilot works program. He viewed the Academy not merely as a training institution but also as a source of new and effective ideas to promote rural development. He therefore accepted all aspects of development in Comilla Thana as the Academy's responsibility. These aspects included agricultural extension, cooperatives, farmer education, local works, and rural administration. In essence, in addition to being an educational institution, the Academy also became a rural experimental station with the thana as its laboratory.

Initially, the Union Councils of Comilla Thana were asked to prepare plans for the projects they wished to see carried out in their areas. The list of such projects included flood control embankments, the opening of silted irrigation and drainage canals, and road building. These plans were then coordinated into a thana plan, in harmony with the Academy's concept of rural development at the thana level. In December 1961 work began, with projects implemented by Project Committees in each Union Council. By May 1962, the pilot project could boast an impressive list of physical accomplishments. An administrative system that took advantage of the capacity of local bodies to plan and execute local development projects had been successfully designed and tested. The Pilot Project also clearly demonstrated the willingness of villagers to participate in such a program.

During the experimentation period, the East Pakistan Secretary of Basic Democracies and Local Government was interested in finding a way to give the local councils a larger role in local development. When the pilot works program at Comilla was called to his attention he recognized the potential of such a program implemented on a province-wide basis through the Basic Democracies system.

For over six months in 1962 the Secretary of Basic Democracies and Local Government argued at all levels of government, without success, that a works program should be established. The government was reluctant to commit resources to East Pakistan and to assume the risks of administrative innovation. In September 1962, however, serious floods inundated East Pakistan. President Ayub responded by flying to the area and announcing that he would provide Rs. 10 crores ($21 million) for flood relief, to be administered through the Basic Democracies. Aware that the floods had affected almost every district in the province, the Secretary determined to use the funds at his disposal to begin a province-wide works program. He intended that the program would not only alleviate the distress caused by the current flood but also help, by the construction of water control systems, to mitigate future disasters. Consequently, in late September 1962, instructions were issued to all local councils setting forth the procedures under which the Works Program would operate. In November, with the expectations thus created throughout the province putting pressure on the government, official sanction was reluctantly given to the Program and the Rs. 10 crores were released. That same month the first allocations to rural councils were made and the works program was officially begun.

The Politics and Performance of the Works Program

Any analysis of the contribution of the Works Program to East Pakistan's economy must be made in the perspective of its two distinct phases. Indeed, a failure to distinguish between time periods has been a major source of the conflicting views about the program. These periods can be broadly characterized as the economic and the political eras. The initiative of a Secretary of the Government of East Pakistan had brought the Works Program into existence. Although it received government sanction in its early days, it had little support and aroused little interest on the part of national leaders. As the Program grew in size in 1963, 1964 and 1965, it was widely acclaimed a success and the interest of national leaders grew accordingly. Throughout this period, the program was firmly controlled by the Basic Democracies and Local Government Department, which adhered to economic priorities rigorously, enforced standards of honesty, and dismissed those who violated them. The administrative operation was frequently adapted in the light of experience to meet changing conditions. During this period, innovations such as thana planning and the position of Thana Circle Officer (in charge of coordinating and directing thana development) were introduced.

In 1965 elections were held. Under the Basic Democracies system, the voting public was to select local council members, who were to form an electoral college to elect the president. As elections approached, pressures to use Works Program funds for support of the government in power grew, but these were generally resisted. East Pakistan, the center of opposition to the government, was expected to vote against President Ayub. In fact, however, the government carried the province by a small majority. The *New York Times* in its report on election results from Pakistan expressed the widely-held view that the Works Program had influenced the outcome of the election. "The failure of any real anti-Ayub vote to emerge in East Pakistan is viewed as a triumph for the three-year-old Rural Works Program, which has pumped much needed funds into farm communities and brought many improvements in rural life."[18] After the election of 1965 the political potential of the Works Program was fully perceived, and the Ayub government moved to employ it for its own political ends.

During 1965 and 1966 the Governor of East Pakistan, Abdul Monem Khan, who was the chief political organizer for the Ayub government in East Pakistan as well as the administrative head of the provincial government, sought to shape the Works Program to serve the political purposes of the regime. The conflicts between the Governor and the Secretary of Basic Democracies over the operation of the program led to the Secretary's removal from office in 1966 and his replacement by another officer more amenable to using the Works Program for political ends.

As a result, since 1966 political considerations have been increasingly important and economic considerations less and less so in the operation of the Works Program. In many instances, misuse and even outright diversion of funds remained unpunished if the local council member had the right political affiliations. As soon as this shift was perceived by local officials, widespread abuse became inevitable, for the necessity to produce economic results was obviated and political support alone was sufficient to justify receipt of funds. Increasingly after 1966, local politics became dominant in local project decisions, and checks on performance and audits of local council accounts became noticeably less frequent.

Concurrently, in the second half of the sixties, opposition to the Ayub regime grew rapidly in East Pakistan and culminated in the violence of 1969 that led to the overthrow of the regime. During this period the system of indirect elections was widely regarded as an oppressive tool for maintaining government power. The Works Program gradually came to be viewed by the urban-based leaders of the opposition as the payoff to the local councillors for their political support of the regime. This view is reflected in the work of Rehman Sobhan already cited. The result was wide-spread, bitter, and often emotional criticism of the Works Program by those who could see it only as a corrupting means of buying political support in the rural areas.

Since the overthrow of the Ayub government the Works Program has

18. *The New York Times*, January 3, 1965, p. 1.

not fundamentally changed, although in 1969 and 1970 allocations dropped by approximately 30 percent to $20 million annually.[19] Even though political support for misuse of funds is gone, it will take a major new effort to correct the corrupt habits that have developed. The new government has not yet made this effort. In the meantime, the structures previously created deteriorate further and the progress of the early 1960's is being lost.

Performance of the Works Program

Given the size of the expenditure on the Works Program, notable physical progress should have been possible. Table 7.1 summarizes the achievements as reported in the documents of the Government of East Pakistan. Also included is a series of revised estimates, based on an eight-thana study[20] carried out in 1967, that modifies, but generally substantiates, the official statistics. A few qualifications are necessary, however. In almost all classifications of Works Program activities there are large achievements in the "repaired" category. Under East Pakistan weather conditions, annual repairs are necessary on most earthwork structures, and the result is that the annual report of mileage repaired is high. The definition of roads is not standardized and up to 60 percent of Works Program roads might better be defined as paths. While these "roads" are quite appropriate for rural conditions, an understanding of the Program's achievements requires knowledge of their size.

Considerable question has been raised about the reliability of the official statistics on the performance of the Program. Critics like Sobhan speak of the "deplorable quality of official statistics relating to the Works Program"[21] Allowing for the divergence of views, the physical

19. In 1969 and 1970 funds for the Thana Irrigation Program have been included under the budget for the Works Program. The figures cited here are net of Thana Irrigation Program funds.

20. Available data on the Works Program and the consequent changes in the rural economy offer little basis for evaluating the contribution of the Works Program. Not only are data limited to agricultural production statistics, occasional sample surveys, and figures on total physical accomplishments, but they also contain many inaccuracies and frequently bear little relevance to analysis of the benefits of the Works Program. Therefore, this evaluation of the Works Program is based on a new set of data developed for the purpose. The data were obtained through a detailed study of eight of East Pakistan's 413 thanas conducted during 1967. The eight thanas were selected in part for geographical distribution throughout East Pakistan, with two thanas in each of the province's four divisions. They were also selected to include samples of the varying physical conditions of the province, while yet attempting to be representative of East Pakistan as a whole.

21. Rehman Sobhan, *Basic Democracies*, p. 201.

Table 7.1. Summary of accomplishments, East Pakistan Works Program, 1962–1968

Totals	Hard-surfaced roads (in miles)		Dirt-surfaced roads (in miles)		Embankments (in miles)		Drainage-irrigation canals (in miles)		Acres Benefitted by columns 5, 6, 7, 8	Community Buildings	Employment created (man-days in thousands)	Total allocation (millions)
	New	Repaired	New	Repaired	New	Repaired	New	Re-excavated				
	1	2	3	4	5	6	7	8	9	10	11	12
1962–67	647	1,835	17,830	80,706	2,883	6,675	3,182	7,944	7,191,403	6,389	153,940	Rs. 710 $ 149
Revised estimates based on 8-thana study, 1967	–	–	12,381	71,036	–	–	–	–	2,955,000	3,195	208,500	–
1967–68[a]	323	355	3,095	13,580	860	920	849	2,022	–	646	19,018	Rs. 215 $ 47.3

Source: Government of East Pakistan, Basic Democracies and Local Government Department, Performance Report(s) on the Rural Works Program, 1963–64, 1964–65, 1965–66, 1966–67 (Dacca). Figures consistent with findings of eight-thana study except as noted.

[a] Figures for 1967–68 were the most recent available in Dacca as of February 1970.

achievements of the Program are examined in detail in Appendix A. Despite some obvious inconsistencies and a few incorrect figures in the official statistics, the weight of evidence in the eight-thana study seems to support the conclusion that the Works Program has made notable progress in developing rural infrastructure.

Maintenance is an important consideration in a climate where heavy monsoon rains cause continuous deterioration of earthwork construction. In the early phases of the Works Program, each Union Council was required to insure that structures erected were maintained. To enforce this regulation Councils were required to spend 25 percent of their total revenue on maintenance. In addition, Councils were instructed that maintenance was to receive priority over new construction. When these regulations were not adhered to, allocations were withdrawn.

In the eight-thana study of 1967, it was found that about 80 percent of the road mileage had been maintained. In two cases roads had been allowed to deteriorate because their location had proven uneconomic and the council had decided that the marginal value of the land's use was higher for agriculture than for a road. The other problem encountered was that approximately 20 percent of the bridges in Works Program roads were of a lower carrying capacity than the roads thereby limiting usage of the roads to those vehicles that the bridges could accomodate. Drainage canals, in all cases observed, had been maintained, presumably because of the high return resulting from improved drainage. Insufficient maintenance of Works Program projects had occurred most frequently with flood control embankments. In the wedge-shaped flood plain extending from northern to south-central East Pakistan, the flooding is so great that small piecemeal embankments are inadequate to divert major flood waters. Embankments in this area had prevented damage from high water, but when overflowed and partially destroyed by major floods, they had not been repaired.

Subsequent observation in 1969, although much less systematic than the eight-thana study, indicated that most Works Program facilities had deteriorated very badly. This suggests that there has been little maintenance work in recent years and that, unless immediate action is taken, many of the new facilities will deteriorate to the point where benefits from them will be sharply diminished.

The Works Program and Organization for Rural Development

One of the most significant dimensions of the Works Program is the decentralized form of organization for economic action which evolved during the first years of its operation. It was based on the following views.

1. The rural people, though generally uneducated, have the knowledge of their own needs and of local conditions to enable them to plan and carry out a program for the development of their own areas.

2. The appropriate role of government in the process of local development is to provide the people with (a) the resources to carry out their own development effort and (b) a clearly defined system within which the work is executed.

3. The system provided by government for carrying out local development should (a) be determined by experience and subject to change on the basis of pragmatic analysis; (b) limit local efforts to those programs for which there is clear evidence of need and available capacity to meet that need; and (c) use the pressure of a fully informed populace to ensure that resources are not misused.[22]

Many of the Works Program projects could not have been carried out without the decentralized form of organization that has used local knowledge to identify the areas that could be drained with simple gravity-flow canals, the most economic location of farm-to-market roads, or the places where rivers most regularly overflow their banks. Nor would it have been feasible for a centralized organization to implement the many small projects in remote locations. Thus, the form of organization used by the Works Program has been effective for a variety of small, but important, local development projects.

The Works Program has increasingly utilized the thana, which has proved an appropriate focus for the organization of its development activities. In the first year of the Works Program there was considerable caution about the capability of the Thana Council to implement projects, largely because the thana had never been an important level of administration. As a result, in 1962–63 Works Program funds were allocated to only 54 of the 413 thanas, one in each subdivision, with only 6.5 percent of total funds going to Thana Councils. The performance of the Thana Councils was so good in that year, however, that in 1963–64 all thanas participated and received 36.2 percent of the funds. This trend has continued, as Table 7.2 indicates, and the thana has become the basic unit of Works Program administration.

The Thana Councils' demonstrated competence as agents for promoting development has been utilized and enhanced in at least two ways. First, a system of thana five-year Works Program plans has evolved. In 1964, each thana was given a Thana Plan Book in which to prepare five-

22. A summary of Works Program procedures is available in John Woodward Thomas, "The Rural Public Works Program and East Pakistan's Development," (Ph.D. thesis, Harvard University, 1968), chapter III.

Table 7.2. Allocation of Works Program funds (thousands of rupees)

Recipient of funds	1962–63[a]		1963–64[b]		1964–65[c]		1965–66[a]		1966–67[d]		Average for five year period
	Actual	%	Actual	%	Actual	%	Actual	%	Actual	%	
Union Councils	20,317	20.3	43,773	21.9	40,257	28.3	25,339	21.1	20,027	13.5	21.0
Thana Councils	6,467	6.5	72,331	36.2	53,418	37.6	60,266	50.2	87,167	58.1	37.7
District Councils	50,290	50.3	60,250	30.1	28,958	20.4	19,713	16.4	22,353	15.0	26.4
Municipal and town committees	19,272	19.3	20,100	10.0	11,644	8.2	8,359	7.0	8,971	6.0	10.1
Administration	381	0.3	379	0.2	6,895	4.8	4,226	3.5	6,403	4.3	2.6
Special experimental projects	3,275	3.3	3,266	1.6	1,000	0.7	2,183	1.8	4,697	3.1	2.1
Total expenditure	99,999	100.0	200,099	100.0	142,172	100.0	120,086	100.0	149,681	100.0	99.9%

[a] Figures compiled from *Performance Report on the Rural Works Programme, 1965–66* (Basic Democracies and Local Government Department, Dacca, 1967), pp. 246–247, table A-1.

[b] Figures compiled from *East Pakistan Rural Works Programme Report, 1963–64* (Basic Democracies and Local Government Department, Dacca, undated), p. 17.

[c] Figures compiled from *Performance Report on the Rural Works Programme, 1964–65* (Basic Democracies and Local Government Department, Dacca, 1966), p. 11, table 2, p. 13, and pp. 250–251.

[d] Figures compiled from *Summary of Physical Achievement on Works Programme, 1966–67* (Basic Democracies and Local Government Department, Dacca, 1968), p. 6.

year plans for the thana's roads, drainage, and embankments. The Plan Book has become an important means of organizing the tasks to be done under the Works Program over a period of years, and of assuring systematic planning of local development based on collection of all relevant data before projects are undertaken.

Second, the thana has increasingly become the focal point of all development activities. The physical manifestation of this is the Thana Training and Development Center being constructed in each thana under the Works Program. These centers provide, for the first time, centrally located offices for representatives of the government departments concerned with rural development. Centralization makes the absence of one representative conspicuous; it makes coordination functions easier; it gives the thana citizens access to all these officers in one visit; and it gives concrete reality to the thana as a center of local development efforts.

The reasons for the effectiveness of the thana-level organization are threefold: (1) the thana is sufficiently large to make planning and implementing the projects within its boundaries technically efficient, and large enough for government agencies to afford to assign it an officer from the technical departments concerned with development, such as Agriculture, Education, or Family Planning; (2) it is sufficiently small to allow any thana citizen to travel easily to thana headquarters and return home in a day, and small enough for a broad spectrum of the people of the area to partitipate in thana activities and to identify with its work; (3) it is an established unit of economic and commercial activities. The thana headquarters town is normally the site of the principal market in the area serving small bazaars scattered through the area and is also the location of commercial services, supply outlets, and the transportation center of the area. The thana-level organization which has evolved through the Works Program has provided the East Pakistan Government with a means of influencing and involving its rural inhabitants in the process of development. This innovation in the administration of development, if understood and correctly used, constitutes an important organizational tool for the future development of East Pakistan.

The Potential for Rural Political Change

The designers of the Works Program perceived the nature of the association between government and its constituents as the critical factor in political development. Their efforts were focused, therefore, on gaining the participation of the people in the achievement of state goals and on creating the institutional framework to guide and structure this participation. The Works Program was well designed to promote this approach to political development.

With the initiation of the Works Program, its planning and conduct became the most important function of the local councils. Because the projects affected the economic well-being of an area, the use of Works Program funds became a matter of widespread local concern. This concern had political significance because it provided the community with specific, rational, non-ascriptive criteria on which to judge the performance of local, elected officials, as long as economic and not political standards were employed. The rural people began to use such criteria to judge incumbents and candidates for local positions. (This could happen because there was some tradition of local self-government and some degree of politicization.)

The Works Program also began to increase the participation of the general public in local government and development. Early efforts to publicize its activities made the Works Program a subject of lively debate in the rural areas. Tea-stall owners and barbers reported that the Works Program was frequently discussed on their premises, and others reported that the Program was frequently a topic of village conversations.

The Program was designed specifically to benefit the poorest classes of people in the rural areas—the landless laborers and the farmers with marginal landholdings. Between 600,000 and one million laborers from this group have annually been given some employment on Works Program projects. This group has traditionally been outside the local political process. With implementation of the Works Program, the members of the low-income group found a new and critical interest in local council actions, although this group's influence in local affairs has remained disproportionately smaller than its size. However, as political loyalties became more important than economic criteria in determining the allocation of funds, the local council members, some of whom were misusing or diverting funds, became less willing to allow an element of public involvement in Works Program affairs.

The public interest in the Works Program and its conduct constituted a first step in political participation. With the shift from an economic to a political emphasis in the Works Program in the middle sixties, however, the potential for a major political change in the rural areas was lost. Nevertheless, the Works Program and the rudiments of political participation and concern that it engendered have increased economic and political expectations in the rural areas. These expectations, manifested in the political turbulence of 1969, cannot be overlooked or neglected in the 1970s.

P.L. 480, the Works Program, and Local Revenues

Underlying the concept of the Works Program was the role it was to play in ensuring the consumption of P.L. 480 aid commodities. As already noted, one of the main questions about the expanded P.L. 480 program, which involved the large-scale import of wheat, was whether or not the rice-eating East Pakistanis could be persuaded to eat wheat. During the pilot project in Comilla, two difficulties in encouraging wheat consumption had been discovered. First, the problems of getting wheat to the work sites, storing it, and distributing it to the laborers involved difficult administrative procedures which would greatly encumber the Works Program on a province-wide basis. Therefore, after the pilot project, the idea of paying wages in wheat was rejected. Second, the pilot project had also demonstrated the difficulty of gaining acceptance of wheat unless the rice/wheat price ratio provided substantial incentives for the consumption of wheat.

In the early days of the P.L. 480 program, the government, hoping to sell wheat at not less than the P.L. 480 procurement price, released it at Rs. 18 per maund (82$\frac{2}{7}$ pounds), only two to three rupees less than the price of rice. The resulting sales of wheat in East Pakistan were so small that the central government became concerned about the financial implications of the situation. Therefore, in April 1964, the government accepted a favorable wheat/rice price ratio to encourage consumption and reduced the release price from Rs. 18 per maund to Rs. 12.50 per maund. Since that date, wheat consumption in East Pakistan has risen rapidly and the question of whether or not East Pakistanis would eat wheat has been settled. By offering the right price incentives, the government was able to modify a habitual food preference and ensure the consumption of P.L. 480 wheat.

Increased government resources in a developing economy are important, at least partly because they permit maintenance of capital structures. The administrators of the Works Program have been aware that the provision of funds to the Union Councils[23] might cause them to be less diligent in the collection of revenues. Specific instructions were therefore issued to all Union Councils requiring them to make sure that their own revenues did not decrease as a result of the new funds from the Works Program.[24] Despite this effort, there is evidence (see Table 7.3) that revenues have declined over the period of the Works Program. One can conclude that even though the period 1962 to 1967 was one of a slight increase in pros-

23. The Thana Councils have no authority to raise revenues.

24. Government of East Pakistan, Basic Democracies and Local Government Department, *Circular No. 44* (Dacca, July 1, 1963).

Table 7.3. Income and expenditures of the Union Councils in 16 thanas (thousands of rupees)

Year	Total revenue collected from taxes, fees, rates, etc.	Total expenditures on establishments, communication, education, etc.
1961–62	2,194.6	1,914.6
1962–63	1,969.6	1,809.1
1963–64	1,906.6	1,599.2
1964–65	1,768.8	1,671.9
1965–66	1,813.7	1,668.7

Source: Government of East Pakistan, Basic Democracies and Local Government Department, "Study of Union Council Revenues" (Dacca, unpublished).

perity in the rural areas, the availability of Works Program funds did lessen the incentive and willingness of Union Councils to assess taxes and collect revenues.

Development Benefits from the Works Program

The Contribution of Works Program Roads

Approximately 75 percent of Works Program funds have been used for the construction of roads. The miles of roads reported built and repaired under the Works Program are listed in Table 7.1. In 1963 there were reportedly 3,411 miles of road, both dirt and paved, in East Pakistan, excluding roads unusuable because of disrepair.[25] The 18,477 miles of new roads reportedly built, plus those made usable by repairs[26] since 1963, represent a quantum jump in the number of miles of usable roads. (It should be noted, however, that only the Thana Council roads, of which 8,000 to 12,000 miles are mostly dirt, are comparable in carrying capacity to the pre-Works Program roads reported for 1963.) By 1967, East Pakistan had approximately 1.1 miles of road, usually dirt, for every square mile of land under cultivation. Although the western nations have from 3.5 to 4 miles of road, usually paved, per square mile of cultivated land,[27]

25. Government of East Pakistan, Bureau of Statistics, *Statistical Digest, 1965* (Dacca), p. 322.

26. There is some double counting in the figure for total miles repaired, since some repair work was on roads previously built or repaired by the Works Program.

27. Government of the United States, President's Science Advisory Committee, *The World Food Problem,* Report of the Panel on World Food Supply, vol. II (Washington: The White House, 1967), p. 582.

Table 7.4. Change in number of commercial vehicles in eight thanas of East Pakistan, 1962–1967[a]

Year	Rickshaws	Animal carts	Trucks	Scooter-taxis	Bicycles	Buses[b]
1962	110	3,159	10	0	1,200	15
1967	491	4,607	65	40	2,250	90

Source: Figures obtained from Union Council registration records.

[a]The figures include only commercial vehicles and not animal carts or rickshaws operated by the owners for their own use, although there has evidently been a substantial increase in these also. The rickshaw is not solely for carrying passengers; it also serves as a conveyance for small quantities of produce. Rickshaws are reported to be capable of carrying up to 5 maunds (410 pounds) and one passenger. Trucks and buses do not usually operate on Works Program roads. They customarily load at the thana headquarters and travel over a provincial highway to areas outside the thana.

[b]Including minibuses.

and although many of Pakistan's roads need to be improved to increase their carrying capacity, it would appear that in the 1960s East Pakistan laid the foundation for an adequate network of rural roads. The dirt-surfaced roads built by the Thana Councils can accommodate most conveyances except heavy trucks; the remainder, built by Union Councils, are smaller and are frequently limited in capacity to foot, bicycle-rickshaw, and light animal-cart traffic. The impact of the rapid development of roads can best be understood in terms of the change in a typical thana. In 1963 there was an average of 8.2 miles of usable road per thana; by 1967 the average was 60.5 miles per thana.

One major consequence of the construction of roads has been an increase in the facilities for carrying agricultural produce, which has enabled farmers to obtain higher prices. Table 7.4 shows the increase in numbers of vehicles in the eight thanas, while Figures 7.1 and 7.2 illustrate the development of the road network for one particular thana—Kaliganj in the Jessore District.

With the increase in roads and commercial vehicles in the thanas, transportation costs have diminished, even though prices generally, and urban transportation costs specifically, rose between 1962 and 1967. (For instance, the cost of transporting construction materials to four urban locations rose an average of 9 percent between 1960 and 1963.[28]) Analysis of the changes in rural transportation costs is complicated because

28. Government of East Pakistan, *Report on the Survey of Prices of Building Materials, Transport Costs, and Wage Rates of Construction Labor at Dacca, Chittagong, Khulna and Rajshahi,* Second Round, December 1961 to March 1963 (Dacca, 1965).

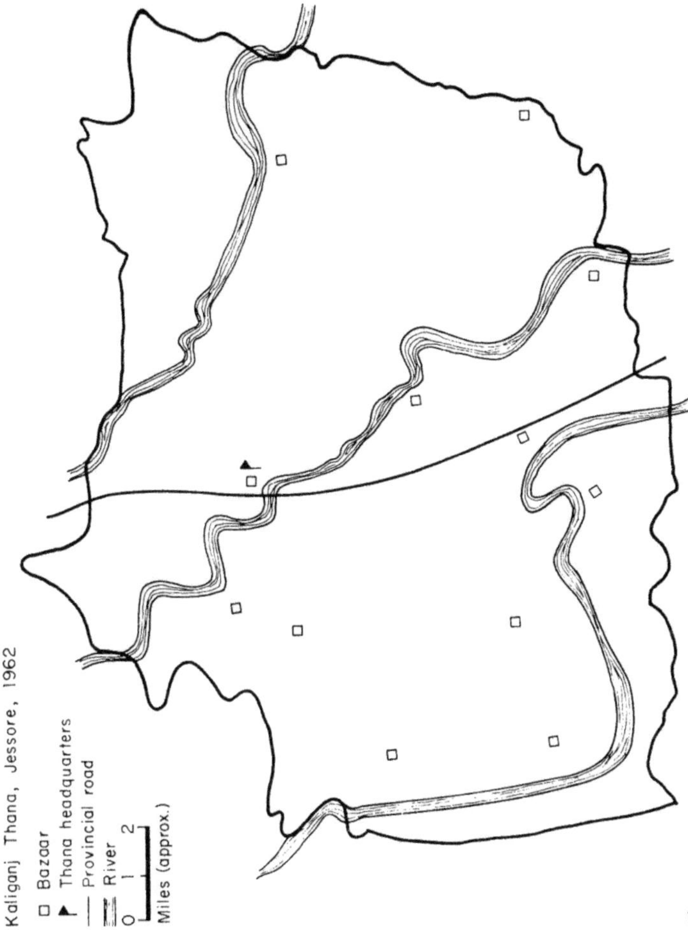

Figure 7.1. Aliganj Thana, Jessore, 1962

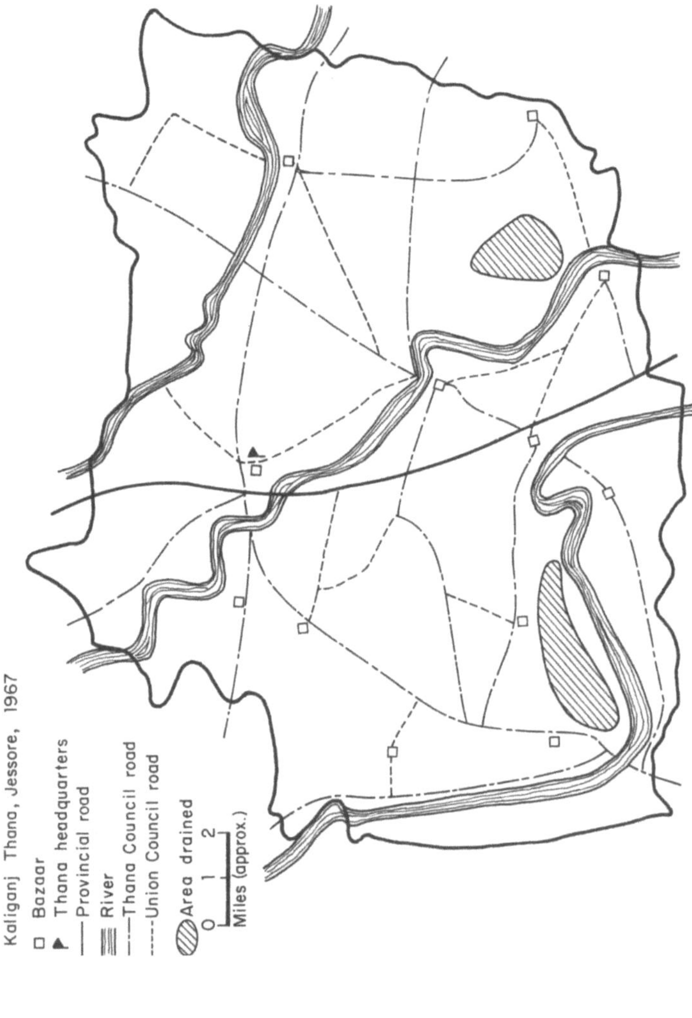

Figure 7.2. Aliganj Thana, Jessore, 1967

Table 7.5. Changes in the cost of commercial transportation of paddy

Year	Average cost per maund/ mile (rupees)	Average cost to primary market per maund (rupees)	Average cost to secondary market per maund (rupees)	Transportation cost as percent of market value of paddy in primary market	Transportation cost as percent of market value of paddy in secondary market
1962	0.38	0.84	2.01	4.0	8.6
1967	0.24	0.53	1.27	2.5	5.5
Saving	0.14 (37 percent)	0.31	0.74	1.5	3.1

Source: These calculations are based on data obtained in the eight-thana study.

the means of transportation vary widely. Farmers may send rice to market by commercial headload or bullock cart; they may have a salaried farm laborer carry their produce to market; because of newly available roads, they may purchase carts and use their own farm animals to haul their produce to market. Carriage is often by headload to a road and then by bullock cart. Roads, moreover, have encouraged farmers to sell produce in the primary, union market as well as in the secondary, thana market. The figures given in Table 7.5, derived from detailed reports of individual farmer experience, are a composite summary of transportation costs.

The eight-thana study, in showing the changes reported by farmers, provides evidence that rural transportation costs declined by roughly 40 percent between 1962 and 1967. If, however, one calculates the reduction of costs as a consequence of the change from headload to bullock cart, made possible by the existence of roads, the decrease in costs is even more impressive. The cost by headload[29] in 1963 averaged Rs. 0.40 per maund; the cost by bullock cart in 1967 was Rs. 0.19, a reduction of 52 percent. Although 37 percent and 52 percent represent substantial savings, their importance is reduced by the relatively short farm-to-market distances.[30] On the other hand, these figures are in current prices. If allowance is made for the price increase during this period, the savings to the farmer are even larger.

The existence of roads, increased transportation facilities, and reduced transportation costs have made it possible for farmers to derive sub-

29. Despite the abundance of rivers and minor waterways, water-borne conveyance has not provided a major means of transporting goods from farm to market in an area of numerous small land holdings. The economically feasible minimum load on boats and the location of waterways have made river transport much more important for inter-thana and district hauling.

30. Although only a few Works Program roads are solid enough to accommodate trucks, in the few areas where trucks are in use the cost of hauling rice to market has been cut by about 65 percent.

Table 7.6. Percentage increase in sale value for produce sold in the market over sale value at the farm

Commodity	At primary market	At secondary market
Paddy	13	14
Jute	13	17
Sugarcane	26	65
Vegetables	34	40
Oilseeds	14	16
Spices	15	13
Tobacco	8	20

Source: Government of East Pakistan, Bureau of Statistics, *Master Survey of Agriculture in East Pakistan,* Sixth Round, (Dacca, 1966).

stantial benefits by selling in primary or secondary markets, instead of selling to traders who come to the farm. These benefits are indicated in Table 7.6, although the cost of transportation and any loss in transit must be deducted from the higher prices available in the primary and secondary markets in calculating the farmers' increased profits. The percentages given clearly indicate the advantages to the farmers of selling produce directly in the market rather than to a middleman.

One way of appraising the general benefits of the roads is to examine changes in the value of land contiguous to new Works Program roads. In six of the eight thanas studied where there were major road building projects, during the period of road construction (1963–1967) land not located close to Works Program roads increased in value by 44 percent, whereas the average value of land adjacent to a Works Program road rose by 154 percent. Whether adjacent to a repaired road or a new one, land increased in value by approximately the same amount. Since there is as yet little demand for commercial sites along these Works Program roads, the increase in land value suggests that the roads offer substantial benefits to the farmers located near them.

Changes in the Rural Economy

The study of the eight thanas in East Pakistan was designed not only to assess the direct benefits of the Works Program, but also to identify changes in economic organization and patterns of economic activity in the rural areas where the Works Program has been in operation.

With the low level of per capita income, the fragmentation of land holdings, and the high population density in rural areas, East Pakistan's agriculture is primarily subsistence farming. For decades the East Pakistan farmer has grown rice for his own consumption. To meet the need for items that he could not produce, he has traditionally planted a small field of jute, which yields a few pounds of fiber. This he has bartered to the itinerant trader (*faria*), who has offered basic household necessities in exchange. The traders have usually agreed to work in certain areas not within one another's jurisdiction. As monopsonistic buyers, they have offered farmers the lowest possible prices. With limited means of travel to local markets, farmers with only small quantities for sale have been virtually helpless. With price incentives only partially operative, the government's instruments for encouraging growth in the agricultural sector have been limited.

There is substantial evidence that this system is slowly being replaced by a rural market economy in which farmers produce a larger percentage of their total crop for sale in the market. Although any economy in a state of transition offers a confusing picture, there is indication of a concurrent functioning of both the old and the new systems. In the eight-thana study, 128 farmers were asked whether they were then producing or selling crops that they had not produced or sold in the early 1960s and if they had changed the manner in which they sold goods. Their responses, summarized in Table 7.7, show an increase in sales of rice, a major increase in the number of farmers selling in the markets rather than to traders, and a shift in cropping patterns to more cash crops.

A substantial change occurred between 1962 and 1967 in the number of farmers growing vegetables, sugarcane, and minor crops for sale, which suggests a sizeable increase in the total number growing these crops as against the two traditional crops, rice and jute. There was also an increase from 36 percent to 57 percent in the proportion of farmers selling some portion of their rice crop. More important is the shift from the use of itinerant traders toward direct sale in the markets. In 1967 some 82 percent of the farmers selling rice sold it directly in the market, in contrast with 36 percent in 1962. Similarly, with respect to jute, whereas in 1962 approximately two-thirds of the farmers used traders, in 1967 approximately two-thirds used markets. Nevertheless, the percentage of jute sold in the market is smaller than the percentage for any other crops. This is probably a consequence of the traders' traditional domination of the jute market. A farmer just beginning to market jute, of whom there are few, would find it easy to take his crop directly to the marketplace, whereas one who has grown jute for a long time might find it difficult to break a long-standing relationship with a trader.

The trends away from subsistence farming and from marketing through itinerant traders, indicated in the eight-thana study and summarized in

Table 7.7. Change in 123 farmers' production and marketing patterns of selected crops in East Pakistan, 1962–1967

Commodity	Number growing commodity	Number growing for sale		Number of those selling who sell primarily in the market	
	(1)	(2)	(2/1) (in percent)	(3)	(2/3)
Rice					
1962	123	45	(36)	16	(36%)
1967	123	70	(57)	57	(82%)
Jute					
1962	81	81	(100)	27	(33%)
1967	81	81	(100)	56	(69%)
Vegetables[a]					
1962	–	13	–	5	(38%)
1967	–	50	–	48	(96%)
Sugarcane[a]					
1962	–	8	–	5	(62%)
1967	–	21	–	16	(76%)
Minor crops[a]					
1962	–	15	–	4	(26%)
1967	–	36	–	30	(83%)

Source: Basic data is from the eight-thana study.

[a]Figures for the total number growing vegetables, sugarcane, and minor crops are not available.

Table 7.7, are corroborated by data on the growth of primary and secondary markets. In Pakistan, the government auctions each market site annually to a leaseholder. (Although there is occasional collaboration between government officials and bidders for market sites, bidding is usually competitive.) Many of the leaseholders maintain records of the number of traders who have paid the daily rental fee, and are willing to reveal the records.

Table 7.8 shows that in 158 markets the rate of increase in the number of merchants (an average of 96.6 percent) corresponds roughly to the rate of increase in rent (90.1 percent), which would appear to confirm the validity of both sets of figures. However, because rents are given in current prices and there has been some inflation over this period, as well as a population growth of approximately 3 percent per year, the increase must be discounted somewhat.

Table 7.8. Increases in size of 158 markets (bazaars) in six[a] thanas in East Pakistan, 1962–1967 (in percent)

Thana	Rate increase of rent[b]	Rate increase of traders
Baniyachang, Sylhet	46.1	23.5
Godagari, Rajshahi	98.9	103.0
Kaliganj, Jessore	85.4	125.4
Muktagacha, Mymensingh	215.9	60.7
Palasbari, Rangpur	82.3	140.9
Satkania, Chittagong	52.5	89.1

Source: Data obtained from Thana revenue officers in the eight-thana study.

[a]Data was not available for two of the eight thanas studied. In Baidyer Bazar Thana, Dacca, the Circle Officer (Revenue) had gone on sick leave and was absent from the thana from the time of the first visit to the thana in July through completion of work at the end of October 1967. The records of market rentals were locked in his office and no key was available locally. In Babuganj Thana, Barisal, serious communal conflict had arisen in 1963. Until that time Hindu traders had controlled the marketing in the thana. As a result of the conflict, many Hindus left the area and the trading system was disrupted. Records of market revenues were reported lost at that time and records for the subsequent period reflect only the rebuilding of the market structure.

[b]In cases where the rent of one or two of the markets in a thana (the average number of markets per thana is 24) appeared questionable, the figures were not included in the calculations.

The Works Program's Drainage Projects

Drainage projects have received only 5 percent of the total allocations of Works Program funds, yet the benefits have been particularly high because drainage projects are not difficult to implement and the Works Program form of organization is uniquely suited to this type of work. In a deltaic plain like East Pakistan there are many depressions where water collects and stands after rains or flooding. This situation can be corrected by simple gravity-flow drainage channels that carry the water into nearby waterways. Drainage canals can also serve as sources of irrigation water or as minor waterways for transportation. Because waterlogged areas are located at widely scattered points throughout East Pakistan, a decentralized effort, utilizing local knowledge, is necessary. Many small, widely scattered projects would be difficult for a government agency to identify and inefficient for it to implement.

In the eight-thana study it was ascertained that, on the average, a mile of drainage canal would drain 48 acres (i.e., one acre inland on each side of the channel). Multiplying the 11,123 miles of drainage canal built by the Works Program by the 48 acres that each mile of canal will drain, the estimated number of acres drained is 533,904. This constitutes 2.8 percent of the total 18.9 million acres of land under cultivation.[31] Farmers report that waterlogged land usually produces about one-third of the normal yield per acre, whereas after drainage it produces as much or more than other land in the same area. If drained land produces the normal two crops with the provincial average yield (1,055 lbs. per acre for *aman* —autumn rice—and 990 lbs. per acre for *aus*—summer rice), the annual increase in output would amount to 1,364 lbs. per acre and 364,123 tons for the whole area estimated as benefitting from drainage. In 1967–68, the estimated increase was 3.5 percent of the total production. The claim by the farmers in the survey that drainage increases production by 200 percent is substantiated by a 326 percent increase in the value of drained land, as compared with a 44 percent increase in the value of land not affected by the Works Program. Furthermore, drained land was usually valued at a price as high or higher than that of surrounding crop land without water problems.

The payoff on drainage programs in relation to the amount invested has clearly been high. Unfortunately, the opportunity for this type of work is limited by the number of areas where waterlogging conditions can be remedied by gravity-flow drainage canals.

The Works Program Flood Control Embankments

Five percent of total Works Program funds have been spent on flood embankment projects. Table 7.1 shows an estimate of 3 million acres benefitted by the Works Program drainage and flood control projects. Of this total, the number of acres drained is 800,000, and the number of acres protected by flood control embankments is 2.2 million. The benefits from embankments must be stated in terms of agricultural production saved and losses of personal belongings, animals, farm supplies, and working time prevented.

Satisfactory water control in East Pakistan will require massive works and billions of dollars. The Works Program has made only a limited contribution. Of the total land area of East Pakistan only 6.2 percent has benefitted from the flood control program. Yet the seriousness of the annual flood loss makes the contribution of the Works Program embankments significant. It is estimated that the annual saving from these embankments amounts to Rs. 100.4 million. (More detail on this calculation is provided in Appendix B.)

31. Haroun ur Rashid, *East Pakistan: A Systematic Regional Geography and its Development Planning Aspects* (Lahore: Sh. Ghulam Ali & Sons, 1965), p. 113.

The value of the embankments was emphatically demonstrated in Satkania Thana. A part of Chittagong District, this thana lies in the coastal belt between the Chittagong Hill Tracts and the Bay of Bengal. One major river, the Dalu, and several minor rivers flow through Satkania. If there are rains in the hills, these rivers can build up to flood stage in twenty-four hours. One hundred and seventy miles of embankments have been constructed by the Works Program in Satkania. When the Thana Council was slow in repairing a washed-out section of a Works Program embankment along the Dalu River, the inhabitants of the area repaired it themselves at their own expense. In August 1967, thirty-six hours of heavy rain caused the Dalu river to rise fourteen feet to a level less than one foot below the top of the embankment. Without the embankment the entire thana headquarters would have been under several feet of water and huge losses would have been sustained. The savings in this one situation alone more than offset the cost of the embankment.

The Impact of Works Program Expenditures

The cash wages paid to laborers on Works Program projects amounted to Rs. 452 million ($94.5 million) in the first five years of the program. Table 7.9 shows the consumption preferences of 120 laborers.

One of the program goals was to provide a new demand for food items, thereby creating the absorptive capacity for increased P.L. 480 imports while concurrently raising the level of nutrition among the poorest and most undernourished rural people and increasing their productive capacity as laborers. Table 7.10 shows the increase of wheat imports from 1958 to 1967. During the same period the import of other foodgrains remained approximately constant.

The 74 percent of the Works Program wages spent on food commodities from 1962 to 1967 represent Rs. 334.5 million worth of food commodities purchased. During this period sales of imported wheat totaled Rs. 991.6 million. The expenditure of Works Program wages on food, if spent on P.L. 480 wheat, would represent 34 percent of the total wheat

Table 7.9. Use of Works Program wages by 120 project laborers (in percent)

Food	74	Transport	1
Payment of debts	10	Education	1
Manufactured household items	8.5	Land	0.5
Agricultural supplies	5		

Source: Calculations based on responses of laborers interviewed in the eight-thana study.

Table 7.10. Wheat imports into East Pakistan under P.L. 480, 1958–1967

Date	Thousands of tons
1958–59	87
1959–60	148
1960–61	234
1961–62	202
1962–63	894
1963–64	656
1964–65	250
1965–66	543
1966–67	830

Source: Government of East Pakistan, Finance Department, *Economic Survey of East Pakistan* (Dacca: East Pakistan Government Press, 1967), table 2, p. 46.

sales, indicating that Works Program wage payments did help to create a demand for the new wheat. However, from 1960 to 1967, the population grew by 9.5 million. As a result, the per capita foodgrain consumption did not rise noticeably. Although the combination of P.L. 480 commodities and a Works Program did not result in an increase in per capita consumption, it did prevent a decrease in a period of rapid population growth, and may have improved the relative position of the poorest class of people, the landless agricultural laborers.

There were also important expenditures of Works Program wages on manufactured goods (see Table 7.9). In addition to the 8.5 percent of wages spent directly on manufactured goods, part of the debt repayment, transport expenditure, and purchases of agricultural supplies was spent for manufactured supplies. Therefore, some 15 percent of Works Program wage payments, an average of Rs. 13.6 million annually, may represent additional demand for manufactured goods over the five-year period. Direct, nonlabor expenditures of the program amounted to Rs. 258 million ($54.5 million) or Rs. 52 million annually. If the estimated foreign exchange component of these costs, 7.5 percent,[32] is deducted, the Works Program has created an estimated annual demand of Rs. 60 million for domestic manufactured goods. In 1964–65 this represented about 4 percent of the value added by manufacturing in East Pakistan. Although some of this probably represented a diversion of potential exports, it also constituted a small stimulant to domestic manufacturing.

32. Richard V. Gilbert, "The P.L. 480 Program for the Third Plan" (mimeo, Harvard Development Advisory Group, Karachi, March 9, 1964).

Works Program Employment Effects

One of the principal purposes of the Works Program was to create employment, especially because voluntary and involuntary unemployment was estimated at 33 percent of total available man-days.[33]

Table 7.1 gives the figures for employment as modified by the eight-thana study. Converting these estimates into man-years, on the basis of 240 working days per year, one gets a figure of 866,000 man-years of employment created in a five-year period by the Works Program, or an average of 173,200 man-years of employment annually. Although this seems an impressive figure, employment on this scale would mean a mere 3.4 percent decrease in annual agricultural unemployment.

These figures, however, understate the real impact of the Works Program on rural unemployment. In East Pakistan, unemployment is primarily a seasonal phenomenon. During the planting and harvesting seasons, which occur four times a year, it is rare to find anyone physically able and desiring work who is without employment. Between these seasons unemployment rises, particularly among the landless agricultural laborers, and probably reaches a rate of between 40 and 50 percent. After the harvest of the fall crop comes the slack season, January to May. During this interval, when there is no rain and when the temperature reaches its annual peak, there is almost no agricultural activity, and unemployment probably reaches 60 to 70 percent of the agricultural labor force. The Works Program provides employment in these three or four months, when it is most needed. Calculations based on the eight-thana study indicate that the Works Program employs from 600,000 to 1 million men annually for periods varying from two weeks to four months. Thus, the Works Program employment, concentrated as it is in the slack season, does spread the benefits of the program more broadly than the figure for total man-years of employment would suggest. For an individual thus employed, the benefits are obvious. If there are eighty-four working days in the slack season and a laborer can earn Rs. 2 a day, his annual income is increased by Rs. 168—an important addition for members of a group in which per capita incomes are approximately Rs. 200 per year.

If second round, or indirect employment benefits could also be calculated, the impact would appear even greater. Although it is only a partial solution to the unemployment problem, the program, in providing a substantial increase in income for up to 1 million workers annually, has re-

33. Wouter Tims, "Employment."

lieved some of the most serious social inequities and political pressures resulting from the unemployment situation.

Community Buildings

Approximately 15 percent of Works Program funds have been used for the construction of community buildings. The most important of these is the Thana Training and Development Center, which has already been discussed. While the effectiveness of the community buildings in fulfilling the purposes for which they have been intended cannot be measured, it is possible to compare the costs of building them under the Works Program and under the direction of the government. The average building constructed by the Works Program contains 1,596 square feet of floor space, at a cost of Rs. 13.84 per square foot. The Works Program uses standard government plans for the construction of union and town community centers. In these plans building costs are estimated at Rs. 21 per square foot. The saving in the Works Program costs is achieved by the absence of supervisory costs and contractor profits and, occasionally, by the donation of supplies. From these figures the saving of Works Program construction over the standard construction can be calculated at Rs. 35.7 million.

Through the Works Program, a new and effective form of organization has evolved. Community buildings are an important part of this organization and are symbolic of the government's goals even if the economic contribution of the buildings cannot be measured directly.

A Benefit-Cost Analysis of the Works Program

There have been continuing doubts as to whether the investment in the Works Program has been productive in economic terms. These doubts were expressed by the Planning Commission when it became necessary to revise the Third Plan. In cutting the plan allocation for the Works Program from Rs. 2,500 million to Rs. 1,820 million, the Planning Commission stated that "efforts will be made to devise a more directly productive programme."[34] Because there are some directly productive returns from the Works Program, it is useful to analyze the program as an investment by comparing the benefits and costs.

The following is a summary of the calculation of a benefit-cost ratio for the Works Program. Full details of the calculation are provided in Appendix B. The savings accruing to farmers who market produce and can benefit from the lower transportation costs resulting from the con-

34. Government of Pakistan, Planning Commission, *Revised Phasing, Sectoral Priorities and Allocations of the Third Five Year Plan, 1965–70* (Rawalpindi, March 1967).

struction of roads are calculated at Rs. 157.5 million annually. From these savings is deducted the loss of production resulting from the agricultural land taken for roads. This loss is estimated at Rs. 26.8 million annually, resulting in an annual benefit from roads of Rs. 130.7 million.

Increases in agricultural production on land drained by Works Program projects can be calculated roughly at an average of Rs. 212.2 million annually. Benefits from flood control works are much more difficult to calculate, but an estimate of Rs. 100.4 million annually is made. Because there is no easy way to calculate the benefits of community buildings, these have not been included in the benefit calculations. The total annual benefits are therefore estimated to be Rs. 452.3 million.

From this amount the annual maintenance costs must be deducted. These are calculated at Rs. 64.8 million annually, resulting in net annual benefits from Works Program roads, drainage, and embankments of Rs. 387.5 million. The benefits and maintenance costs are summarized in Table 7.11. Costs are defined as the annual allocations of the government to the Works Program. To these benefits and costs a discount rate of 12 percent is applied. The result is a benefit-cost ratio of 3.4. This figure is not sensitive to minor variations in assumptions about any of the above components. This high ratio of benefits to costs provides ample evidence of the favorable return to East Pakistan's investment in a Works Program.

Table 7.11. Calculation of net annual benefits from Works Program projects (millions of rupees)

Benefits		
1. Road-user savings (for carrying agricultural produce only)	157.5	
Less production loss, land used for roads: 44,155 tons	−26.8	130.7
2. Increased production from land drained		221.2
3. Flood protection: 1.7 million acres		100.4
		452.3
Less Maintenance		
Roads at Rs. 560 per mile		56.6
Drainage, re-excavation every 5 years		4.4
Embankments, 7,168 miles maintained at Rs. 560 per mile		3.8
		64.8
Net Annual Benefits	Rs.	387.5

Source: Calculated from data obtained in the eight-thana study and data from the documents cited in footnotes (B1), (B2), (B3).

The Rural Works Program in West Pakistan

A Rural Works Program[35] similar in design and objectives to that of East Pakistan was launched in West Pakistan in 1963–64. Because social, political, and economic conditions in West Pakistan are substantially different from those in East Pakistan, the transfer of the program provides an opportunity to analyze the degree to which East Pakistan's experience is more broadly applicable.

In West Pakistan civil administration has traditionally been strong, and there has been little scope for the development of local politics. The highly structured class system has not given rise to political participation and activism. The civil service, particularly the Deputy Commissioner of each district, and the powerful Muslim landowners have, over time, established a rough alliance maintaining the status quo.

The differences between East and West Pakistan have been well summarized by one political analyst. "Only in East Pakistan is the intelligentsia actively involved in politics. East Pakistan is, as was shrewdly observed by Burton Marshall, all politics and West Pakistan all government. . . . East Pakistan is socially egalitarian; its economy characterized by a sharing of poverty. West Pakistan is socially stratified, distinguished by extremes of wealth and want with little desire on the part of the wealthy to share their riches with the multitude. The pattern of inequality [is] inherited from its feudal past.[36]

At the time of the launching of the Rural Works Program in West Pakistan, the level of development in the two provinces was also significantly different, as were the most pressing economic problems. In 1964–65, per capita gross domestic product for East Pakistan was Rs. 327 ($69), while in West Pakistan it was Rs. 464 ($98.).[37] In West Pakistan real industrial growth had taken place, and, compared with East Pakistan, there was less dependence upon agriculture. The better state of rural facilities and the geography of West Pakistan resulted in fewer obvious high-priority development projects that could be carried out by simple, labor-intensive methods. The density of population in the East was much greater[38]; it was overwhelmingly rural; and 33 percent of the agricultural

35. The program has generally been called the Rural Works Program in West Pakistan. To differentiate between the programs in the two provinces, that name will be used here.

36. Mushtaq Ahmad, *Government and Politics in Pakistan*, 2d ed. (Karachi: Pakistan Publishing House, 1963), p. 285.

37. Gustav F. Papanek, *Pakistan's Development–Social Goals and Private Incentives* (Cambridge: Harvard University Press, 1967), p. 317.

38. Government of Pakistan, 1961 *Population Census of Pakistan*, p. 13.

labor force were unemployed compared to 19 percent in West Pakistan.[39] Because of these variations, priorities for rural development differed between East and West.

Finally, the administration of the Works Program in East Pakistan has been greatly simplified by the physical, cultural, linguistic, and social homogeneity of the province. Diversity, however, typifies West Pakistan. Therefore, the program carefully formulated to meet the needs and conditions of East Pakistan was now being transplanted to an area in which it would have to operate under a variety of different conditions.

A fundamental decision had to be made in implementing the Rural Works Program. Should the program attempt a major social reform by placing the program's funds and the power to determine their use with the union and the *tehsil* (the rough equivalent of the thana), thereby circumventing the existing power structure in the hope of reaping some of the political and social benefits that the program achieved in East Pakistan? Or, alternatively, should the program attempt lesser objectives and use the existing power structure in the hope that economic gains would eventually lead to larger political and social gains?

After debate within the government, the latter approach prevailed. The key role in the program was given to the Deputy Commissioner. One economic advisor explained why this was considered necessary: "because of powerful landlords and [the] semi-feudal structure of society, the tradition of the people is to be organized from above rather than to act on their own initiative."[40] Without the leadership of the Deputy Commissioner, supported by the landowners, it would not have been possible to organize and carry out the program. Moreover, the Deputy Commissioners were regarded as the only officers with sufficient power and authority to ensure that the landlords did not use available funds entirely for their own purposes.

Because different areas in West Pakistan had widely differing needs and capabilities, it was also considered necessary to have a large variety of Rural Works Program projects and varying methods of implementation. Local councils were encouraged to implement projects themselves; government agencies were authorized, when necessary, to carry out projects under the Rural Works Program. Deputy Commissioners and local councils were also authorized to hire private contractors to implement projects whenever it was felt that contractors could do the work more satisfactorily than the councils.

39. Wouter Tims, "Employment," p. 2.

40. Wilfred Salter, letter to Richard V. Gilbert, April 10, 1963.

Because the government wished to begin a Rural Works Program as rapidly as possible, and because operational procedures of the program would not be uniform throughout West Pakistan, thereby rendering a single pilot project meaningless, the Rural Works Program was launched in 1963–64 on a province-wide basis.

During the five years the Rural Works Program has been in operation, the government has allocated to it Rs. 378 million ($79 million). In addition, the rural people have contributed land, labor, supplies, and local revenue valued at Rs. 72 million ($15 million), bringing total inputs into the program to Rs. 450 million ($95 million). This investment has resulted in the following new facilities:[41]

2,700 miles of new hard-surface roads
6,000 miles of new dirt-surface roads
2,000 miles of roads repaired
1,340 health centers or dispensaries constructed
12,500 community water supply systems developed
8,000 schools constructed
2,000 community centers constructed.

The range of projects carried out is large. In a report covering the West Pakistan Program through 1965–66, a total of thirty-nine different types of projects are identified.[42]

As planned, the program has been administered through the traditional administrative system with no important decentralizing effects. Responsibility for its implementation has increasingly been placed on a higher level (District Councils) while allocations to the lower councils have been reduced, as Table 7.12 shows. In the first year of the Rural Works Program, the Union Councils spent 71 percent of the funds, while the District Councils spent only 28 percent. By 1965–66 the roles had been reversed and the District Councils spent 55 percent while the Union Councils spent 35 percent. This same trend away from direct local participation is also demonstrated by the trend toward the use of contractors, with the result that, by 1965–66, 75 percent of Rural Works Program

41. S. M. Wasim, *Review on* (sic) *Basic Democracies and Local Government in West Pakistan*, Speech (mimeo, undated, 'presumably 1968'). The expenditure and accomplishment figures cited here are approximations and are the only up-to-date figures available at the time of this writing. There was no attempt to verify these figures, as in East Pakistan, and there is thus no claim concerning their accuracy. The above listing includes only major categories of projects undertaken.

42. Government of Pakistan, Ministry of Information and Broadcasting, *Use of P.L. 480 Funds for Rural Development Through the Basic Democracies* (Rawalpindi: Government of Pakistan, undated).

Table 7.12. West Pakistan Rural Works Program

Funds	1963–64	1964–65	1965–66
		percents	
Spent by			
District Councils	28.4	41.2	55.2
Tehsil Councils	–	7.7	5.7
Union Councils	71.6	50.7	35.7
Other uses	–	0.4	3.4
Paid to			
Contractors for implementation of projects	45.4	59.0	75.2
Spent by local councils on			
Skilled labor	11.7	a	2.5
Unskilled labor	17.0	a	3.5
Total	28.7	12.5	6.0

Source: Data for 1963–64 is derived from Government of West Pakistan, West Pakistan Rural Works Programme Evaluation Report, 2nd ed. (Lahore, 1964). Data for 1964–65 is from a published letter to the West Pakistan Members of the Provincial Assembly from the Basic Democracies, Social Welfare and Local Government Department, February 23, 1967. Data for 1965–66 is from Government of West Pakistan, Basic Democracies, Social Welfare and Local Government Department, 1966, Statistics on the Rural Works Programme (Lahore: unpublished, 1967).

[a] Detail of expenditure not available.

funds had been turned over to contractors. Therefore, the administrative talents existing among the local people have not been utilized and a sense of identification with the work carried out has not been present to the same degree as in East Pakistan.

The Rural Works Program has focused on provision of community facilities rather than on economic objectives. The limited number of road projects have usually served economic ends, and many have yielded very high returns, particularly in the productive agricultural areas of the Punjab.[43] Nevertheless, between 1963 and 1966 over half of the program's funds went into health, education, and social welfare projects. This emphasis on community facilities is in sharp contrast with

43. For one calculation of the high benefits from road building in a few unions in the Punjab see Shahid Javed Burki, "The Economic, Social, and Political Significance of the West Pakistan Works Program," paper presented to Economics 267 seminar at Harvard University, 1967, p. 28.

the priorities of the program in East Pakistan. There are a number of reasons for this emphasis. First, in the absence of a pilot project, the government did not carefully determine the types of projects that would contribute most to development. This decision was left entirely to district and local government officers. Second, the new program of rural development was in the community development tradition, stronger in West than in East Pakistan. Former community development workers were employed by the Basic Democracies Department, which was implementing the program, and by the local councils. Third, many of the facilities for the promotion of agricultural development were already being provided from other sources: private investment in irrigation, and government investment in large drainage and water control works. Nevertheless, with appropriate experimentation, projects with a greater economic contribution could have been found for West Pakistan. Field channels, for example, were required for the irrigation works being carried out on a large scale in the province. With the rapid rise in agricultural production, rural roads for farm-to-market hauling and local storage depots were increasingly necessary. These and other projects might have been developed to make the program serve economic priorities more directly.

One other important difference between the programs in the two provinces is the amount of labor used. The labor component of West Pakistan's program has constantly declined, primarily because of the extensive use of contractors and their tendency to avoid management difficulties by using capital-intensive methods. The outcome has been a substantial diminution of the program's employment-creation effects.

What can be learned from the experience of transferring the Works Program to West Pakistan? First, this experience illustrates the difficulties of such transfers. A successful program must be consistent with economic conditions and priorities, and with administrative and political traditions of the area in which it is to be implemented. The low utilization of labor and the tendency to develop community facilities in West Pakistan illustrate some of the hazards of ignoring this point.

Second, preliminary testing on a small scale would appear to be a prerequisite for undertaking a program. If the program is built around the solution of specific priority problems, its chances of success would obviously be greater than those of a program essentially borrowed from another area and adapted for implementation. At times this prescription might require the design of several different approaches for areas within a nation or province in which conditions are not homogeneous.

Third, the West Pakistan experience emphasizes the critical nature of the unit of decision-making and administration. In East Pakistan the thana was found to be a suitable unit. In West Pakistan the choice of the district strongly affected the ultimate results of the program. Similarly, giving the Deputy Commissioner a key role in West Pakistan assured that the program would not alter the status quo, while the creation of a new cadre of Circle Officers to serve the thana in East Pakistan had an innovative effect.

Fourth, because of the great difficulties in predicting results and effectiveness of procedures, a program's administration should be flexible. In East Pakistan an approach to rural development that allowed important changes in procedures or the addition of a new irrigation program as priorities in the rural areas shifted was central to the effectiveness of the program. West Pakistan's program has lacked the same degree of flexibility.

Concluding Observations

The success of the East Pakistan Rural Public Works Program in the first five years of its operation, from 1962 to 1967, is clear. In that period both the economic benefits and the political potential were demonstrated. However, in the years following 1967, the vulnerability of the Program to political misuse and corruption has also been demonstrated.

The failure to achieve continuing economic growth in the rural area of East Pakistan during the 1960s demonstrates an often overlooked fact: without other successful programs of agricultural development such as the supply of new seeds, water and modern inputs, a Works Program cannot insure growth. The reverse is also true: a necessary part of growth in the rural areas of East Pakistan is a Works Program, both as an effective instrument for building rural infrastructure and as the only major effort to improve conditions among landless laborers.

To achieve a Works Program that is again highly effective will take concerted and determined action on the part of the government, probably including the following steps: (1) election of a new group of local officials; (2) a change in the name of the program to remove the remaining political opprobrium; (3) a major new effort at the Provincial level to institute procedures, rules and checks to rebuild the operational system of the program and reimpose discipline in its administration; (4) designation of funds for maintenance for a year or two so that previous facilities, now in disrepair, can be made operational once more. Unless this effort is made it would be better to end the program and to use the resources elsewhere.

The problem of organizing, financing, and promoting rural development has proved to be as intractable as any other in economic and social change. Despite the misuse that has crept into the Program and now jeopardizes its effectiveness, the Works Program in East Pakistan evolved an effective tool for accelerating rural development. A program that has found some answers to these difficult problems merits close examination for its relevance to other nations. The problem and the goal are always the same: to influence, mobilize, and motivate millions of individuals whose decisions will determine the success or failure of rural development and whose capacities may represent one of the largest pools of under-utilized resources available to the nation. On the basis of the foregoing analysis of the East Pakistan Works Program it is possible to make the following generalizations.

1. The approach to the formulation of such programs must be pragmatic, not doctrinaire. This is the most significant lesson of the East Pakistan experience. This experience provides neither a model nor a new technique of rural development that other nations can apply to the solution of their problems. Rather, the Works Program suggests an approach that begins by identifying priority needs, links these to potential sources of financing, tests the approach before undertaking it on a large scale, evaluates efforts honestly and critically at all stages, and maintains flexibility in the administration of the program.

2. Aid in the form of surplus commodities (e.g., via P.L. 480), frequently considered "surplus dumping," can be as productive as other forms of assistance. Although it is important that programs using such resources be tailored to the unique requirements of surplus commodity aid, they can be highly productive with appropriate planning and design. Surplus commodities are a form of assistance that is relatively attractive to donor nations and holds promise in a period when they are disenchanted with the role of aid-giving.

3. Programs such as the Works Program create employment much more cheaply than is possible in the urban-industrial sector of the economy. Industrial employment usually requires heavy investment in housing and urban infrastructure, avoided by rural-works-type employment. In Pakistan one new man-year of employment created by the urban-industrial sector costs twenty-three times as much as one created by the Works Program.[44] Given the magnitude of the problems of rural-urban migration in many countries, a program that creates new rural employment and reduces the flow into the urban areas is highly beneficial.

44. Government of West Pakistan, Directorate of Rural Works Program, Basic Democracies, Social Welfare and Local Government Department, *West Pakistan Rural Works Program: Evaluation Report, 1963–64* (Lahore, undated), p. 34.

4. If the appropriate method and structure can be found, there are substantial benefits in decentralizing the administration of some development programs. Decentralization permits the use of local managerial talents not otherwise utilized. It can solve the problems of organizing labor-intensive programs and implementing small, widely scattered projects. It also provides sources of information not available at the national level. This is particularly important for the identification of small, high-return, local projects.

There are also negative aspects of decentralization. The possibilities for inefficiency, or the outright misuse of funds, are often greater at the local level than at the national level. If communities are dominated by a few powerful individuals, local decision-making can be controlled by them to their own advantage, reinforcing their authority. The question of equity versus ability to use funds effectively may present some difficult political questions for those responsible for allocating funds. In an area where regional differences are more pronounced than in East Pakistan this issue may become serious. However, East Pakistan's experience suggests that ways to circumvent these problems can be found and that the benefits of doing so are high.

5. Mobilizing rural people for participation in the affairs of the nation can provide new resources for development. By making economic improvements widely visible, it can also help to create popular identification with the nation and support for the government. Participation may help build support for the nation's public requirements, ranging from voting in elections to revenue collection.

Critical to the process of mobilizing the rural people are supporting services and supplies, which it is the government's function to provide. This was one of the strengths of the Works Program. It concentrated on a few activities and made certain that organization, training and supplies were adequate.

6. Contrary to widespread assumption, labor-intensive projects can be highly productive and a significant spur to development, if properly conceived and designed. The most important consideration is that the technology of the projects must be suitable for the skills of both labor and management.

7. Where funds are being used by local councils, it is important to provide a well-defined set of conditions under which the councils are to operate. This should include limitations on the type of projects to be undertaken, in order to ensure that they are not only important to the national development program but also within the technical capacity of the local councils. As the units of local government demonstrate their

capacity to make responsible decisions and to implement them, increasing responsibility can be granted. Freedom for local governing bodies to make decisions and to implement programs within a framework carefully structured by the national government has been a successful mode of operation in East Pakistan.

8. There have been few agricultural success stories in areas where farmers are confined to small land holdings and have neither the capital to invest nor enough land to justify expenditure on improved inputs and techniques. In such situations, rapid expansion of agricultural output will come only as organizational means are found to influence farmers and to permit the cooperative use of facilities. In East Pakistan such a system of organization is evolving. Thana Irrigation A new Expanded Works Program relies on cooperation among small farmers and should, over the next few years, provide a major impetus to development.

9. There appears to be a minimum scale for a program of this type. The political value, as well as the economic gain, will be largely lost unless the funds for each governmental unit enable it to undertake work of sufficient magnitude to make the population aware of the program and of its benefits. If the size of the program is inadequate to convince local leaders that it is worthy of their time and energy and that their prestige is involved in its success, there is little chance for a favorable outcome. Furthermore, there should be an assured flow of funds so that the local councils can plan ahead and undertake works that can be improved and extended in succeeding years. A clear danger in a Works Program is that it will receive only small amounts of money and that political forces will press for distribution of available funds equitably among all local units with the result that none of them will have sufficient resources to carry out any significant work.

10. A works program creates expectations of progress. If it produces rapid development of rural facilities it will build considerable support among the rural people for the sponsoring government. Once this has occurred, the government can overlook its rural inhabitants only at its own risk. This means that the initiation of such programs tends to commit resources to the rural areas for a considerable period of time, for to encourage expectations and then leave them unfulfilled is to invite political disaster.

Appendix A

Physical Achievements of the Works Program

Because the physical achievements of the Works Program are a source of considerable controversy, it is necessary to comment on the figures contained in Table A.1 in greater detail. Some of the limitations in the official figures have been pointed out in the text. These include the listing of all embankments in the road category as well as under embankments and the reporting of repairs each year even though the same facilities are being repaired. The revised estimates are based on data obtained in the eight-thana study in 1967. In this study the exact sizes and lengths of roads, embankments, and drainage or irrigation canals were recorded. These were averaged and a projection, based on these figures, was made for the 413 thanas. The resulting figures generally substantiate those reported by the Government of East Pakistan as listed in columns 1, 2, 5, 6, 7, and 8 of Table A.1. In the category of dirt-surfaced roads the projections indicate a somewhat smaller achievement than has been claimed. Column 9 gives the government's figures for acres benefited by flood embankments and drainage canals. Data gathered in the eight thanas do not confirm these figures but indicate an area substantially smaller. The disparity is probably caused by the government's use of figures for maximum possible acreage benefited whereas in the eight-thana study the figures for the usual or normal acreage benefited were used. Since the eight thanas were assumed to be roughly representative of the province, the average area benefited in these thanas was projected for all thanas and suggests that the total area benefited was approximately 3 million acres.

In the case of community buildings, the government estimates (Table A.1, column 10) that 6,389 buildings have been constructed. This would indicate that one building has been constructed in each of the 4,053 unions and 413 thanas and that a substantial number have been built by municipal and town committees. The eight-thana study did not provide evidence to support this claim, nor did it provide a good basis for an alternative estimate. It was assumed that the Works Program reports include any building that is under construction. Since the average building construction time is two years, it was decided, arbitrarily, to halve the figure for the number of buildings, and to suggest that 3,195 buildings have been constructed.

The figures for man-days of employment on Works Program projects, as provided by the Basic Democracies and Local Government Department (Table A.1, column 11), proved to be inaccurate. Discussions in the eight thanas with clerks who actually report the employment figures showed that at least three standards were being used. Some clerks were

Table A.1. Summary of accomplishments, East Pakistan Works Program, 1962–1968

Year	Hard-surfaced roads (in miles)		Dirt-surfaced roads (in miles)		Embankments[a] (in miles)		Drainage-irrigation canals (in miles)		Acres benefited by columns 5, 6, 7, 8	Community buildings	Employment created (man-days in thousands)	Total allocation (millions)
	New	Repaired	New	Repaired	New	Repaired	New	Re-excavated				
	1	2	3	4	5	6	7	8	9	10	11	12
1962–63	0	0	3,600	8,700	0	360	1,300	450	–	0	10,200 (34,000)[e]	Rs. 100 $ 31
1963–64	27	37	3,308	20,882	364	848	168	1,147	110,346	2,630	50,680 (60,000)	Rs. 200 $ 42
1964–65[b]	325	755	5,454	22,956	1,132	2,522	1,081	4,275	3,266,069	1,952	52,929 (41,500)	Rs. 140 $ 29.4
1965–66	161	730	3,149	18,261	909	1,880	318	826	1,236,490	1,006	18,264 (32,500)	Rs. 120 $ 25.2
1966–67[b]	134	313	2,391	9,907	478	1,065	315	1,246	2,517,898	801	21,867 (40,500)	Rs. 150 $ 31.5
Totals	647	1,835	17,830	80,706	2,883	6,675	3,182	7,944	7,191,403	6,389	153,940	Rs. 710 $ 149
Revised estimates, 1967[c]	–	–	12,381	71,036	–	–	–	–	2,955,000	3,195	208,500	–
1967–68[c]	323	355	3,095	13,580	860	920	849	2,022	–	646	19,018	Rs. 215 $ 47.3

Source: Government of East Pakistan, Basic Democracies and Local Government Department, Performance Report(s) on the Rural Works Program 1963–64, 1964–65, 1965–66, 1966–67 (Dacca). Figures consistent with findings of 8-thana study except as noted.

[a] Embankment tops frequently used as roads and reported as roads and embankments.

[b] Division into New and Repaired (Re-excavated) categories estimated by author.

[c] Based on eight-thana study.

[d] Figures for 1967–68 were the most recent available in Dacca as of February, 1970.

[e] Figures in parentheses are revised annual estimates based on findings of eight-thana study.

reporting man-days; others were reporting the number of men employed regardless of the amount of time they worked; and still others were reporting the number of men paid at each pay period. Therefore it was concluded that the official figures were unreliable. Revised estimates suggested by the eight-thana study are provided at the bottom of column 11. These estimates suggest that employment created actually exceeded that officially reported. These estimates were obtained by calculating the labor component of the total Works Program expenditures from official reports, which ranged from 60 percent to 70 percent of expenditures. The actual amount paid in wages was divided between skilled (5 percent of the total employed) and unskilled laborers at the average wage rates for each group as ascertained by the eight-thana survey. Calculations were then made of the number of man-days of employment created by the Works Program. According to this estimate, the Works Program has provided 208.5 million man-days of employment for skilled and unskilled workers.

Appendix B

The Calculation of a Benefit-Cost Ratio for the Works Program

The transportation savings for farmers carrying agricultural goods to market were calculated in the economic benefits section. From these figures one can estimate the total annual savings from Works Program roads. Rice production in 1967–68 was 10.6 million tons; jute production was 1.2 million tons, and sugarcane 7.6 million tons.[B-1] Approximately 80 percent of the rice is normally consumed at the farm and 20 percent is marketed. All of the jute and 90 percent of the sugarcane are marketed. Therefore, roughly 2.1 million tons of rice, 1.2 million tons of jute, and 6.8 million tons of cane are marketed annually, a total of 10.1 million tons of produce.[B-2] It is estimated that 75 percent of the rice and 80 percent of the jute marketed travels on Works Program roads because, with the exception of headload, there are few alternative methods of transportation. Because cane is grown in drier areas, the percentage carried to market by road is higher than for rice and jute, approximately 90 percent. Calculated on the basis of these percentages, 8.7 million tons of agricultural produce move over Works Program roads annually. Assuming conservatively that these crops must travel only to secondary markets (there to be transferred to non-Works Program roads or to boats), Works Program roads have reduced transportation costs from farm to secondary market by Rs. 18.11 per ton, resulting in an annual saving of Rs. 157.5 million on marketed produce.

From these savings must be deducted the loss of production from the land taken from agriculture for roads. In East Pakistan all roads must be built on embankments. To build roads from 10 to 23 feet wide (Thana Council roads are usually 15 feet wide and District Council roads 23 feet) embankments must be from 14 to 27 feet wide at the base. The average road is 15 feet wide or 19 feet including the embankment, which means that every mile of road takes, on the average, 2.3 acres of productive farm land. On this basis it is calculated that 42,297 acres of farm land have been lost to roads since 1963. If two rice crops could have been grown on this land annually, at the average yield for the province, and a third crop grown on 5 percent of it (the provincial cropping average), the roads have resulted in the loss of production of 44,155 tons of rice annually. Calculated at the 1967–68 market price for cleaned rice in secondary markets, Rs. 25 per maund (82 pounds), this loss amounts to Rs. 26.8 million annually. If this figure is deducted from the road-user savings, the

B-1. Government of Pakistan, Central Statistical Office, *Monthly Statistical Bulletin*, (Karachi, August 1968), p. 1492.

B-2. The percentages are based on statistics on cropped areas given by Haroun ur Rashid, *East Pakistan*, pp. 179–192.

net benefit from the roads is Rs. 130.7 million annually. This calculation understates the benefits from roads because it does not include the savings on goods moving from the market to the farm, which are also substantial. On the other hand, this calculation does assume that decreased labor spent on transporting goods had alternative uses (i.e., that the opportunity cost of labor was not zero). Were the latter the case, the benefits as calculated would have an upward bias.

Increased production resulting from Works Program drainage projects is estimated at 364,123 tons annually. Figured at Rs. 25 per maund, this amounts to Rs. 221.2 million annually. Because the drainage is gravity flow and the production increase is calculated without the inclusion of any new inputs, there are no additional costs to be deducted from these benefits.

The calculation of the annual benefits resulting from flood protection embankments constructed by the Works Program is even more crude than the estimates for roads or drainage. First, it is impossible to determine how many of the acres benefited are agricultural lands and how many are population centers. This distinction could be important because the potential flood losses in a human settlement are higher than on agricultural land. Second, the only available estimates of annual flood losses in East Pakistan, or even of the losses in the areas subject to recurring floods, are probably based more on informed guess than on hard data. The only data available indicate that serious flooding in East Pakistan occurs at approximately two-year intervals.[B-3] Major floods occur less frequently. Calculating from the Planning Department report, the biennial floods damage 6 million acres of land that are not affected by normal monsoon-season high water. The losses due to the biennial floods amount to Rs. 710.2 million, or Rs. 355.1 million annually.

The eight-thana study provides the estimate that 2.2 million acres are benefited by flood embankments but that only 75 percent of the embankments are maintained, which reduces the area benefited to 1.7 million acres. This area is 28.3 percent of the land most susceptible to flood damage. Therefore, 28.3 percent of the annual average loss from flooding, or Rs. 100.4 million, is a rough estimate of the annual savings from the Works Program flood embankments.

On the basis of these calculations, it is estimated that the annual benefits from Works Program projects—roads, drainage, and embankments—amount to Rs. 452.3 million annually from 1967–68 on.

B-3. Government of East Pakistan, Planning Department, Agricultural Planning Group, *Flood Damage and Damage Due to Other Causes* (mimeo, Dacca, undated).

From the gross benefits must be deducted the annual maintenance costs of Works Program facilities. In the eight thanas, councils were asked their road maintenance costs; the average was Rs. 560 per mile per year. Multiplying by the total miles of road built and repaired results in a figure of Rs. 56.6 million for annual maintenance costs. Farmers also reported that drainage canals silted up in about five years. Therefore, the annual maintenance cost of these canals is calculated at 20 percent of the total cost of the canals, or Rs. 4.4 million. Because flood embankments are similar to roads and often are used as roads, it is assumed that the maintenance cost of embankments is the same as that for roads. Because only 75 percent of the embankments have been maintained, the cost of maintenance, Rs. 560 per mile, is calculated on three-quarters of the total miles of embankments built or repaired under the Works Program. The resulting figure is Rs. 3.8 million spent on annual repairs to embankments. These calculations produce a figure of Rs. 64.8 million in total annual maintenance costs from 1967–68 on. Although maintenance costs are taken from both the Works Program allocations and from funds provided by local councils, it is assumed for purposes of this analysis that the total maintenance costs are provided by the local councils. They are therefore deducted from the benefits, and the government's annual investment in the Works Program is assumed to contain no maintenance component. On this basis the net annual benefits from Works Program roads, drainage, and flood control embankments are estimated at Rs. 387.5 million from 1967–1968 on. The benefits and maintenance costs are summarized in Table 7.11 in the text.

The gross benefits from road, drainage, and embankment projects are calculated for the year 1966–67. It is assumed that benefits grew at a constant rate over the preceding five years the Works Program was in existence to reach this level. From these benefits annual maintenance costs are deducted. Although a constant rate of maintenance expenditures is calculated from 1962 on, it is assumed that, despite maintenance, by 1976–77 all the works constructed during the period 1962 to 1967 will yield no further benefits. Therefore, benefits are assumed to terminate in 1976–77, and the calculation ends with that year (although the benefit stream theoretically continues somewhat longer).

The costs of the Works Program are taken to be the government's annual investment in the program. Because the future Works Program allocations are not known, the benefit-cost ratio is calculated as if the government investment in the Works Program had ended in 1966–67.

Although 15 percent of Works Program funds have been spent for construction of community buildings, it is difficult to demonstrate any direct

Table B.1. Benefits and costs of the East Pakistan Works Program (millions of rupees; 1967–68 constant prices)

Year	Benefits				Costs	
Year	Gross benefit	Mainten-ance cost	Net benefit	Benefit dis-counted at 12 percent	Gov't. of East Paki-stan investment in Works Program	Cost discounted at 12 percent
1962–63	0	0	0	0	100	100
1963–64	90.4	0	90.4	80.5	200	178.6
1964–65	180.8	16.2	164.6	130.0	140	111.6
1965–66	271.2	32.4	238.8	169.5	120	85.4
1966–67	361.6	48.6	313.0	198.8	150	95.4
1967–68	452.3	64.8	387.5	219.7	0	–
1968–69	452.3	64.8	387.5	196.4	0	–
1969–70	452.3	64.8	387.5	175.1	0	–
1970–71	452.3	64.8	387.5	156.5	0	–
1971–72	452.3	64.8	387.5	139.8	0	–
1972–73	452.3	64.8	387.5	124.7	0	–
1973–74	452.3	64.8	387.5	111.2	0	–
1974–75	452.3	64.8	387.5	99.5	0	–
1975–76	452.3	64.8	387.5	88.7	0	–
1976–77	452.3	64.8	387.5	79.4	0	–
Total benefits				1,969.8	Total costs	571.0

Source: Figures for the benefits are derived from the calculations described in Appendix B. Figures for the costs are taken from Government of East Pakistan, Basic Democracies and Local Government Department, Performance Report(s) on the Rural Works Program, 1963–64, 1964–65, 1965–66 (Dacca). Costs for 1966–67 were recorded by the author from documents shown him by the Basic Democracies and Local Government Department.

economic benefit from this construction. Therefore, nothing is included in the benefit calculations for the buildings. Nevertheless, the construction costs are included in the cost figures because community buildings may have helped make possible the other benefits, for example, by providing a meeting place for councils planning the Works Program.

This analysis is computed in 1967–68 constant prices, although the program began in 1962–63; therefore it is important to ascertain whether inflation during this period may have distorted the results. This does not appear to be the case: the general price index for East Pakistan was 106 in January 1963 and 115 in January 1967. This minor increase is not sufficient to distort the results.[B-4]

B-4. Government of Pakistan, Central Statistical Office, *Monthly Statistical Bulletin* (Karachi, January 1967), p. 112.

Although the marginal productivity of labor is very low in the rural areas during the December-to-May slack season, the benefit-cost ratio is calculated at the actual financial cost of the labor. If the opportunity cost of labor is assumed to be zero, the ratio of benefits to costs in the Works Program (where the labor component comprises 65 percent of the total cost) rises to 10.11. Alternatively, if a shadow wage rate of 50 percent of actual wages is used, the benefit-cost ratio is 5.11.

The choice of an appropriate discount rate for East Pakistan is somewhat arbitrary. There seems to be general agreement that it should be somewhere between 8 and 14 percent. The Planning Commission has established 12 percent as appropriate in Pakistan,[B-5] and this rate is used for discounting both the benefits and the costs. The resulting benefit-cost ratio is 3.4. To test the sensitivity of this analysis to the discount rate used, calculations were also made at discount rates of 8 percent, 10 percent, and 14 percent, which produced ratios of 4.1, 3.7, and 3.1 respectively. Regardless of the discount rate used, there has been a good return, in economic terms, on the Works Program investment. The calculations are shown in Table B-1.

B-5. Government of Pakistan, Planning Commission, *A Manual for the Economic Appraisal of Transport Projects* (Islamabad, June 1969), p. 18.

8 Pakistan's Industrial Entrepreneurs—Education, Occupational Background, and Finance

Gustav F. Papanek

Industrial development in Pakistan contradicted many widely held notions. It proceeded at a pace quite unexpected in a country that began with no industry and no industrial tradition—the modern manufacturing sector expanded from less than 1 percent of the domestic product in 1947 to nearly 10 percent of a much larger product in 1967–68. The entrepreneurs responsible were largely indigenous traders, with little industrial experience. The necessary capital came largely from the entrepreneurs' own savings.

Because Pakistan's rapid industrialization began as recently as 1947, it is especially interesting and easy to study. In other countries with a long history of industrial growth, it is difficult to discover much about the men and money instrumental in the original spurt of industrialization. Pakistan's industrialization process as a whole—the speed, the savings patterns, the economic changes that determined industrial development—has been described elsewhere in broad terms.[1] This chapter examines in detail the background of Pakistan's industrialists and their sources of finance.

The industrial development in Pakistan differed in three fundamental respects from the early stages of the industrial revolution in some of the currently developed countries. Firms were large, most of the technology was transferred from other countries, and the process was rapid as a result of extreme incentives. These characteristics affected the financing of industrialization and the nature of the entrepreneurial group that brought it about. Pakistan provides important lessons for other less developed countries similarly situated.

NOTE: I am grateful for the computational work of Stephen Guisinger and for the comments of J. Tomas Hexner, Hanna Papanek, Joseph J. Stern, and Raymond Vernon.

1. Gustav F. Papanek, *Pakistan's Development—Social Goals and Private Incentives* (Cambridge: Harvard University Press, 1967).

The modern technology that was used typically involves substantial economies of scale. Pakistan's industry therefore was dominated by large units. When modern manufacturing was 6 percent of the national product there were some 3,000 industrial firms, but 500 large firms (minimum assets of Rs. 1,000,000 or U.S. $200,000) contributed about 85 percent of the value added. Sixteen families controlled firms with one-quarter, and 60 families firms with nearly one-half, of all sales of manufacturing units. In short, the number of entrepreneurs required to start a rapid process of industrialization, in a country with a population of 100 million was about a hundred.

The firms that they set up were largely technological carbon copies of firms in the developed world. There are good economic reasons for arguing that the less developed countries should use fundamentally different technologies from developed countries, technologies that are more labor-intensive and less capital-intensive. There are also good arguments on the opposite side, for the use of machine-paced technology in less developed countries. Whatever the merits of these arguments, Pakistan's industry did rely on transferred technology.

The third characteristic of Pakistan's industrial development, the speed of the process in response to extreme incentives, has already been mentioned. Government intervention in the economy was massive and provided extensive protection from foreign competition for the developing manufacturing sector. Profits in industry were therefore high, the rewards of becoming an industrialist were great, and there were substantial disincentives to remaining an importer with a sharply reduced turnover.[2]

These three factors are, or at least can be, duplicated in many less developed countries. One would suppose that they would produce a similar pattern of industrial development in many instances, though for a variety of political, equity, and efficiency reasons an alternative pattern may be preferred. In Pakistan, the size of plants, the use of existing advanced technology, and the speed of the process affected which groups dominated industrialization, the education and technical knowledge they required, and their sources of finance. That Pakistan's industrial entrepreneurs were largely drawn from merchant capitalists, with little education and less technical knowledge, and were financed from trading profits resulted to a considerable extent from these three characteristics of its industrial development.

In order to focus on the development of indigenous entrepreneurs, this study ignores government firms and private industrialists who were

2. Papanek, *Pakistan's Development.*

foreigners or non-Muslims. The latter were largely well-established industrialists, primarily Hindus, whose firms had been set up before Independence. In 1958–59, the date of the survey on which this study is based, roughly two-thirds of industrial assets were in the hands of Muslim private industrialists, the subject of the analysis which follows. It needs to be emphasized that nearly all the data used below relate to the early stage of industrial development, but are important to an understanding of the somewhat different situation in the 1960s.

All the data in this paper came from a sample survey I carried out that included about 9 percent of all firms and 58 percent of the value added in the manufacturing sector (so-called "large-scale" industries) throughout Pakistan.[3] Cross-checks with independent data confirm that the sample represented the universe quite accurately. Most tables in this paper are for the universe, not the sample.

Education and Success in Industry

Because books on development are usually written by teachers, it is not surprising that they tend to stress the importance of formal education. If Pakistan's entrepreneurs did not follow the script, it may be in part because many of them could not read it. The causal relationships between education and success in industry in Pakistan appear to be complex, largely because many of Pakistan's industrialists obtained most of their education from their business-oriented families rather than from the school system.

When industrialists were compared with the population as a whole, most of whom were cultivators, the industrialists were, quite naturally, above average with respect to formal education. But industrialists were less well educated than other elite groups in Pakistan—government officials and large landlords—or than businessmen and industrialists operating comparable enterprises in the developed world.[4] Furthermore, there was no clear relationship between education and success in industry, as can be seen from Table 8.1.

Although educational attainments reported in the survey probably were exaggerated, one-fourth of the industrialists questioned said that they had completed primary school at best, and most of these were in fact without

3. The survey is described in detail in Gustav F. Papanek, "Industrial Production and Investment in Pakistan," *Pakistan Development Review*, 4 (Autumn 1964), 462–490.

4. This statement is not based on surveys or other statistical data, which do not exist, but on such facts as the educational requirements for civil servants and the educational patterns in landlord families.

Table 8.1. Education and success of Muslim industrialists as of 1958

Education	Percentage of no. of firms[a]	Percentage of total[a]	Investment controlled: Total	Traditional industries[b]	Cotton textiles	Nontraditional industries[b]
			millions of rupees[c]			
No formal education	8.0	6.5	180	45	70	65
Primary	18.0	25.5	730	60	360	310
Secondary	18.0	21.0	595	185	250	160
Matric[d]	27.5	19.0	540	80	100	360
College	16.5	18.5	540	220	210	110
Post grad—general	4.5	2.0	55	–	30	25
Technical—below college	1.0	0.5	10	10	–	–
Technical—college	4.0	6.0	170	50	40	80
Technical—post grad	2.0	0.5	10	10	–	–
Total	99.5	99.5	2,830	660	1,060	1,110
Unknown	0.5	0.5	160	–	–	160

Source: The data for all tables in this chapter were obtained in a survey carried out by the author in Pakistan, and described in Gustav F. Papanek, "Industrial Production and Investment in Pakistan," *Pakistan Development Review*, 4 (Autumn 1964), 462–490.

[a] Rounded to nearest half percent.

[b] Traditional industries include the following industry groups: primary processing; import processing—traditional.

Nontraditional industries include the following industry groups: secondary processing; import processing—nontraditional; jute; chemicals, cement, paper; machinery, transport equipment.

For definition of these industry groups, see appendix.

[c] Rounded to nearest Rs. 5 million.

[d] "Matric" is the comprehensive examination at the end of secondary education after 10 years of schooling.

formal education. This poorly educated group controlled one-third of industrial investments, a disproportionate amount.

One might expect industrialists with little or no formal education to be concentrated in the simple processing industries. In fact, however, they controlled a share of cotton textile and other nontraditional industries roughly equal to their share in industry as a whole. On the other hand, firms in traditional industries were concentrated in the hands of the most highly educated decision-makers.

Lack of education seemed to be no handicap to successful performance. All firms in the survey were divided into four roughly equal groups with respect to two success indicators: the rate of growth in assets between 1947 and 1959 and the rate of return in 1958. Industrialists with little education were found in nearly equal proportions in the highest quartile and in the lowest quartile with respect to both success indicators, as

Table 8.2. Performance of firms controlled by industrialists with little education[a] (number of firms)

Performance measured in terms of:	Large firms: Highest quartile	Large firms: Lowest quartile	Smaller firms: Highest quartile	Smaller firms: Lowest quartile	All firms: Highest quartile	All firms: Lowest quartile
Rate of asset growth	7	2	8	11	15	13
Rate of return	2	6	10	7	12	13
Both criteria	9	8	18	18	27	26

[a] Includes industrialists who said they had no formal education or had been to primary school only.

Table 8.2 shows. In other words, industrialists with little education did as well as more educated ones by these criteria of success.

Although education might be considered of particular importance with larger, and presumably more complex, enterprises, the poorly educated industrialists did just as well whether they ran a large or a small firm. Regardless of size, firms headed by decision-makers with little education were as often in the top as in the bottom quartile with respect to the two success indicators. It became clear in the course of interviews that industrialists with little education could handle large enterprises because they hired specialized technical and management talent. They often left management to their assistants and concentrated on organizing capital and obtaining government permits—activities in which they were strong, especially if their background was in trade. In the small firms management functions could presumably have been delegated less easily.

In examining in greater detail the effect of education on the success of industrialists, one has to be careful of sampling errors. The number of firms in some categories is quite small and the two indicators of performance—the rate of growth in assets and the rate of return—are often contradictory. If the total of both indicators is the criterion of success (Table 8.3), the group with secondary education shows the best performance, with substantially more firms in the top quartile than in the bottom one. (Some firms may be counted twice if they are in the top quartile for both indicators, or in the bottom quartile for both, or in the top for one and the bottom for the other, or vice versa.) Industrialists in this group had spent 7 to 11 years in school, but only marginally outperformed their competitors with little or no formal education. Those who received technical training or education beyond high school controlled firms that did much worse than average, with the worst performance by firms in the hands of technically trained industrialists. This is a paradoxical and—at least to educators—discouraging set of relationships.

Table 8.3. Education of industrialists and performance of firms controlled by them (number of firms)

Education	Rate of growth		Rate of return		Total of both indicators			
	Highest quartile	Lowest quartile	Highest quartile	Lowest quartile	Highest quartiles		Lowest quartiles	
No formal education	7	4	4	5	11	27	9	26
Primary	8	9	8	8	16		17	
Secondary	11	8	10	8	21	38	16	29
Matric	9	3	8	10	17		13	
College	3	13	8	13	11	23	26	44
Post grad—general	4	3	4	5	8		8	
Technical	2	4	2	6	4		10	
Total	44	44	44	55	88		99	

There are several explanations for these relationships. First and probably most important, it is a mistake to equate education and formal schooling. Many of the entrepreneurs with little formal education came from traditional trading "communities" (quasi-castes). They had almost always received a remarkably fine business education in their family enterprise. They had been indoctrinated with the importance of economic success, and the need for hard work, thrift, and risk-taking to achieve success. They had also learned about buying and selling. In the early stages of industrialization, these skills and attitudes were more useful than much of the rote learning that was a large part of the formal education system.

A second explanation is that the offspring of the big trading families started with important advantages in terms of access to capital, access to a network of suppliers, and connections, and were therefore among the more successful industrialists. On the other hand, industrialists in 1959 with higher education often came from professional families with less capital, fewer business contacts, and less business experience. If success in industry was partly the result of training and experience in business, and those with much of that training had little formal schooling, it is not surprising that formal schooling and success are not correlated.

Third, formal education may not have been an asset during early industrial development. The educated, especially those with technical training, might have tended to concentrate on management, on technical problems, or on technologically advanced industry. These tendencies were handicaps—at least in achieving a high rate of growth in assets and a high rate of return. The successful industrialists in the 1950's competed intensely, often with little regard for the niceties of the law, for funds and permission from government to invest in industries with a quick payoff and a minimum of technical problems. The successful industrialist, in short, was a promoter, not a skilled technician and manager.

Finally, a lack of relevant education, like any scarce input, could be made good at a price. Especially in its early years, Pakistan's industry was generally high cost. These costs resulted from many inadequacies, of which a poorly educated entrepreneurial group may have been one. Whether the industrialists compensated for lack of education by hiring some specialized skills or by accepting greater inefficiency, inadequate education for the whole group probably contributed to high costs, even if *within* the group of industrialists, formal education and performance are not correlated.

Informal contacts with industrialists indicate that by the middle 1960's the situation had begun to change. As the market expanded and government controls were no longer as all-pervasive as earlier, management became more important and personal contacts with other businessmen and with government officials became less significant. New industries were more complex and required more technical and management skills. Education was therefore coming into its own. A few of the original entrepreneurs were giving increasing responsibility to their educated sons and grandsons. By the 1960's, many of the leading business families, which two or three generations back had often disregarded formal education, wanted most of their sons to have a higher education. Because these families will usually continue to show up as among the more successful, a correlation between advanced education and success in industry is likely to develop. A survey carried out in 1965 would probably have shown that the educated were more important and successful in industry than they had been in 1960, though not necessarily because of their education.

After all these exceptions and explanations, the major outlines still remain. A large share of Pakistan's industry was originally developed by entrepreneurs with little or no formal education, who performed as well as their educated colleagues and who established enterprises with complex technology or substantial capital requirements. Decision-makers with secondary education turned in an above-average performance with respect to growth and profits. The performance of those with college, technical, or other advanced education was below average. A dozen years after the start of industrial development, the situation had begun to change as decision-makers increasingly were trained technicians and managers. In Pakistan, then, education followed rather than preceded industrial development. If Pakistan's experience is any guide, rapid industrial development need not wait for the extensive education of industrialists.

Technical Knowledge and Competence

An examination of the sources of technical information used by industrialists supports the explanation of the success of uneducated entrepreneurs given above, and further clarifies the paradoxical relationship between education and industrial success. Pakistani industrialists controlling complex industries and large firms bought their technical information the same way they hired their transportation or machinery. Even in the late 1950's, when many of the foreigners who had came to Pakistan with the industrial machinery were gone, foreign technicians still played an important role. This role, however, involved significant foreign exchange outlays, even if they were hidden in the price of machinery.

Nearly two-thirds of all firms, according to the industrialists' responses (summarized in Table 8.4), obtained the technical information to operate from some member of the controlling family (including the decision-makers). However, it was mainly the small firms that could rely on this source of technical expertise. In the new industries, which usually had complex technical problems, and among the larger units, over two-thirds of investment was in firms that relied at least partly on foreigners for

Table 8.4. Sources of technical information in 1958 as given by industrialists (percentages of total in each category)

Source of information	All firms	All investment (value)	Large firms[b]-investment (value)			
			Total[b]	Traditional industries[c]	Textiles	Nontraditional industries[c]
Mainly foreigners	1.5	26.0	31.5	-	16.0	54.0
Partly foreigners, mainly outside family	4.5	19.5	22.5	13.5	39.5	13.5
Pakistani outside family	26.0	36.0	39.5	79.0	37.0	27.5
Partly or wholly family	64.5	18.5	6.0	7.0	7.5	4.0
Unknown	4.0	0.5	-	-	-	0.5

[a] Rounded to nearest half percent.

[b] Includes all firms with Rs. 1,000,000 ($200,000.00) or more of investment.

[c] For definitions see footnote (b) to Table 8.1.

technical information. The remaining firms in this group relied primarily on Pakistani technicians drawn from outside the decision-maker's family. (Because they report the situation in the late 1950's, when many firms had already reduced their dependence on foreigners, these percentages understate the role of foreign technicians.)

Before the 1960's, young family members had been training in technical skills for only a few years and most of them had not yet returned to the family firm. From general observation it is clear that in the late 1960's the importance of foreigners in providing technical knowledge declined greatly, while the importance of family members greatly increased.

Industrialists were asked what occupation their children would follow. A large number (one-fifth) did not respond. Of those who did answer, less than one-tenth thought their children would become professionals, traders, or industrialists outside the family enterprise. The rest said their children had entered or were expected to enter the family industrial enterprise, and of these, one-seventh were expected to have specific technical training. One-quarter of 1958 industrial assets were controlled by families that said that they had sent or were sending their children for technical training in industry. In short, a definite industrial class is emerging, distinguishable from the older business or commercial group.

The more successful business houses, with strong family leadership, assign their educated offspring to activities they are best qualified for, discriminating among them on the basis of competence—the most enterprising and intelligent manage major units in the family empire, the least competent handle charities, or represent the family socially. However, the family management is reluctant to discriminate too severely against family members, however incompetent. As the leading firms find it increasingly possible to dispense with foreign and nonfamily technicians, inefficiency could gradually become built in if every educated grandson is entitled to some important position regardless of intelligence or enterprise.

The degree of nepotism, and of the inefficiency that can result from it, will increasingly depend on competitive pressure. Most families hate to discriminate among members, but hate even more to fall behind in expansion and in profits. If the economic system is essentially competitive, the shift to technically trained family members could result in improved functioning of Pakistan's industry. But if there is little effective competitive pressure, the shift to greater reliance on family members could reduce industrial efficiency. To prevent this, nepotism must be taken into account in framing government policy.

The use of foreigners to provide technical knowledge, including management techniques, was substantial. The lack of technical knowledge is widely considered a serious obstacle to the industrialization of less developed countries. It is often argued that this knowledge is available only with investment by foreign private enterprise, since companies from the developed world are unlikely to make their technicians available except to firms they control. (This argument naturally finds favor with companies in the developed world.) Hiring foreign technicians is considered a poor alternative by many industrialists in less developed countries because they generally believe that anyone available must have professional or personal flaws.

Yet the problem of acquiring technical knowledge proved manageable in Pakistan. During the initial period of industrialization most industries had a relatively simple technology that could be acquired quickly by Pakistanis. During the learning period, the necessary technical and managerial skills were often bought together with the machinery. A typical arrangement for a textile mill might call for the Japanese supplier of the machinery to provide the engineers required to erect the machines and to supervise their operation for some time. The supplier, concerned primarily with selling his machines, had an interest in expediting the training of Pakistani technicians so that his people could leave—a situation quite different from one in which a foreign company controls the enterprise and uses it to put its less competent executives out to pasture. If the sales contract required satisfactory operation of the machinery by Pakistanis before the sale was completed, the supplier had some incentive to send good technicians and to provide adequate training. The Pakistani controlling the enterprise was an entrepreneur pure and simple, finding the money, obtaining the government permits, hiring the top Pakistani staff, buying the machines and other imports, and arranging for marketing.

By the time industrialization moved to its second stage, involving industries with complex technology that required a highly skilled technical team, the whole industrial sector in Pakistan had become more sophisticated. There were more technically trained Pakistanis; some industrialists knew a good deal about sources of technical information and could hire foreign firms or technicians without falling into the hands of international carpetbaggers; other industrialists made sophisticated partnership arrangements with foreign companies in order to obtain technical, managerial, and marketing skills. In the 1960's when Pakistan moved into industries of considerable complexity, the lack of technical knowledge still did not impose insurmountable barriers.

The lack of technical knowledge, like the lack of education, was surmountable primarily because firms were large. Pessimists about industrial growth in the less developed countries often seem to see such growth as a replay of the Industrial Revolution, speeded up. In many respects this is a false image. If Pakistan's industrialists had begun as small artisans or merchants who gradually acquired modern machinery and slowly built up an industrial enterprise, a lack of technical knowledge and education could have been a serious drawback. But in industrialization, as in so many activities in this imperfect world, money can often substitute for education and training. The rich Pakistani merchants who became industrialists hired their engineers and some plant managers from abroad and their accountants, lawyers, labor relations officers, and most plant managers from within the country. Fortunately many industrialists were shrewd enough and were under enough competitive pressure to realize that the next generation would need more education and more technical knowledge. Therefore they also used their money to buy a good education for their sons and grandsons. Large units, with the concentration of wealth and economic power this implied in a less developed country with a small industrial sector, were certainly not an unmixed blessing, but they did ease the solution of some problems.

Activist or Business-is-all

It is interesting to examine to what extent the industrial entrepreneurs conformed to the stereotype of the modern businessman. The successful contemporary U. S. businessman or industrialist is often pictured as a go-getter, involved in a variety of social, civic, and political activities as well as in business. In Pakistan, the opposite stereotype is held in government and the universities. The businessman-industrialist is believed to be interested almost exclusively in his enterprise. Superficially the Pakistani stereotype seems more appropriate. Over half of all Muslim industrialists said they had no nonbusiness interests and close to a third said they had "few" such interests. Less than 10 percent said they were "active" or "very active." But nearly 40 percent of assets were in the hands of those "active" or "very active" in nonbusiness pursuits. The big industrialists, with command over resources and in position to hire staff, played an important role not only in industry but also in other areas.

Table 8.5. Nonbusiness interests of industrialists (percentages)

	None	Few	Moderate	Active	Very active	No response
Industrialists	53	29	8	5	4	1
Control of assets	27	18	14	12	26	3

The activists were often leading figures in their communities (quasi-caste and religious groupings) and sometimes in various social organizations. The important industrialists clearly were not content to achieve economic eminence; they wanted to play a role in other areas as well. This tendency is giving them a more important political role—in the broadest sense—than if they involved themselves only in industrial affairs.

The Occupational Background of Industrialists

The importance of trade, and especially foreign trade, in the background of decision-makers has been covered elsewhere,[5] but some of the details of their background shed further light on the process by which traders became industrialists, and also shed some light on widespread assumptions about that process.

The industrialists of Pakistan had been primarily traders before 1947 (those who had been primarily traders controlled two-thirds of 1959 assets). However, many of these traders or their families had had some experience with industry. As indicated in Table 8.6 a very small group of Pakistan's industrialists reported industry as their secondary occupation before 1947. This tiny group, nearly all giving trade as their primary occupation, contributed a disproportionate number of Pakistan's merchant-capitalists and controlled nearly a third of all industrial investment in 1959. Even stronger evidence that Pakistan's industrialists were not complete neophytes in industry is provided by Table 8.7. Over half of all Muslim industrialists, controlling almost two-thirds of industrial investment in 1959, came from families that had some experience with industry before Independence. A relatively small proportion of this experienced group—17 percent of all industrialists—had been primarily in industry and an even smaller group—4 percent of all industrialists—had industry as their secondary occupation. For other industrialists, pre-1947 experience represented a minor, tertiary, aspect of their business activities. Still other industrialists had no personal experience with industry, although some family members, usually a brother or father, had some industrial interest before 1947. The shift from trade to industry as a primary occupation in response to economic incentives was facilitated by the contact with industry, however slight, of many merchant-capitalist families who came to dominate Pakistan's industry.

A sharp contrast emerges from Table 8.6 between the group primarily

5. Papanek, *Pakistan's Development*, chapter 2.

Table 8.6. Prior occupation of Muslims who were industrialists in 1959 (percentages—rounded)

Prior occupation	Previous primary[a] occupation		Previous secondary[a] occupation	
	Industrialists	Industrial investment[b]	Industrialists	Industrial investment[b]
Industrialists before 1947	17	16	4	30
Small industry, handicrafts	18	6	23	7
Traders (incl. govt. contractors)	45	63	69	49
Employees, professionals, others	18	10	4	12
Agriculture	3	6	negligible	1
	101	101	100	99

Source: Gustav F. Papanek, *Pakistan's Development—Social Goals and Private Incentives* (Cambridge: Harvard University Press, 1967), p. 41.

[a]Primary and secondary were determined according to proportion of income received.

[b]Proportion of total industrial investment controlled by each category.

engaged in trade before Independence, which came to dominate post-1947 industry, and another large group involved in small-scale industry and handicrafts. If both primary and secondary occupations are taken into account, 41 percent of all the industrialists in 1959 fall into this category, yet they controlled only 13 percent of 1959 investment. Clearly those whose experience had been in small-scale industry and handicrafts were not nearly as successful during post-Independence industrialization as their trader counterparts.

The importance of economic incentives in occupational shifts is confirmed by Table 8.7. Many of Pakistan's industrialists were from families that first became involved in industry in the 1930's, when there was strong nationalist agitation for breaking British predominance in this field. However, the largest groups entered industry during the Second World War and between 1952 and 1955, two periods when economic incentives were strong because competition from imports was sharply curtailed.

The occupational pattern can be traced back to the industrialists' fathers and grandfathers (Table 8.8). About half of 1959 industrial assets were in the hands of those whose family background was in trade. Among such trade-oriented families, the grandfathers of the 1959 decision-makers were primarily wholesalers, buying and selling in undivided

Table 8.7. Timing of initial entry into industry for the family of Muslim industrialists, as of 1959 (percentages—rounded)

Period	Industrialists	1959 Assets
Before 1920	8.5	12.0
1920–1928	11.0	19.5
1930–1939	13.5	22.5
1940–1947	24.5	16.5
1948–1951	13.5	9.0
1952–1955	22.5	19.0
1956–1959	6.0	1.5

India.[6] The fathers continued in trade, but shifted somewhat to exporting and importing. Some had a secondary interest in industry. This group included the more successful of the industrialists—one-third of all industrialists belonged to it, but they controlled about half of all assets.[7] There is an almost complete overlap between this group and the trading communities, quasi-castes with a long history in trade.

Another substantial group had grandfathers, and to a lesser extent fathers, in agriculture. That some industrialists come from this background is not surprising, since the overwhelming majority of Muslims in pre-partition India were cultivators. However, in relation to their importance in the total population this group furnished a very small proportion of industrialists. Many of the agriculturalists who did become industrialists seem to have been farmer-traders, usually on a small scale, who moved into simple processing activities closely related to their previous trade (cotton ginning, jute baling). A few were large landlords, sometimes local rulers, who moved into such large-scale activities as sugar mills when the advantages of being an industrialist became clear. The clear division between the group of small farmer/traders-industrialists and landlords-industrialists on the one hand and the more important trader/business community-industrialists on the other is highlighted by the fact that practically no industrialists indicated that their fathers' secondary occupation had been in agriculture. Industrialists with a background primarily in trade had no ties to the land.

6. This pattern is substantiated by: G. M. Farooq, *The People of Karachi: Economic Characteristics* (Pakistan Institute of Development Economics, July 1966).

7. Clearly one cannot speak of a "group" over several generations on the basis of a simple statistical table. Statistically a family with a trader grandfather could have a landlord father and a current decision-maker who was an employee before becoming an industrialist. The discussion above on family histories is based on an examination of individual interviews, as well as the statistical data

Table 8.8. Occupation of fathers and grandfathers of those who were industrialists in 1959 (percentages – rounded)

Occupation category	Father: Primary occupation Number[a]	Father: Primary occupation Assets[b]	Father: Secondary occupation Number[a]	Father: Secondary occupation Assets[b]	Grandfather: Primary occupation Number[a]	Grandfather: Primary occupation Assets[b]
Importer	4.5	11.0	3.0	7.5	1.5	3.5
Exporter	7.5	20.5	0.5	1.0	7.0	9.5
Wholesaler	25.5	29.0	4.0	6.0	18.0	35.5
Retailer	2.0	4.0	2.0	1.0	6.5	4.5
Government contractor[c]	5.0	8.0	2.5	3.5	5.0	8.0
Industrialist[d]	6.5	5.0	8.0	27.5	5.0	6.5
Small industrialist[e]	15.5	3.5	5.0	4.5	16.0	6.5
Employee	17.0	7.5	1.5	2.0	8.0	3.5
Agriculturist, etc.[f]	11.0	10.5	1.5	2.0	14.0	11.5
Other, unknown, none	0.0	0.5	72.0	44.5	20.0	10.5

[a]The percentage of the number of industrialists in 1959 whose fathers/grandfathers were in the category.
[b]The percentage of 1959 assets controlled by industrialists whose fathers/grandfathers were in the category.
[c]Mostly traders who procured goods, carried out construction and provided services for the government.
[d]Large and medium-sized industry.
[e]Essentially handicrafts, workshops, and village enterprises.
[f]Includes local hereditary rulers with substantial land holdings.

Only 15 percent of 1959 industrial assets were controlled by industrialists whose fathers or grandfathers were employees, retailers, artisans, or small-scale industrialists. Only about one-third of the present industrialists had been primarily in these occupations before 1947. So far as Pakistan is concerned there is little to the notion that industrialists develop from the ranks of retailers, employees, artisans or small-scale industrialists, where they first learn simple business skills or industrial processes. In many countries from Southeast Asia to Africa governments are attempting to develop indigenous industrialists, by encouraging nationals to become retailers, to set up small industrial or handicraft establishments, or to work as employees in the modern sector. Pakistan's experience indicates that these policies may not be effective: its industrialists did not follow this route.

One reason for the lack of success of small shopkeepers, employees, and artisans may be that they did not have access to the capital, technology, and contacts required by modern industry. The crucial obstacle to industrial enterprise was not some knowledge of particular industrial techniques and a willingness to work with one's hands, which someone in handicrafts or small-scale industry might possess; nor was it a knowledge of sales techniques, which a retailer might have; nor a knowledge of the functioning of existing large-scale organizations plus a good education, which employees might have. The obstacles which early industrialists faced were adequate finance for investment on the required scale and funds to buy the required technical knowledge, plus access to foreign suppliers of machinery and to the government officials who provided permits. Industrialists also had to be willing to take substantial risks. In these respects traders had an edge. There are other less developed countries that face similar circumstances and that have made the political decision to rely on private and indigenous development of industry. Such countries may also find that reserving retail trade or small industry to nationals is not good preparation for national participation in large-scale modern industry. These countries may do better to encourage and assist some of their large-scale traders to enter industry directly.

Some further insight into the process of industrialization is gained by comparing the former occupation of industrialists with the industries they entered. (Given the increasing unreliability of sample surveys as results are disaggregated, one has to interpret a matrix, such as Table 8.9, with caution.)

The pattern of post-Independence industrial interest of those who were already in industry before Independence is striking. Nearly one-third of the investment of this group was in the least sophisticated industries—

Table 8.9. Previous occupation of industrialists by industry groups in 1959 (millions of rupees of investment)[a]

Previous occupation (before entering industry or before 1947, whichever was later)	Industry group[b] in which engaged in 1959							
	Simple processing (e.g., jute baling)	Secondary processing (e.g., cigarettes)	Cotton textiles	Jute	Import processing		Chemicals, machines, cement, etc.	Total
					Traditional	Nontraditional		
1. Importer	40	20	420	140	60	10	150	850
2. Exporter	–	50	190	160	–	–	40	430
3. Wholesaler	70	20	140	–	40	10	10	280
4. Retailer	–	–	20	–	–	–	–	30
5. Govt. contractor	10	90	40	–	130	–	50	340
6. Industrialist	170	50	160	–	20	80	40	530
7. Small industrialist	–	20	70	–	–	80	10	180
8. Employee	60	10	–	–	20	20	30	140
9. Agriculturalist, etc.	–	160	10	–	10	–	–	180
10. First occupation[c]	–	–	–	–	10	–	20	30
Total	350	400	1,060	300	310	200	360	2,990

[a]Rounded to nearest Rs. 10 million. Therefore, figures may not add.
[b]For definitions of industry by groups and examples of industries in each group, see appendix.
[c]Industry was their first occupation.

in simple processing (e.g., jute baling, canning). The owners had probably been in the same industry before Independence and simply continued or expanded their holdings. Another third of the investment of these experienced industrialists was in cotton textiles, again in some part undoubtedly the expansion of their pre-Independence industrial holdings. In short, industrialists whose primary occupation before Independence was already industry were not particularly venturesome in their post-Independence investments.

If all industries are divided into three categories—traditional (simple processing and traditional import processing); cotton textiles (which called for somewhat greater entrepreneurship); and nontraditional (everything else, and on the whole requiring the most entrepreneurship)—it is clear that the smallest proportion of traditional investment was by those previously in international trade. This group dominated textiles and was most prominent in the nontraditional industries. Two-thirds of the most sophisticated, capital-intensive investment in the nontraditional category (chemicals, cement, machinery, transport equipment, paper) was controlled by those formerly in international trade.

Employees who did become industrialists invested primarily in traditional industries (nearly half in simple processing), where capital and technical requirements were modest. These employees do not appear to have been highly skilled or technically trained. Many may have run a cotton gin or jute press for Hindu owners before Partition, and then taken over the business. Those who had been in small-scale industry invested in cotton textiles (mostly in their accustomed activity of cloth printing, etc.) and in nontraditional import processing (mainly simple metal-working, plastic processing, etc.) but most of them never became large-scale industrialists.

Table 8.10. Extent of innovation in industrial investment by previous occupation of industrialists

Previous occupation (before entering industry or 1947, whichever was later)	Occupational category in Table 8.8	Industrial investment in 1959 (millions of rupees)			
		Traditional	Textiles	Nontraditional	Total
Foreign trade	1,2	100	610	570	1,280
Internal trade	3,4,5	250	200	200	650
Industry	6,7	190	230	290	710
Other	8,9,10	100	10	240[a]	350
Total		640	1,050	1,300	2,990

[a] Includes substantial investment in sugar mills.

In short, the disaggregation of the previous occupation of industrialists and especially of the industries they invested in after Independence supports some of the conclusions reached earlier. Investment in less traditional industries, requiring technical sophistication and more capital, was not undertaken primarily by those who might have been expected to have had a better technical background—former industrialists and employees. Such investment was dominated, rather, by those with international connections and capital—importers, and to a lesser extent, exporters. The international traders knew how to obtain foreign talent to run complex industries and they approached their industrial investment decisions with no prior commitment or preconception with respect to industry.

Employees and industrialists, already familiar with an industry, probably found it easiest to continue in the same activity, relying on their own technical knowledge. Those in internal trade approached industry rather cautiously, since they could still pursue their normal trade activity. On the other hand, those in international trade, and especially importers, were suddenly deprived of much of their normal business by import restrictions. Therefore they were more inclined to look around for potentially very profitable, though nontraditional, industrial investments since the whole industrial field was in any case new to them. They knew they could not rely on their own technical knowledge, and might do better in buying technical expertise in completely new industrial fields rather than in activities already undertaken by others.

Although some of the suggested motivation is based on speculation, the actual behavior of the industrial enterpreneurs is clear—in Pakistan's case the entrepreneurs who developed its most sophisticated industries did not have experience in more traditional industry, either as owners or employees, but in large-scale trade. Incentives and capital were more important than technical knowledge or industrial background in explaining innovative activity.

The Sources of Finance

Inadequate finance is supposedly another serious obstacle to early industrialization. In examining this supposition it is worthwhile to distinguish the initial investment in industry (the financing of the initial entrepreneurial decision), from the subsequent financing of expansion. Unfortunately the data in Table 8.11 are for each firm, not for each decision-maker as entrepreneur. The initial investment in a particular firm, therefore, sometimes represents the second or third industrial

Table 8.11. Sources of capital (millions of rupees of 1958–59 assets)

Source	Original investment	Later investment	Later disinvestment (minus)	Final assets
Industry pre-Partition	180	10	–	190
Import trade	250	40	–	290
Export trade	120	30	–	150
Internal trade	140	20	–	160
Govt. contracting	100	–	–	100
Trade—unspecified	5	–	–	5
Land—rural	60	20	–	80
Transport	15	–	–	15
Commercial banks	165	160	10	315
Creditors	35	80	10	105
Scattered shareholders	60	70	–	130
Government credit	–	30	–	30
Pakistan Industrial Development Corp.	130	10	90	50
Government equity	35	–	20	15
Foreigners (incl. Indians)	10	–	30	–20[b]
Others	–	10	10	–
Re-invested industrial earnings	205[c]	1,300	–	1,505
Total	1,510	1,780	170	3,120

[a]Rounded to nearest Rs. 5 million.

[b]A negative figure is not impossible. It simply means that some original investment in a Muslim-controlled firm by an Indian national was reported under a heading like "Industry, pre-Partition" or "internal trade" while later disinvestment was reported in the category of "foreigners."

[c]That is, the profits from one firm were used to finance the initial establishment of another firm.

investment for a particular decision-maker, or his family, and sometimes even the second or third investment in a particular industry. This somewhat obscures, but fortunately does not eliminate, the distinction between initial and subsequent investment.[8]

Pakistan's early industrialization was substantially financed by the investment of profits from trade. Of the funds used to finance the initial establishment of firms some 40 percent came from this source (including

8. Initial investment is defined here as the investment in setting up a firm, regardless of when the firm was established. Subsequent investment financed its expansion, modernization, or improvement. The data, like the rest of the survey results, end with 1959.

government contracting), with nearly one-third provided by international trade.

Banks and credit institutions did not play a significant role in financing the initial establishment of Pakistan's privately owned industry. Only a little over 10 percent of the funds for initial investment came from commercial banks and none from government credit institutions. Roughly another 10 percent was equity investment by government (including the Pakistan Industrial Development Corporation) in privately controlled firms. As one might expect, the commercial banks contributed significantly to later expansion of firms. The government too played the role it had set for itself, and withdrew much of its investment once private firms were well established.

The data also shed some light on the role of the stock market and small shareholders. In setting up enterprises, the family-controlled firms were overwhelmingly important. Less than 5 percent of investment came from scattered shareholders, most of this from directors not associated with the dominant family, who bought a few shares on a reciprocal basis in enterprises controlled by friends. The role of shareholders became more important as enterprises aged. Often the dominant family allowed an enterprise to go public after they had skimmed off the high profits of the early years, thus obtaining funds for new investment in high-profit areas.

The most important source of financing for Pakistan's industry was reinvested industrial earnings, which provided nearly half of the investment in 1958–59. Trade, and especially import trade, started private industry, together with some contributions by the government and the banks, the latter mainly for working capital. Subsequently, the government withdrew most of its funds, the banks expanded their financing, and assets doubled as profits were reinvested.

Some Conclusions

The three major characteristics distinguishing Pakistan's industrialization from that of the Western world have been mentioned earlier: a very rapid process, based on a limited number of large units and on imported technology. The consequences of these characteristics for the development of Pakistan's industrial entrepreneurs can now be summarised.

Because much industrial investment was in large units, substantial capital was required. Would-be industrialists with a substantial sum to invest therefore had a crucial advantage over their less wealthy rivals, especially because neither the commercial banks nor government investment or credit institutions were very venturesome in providing capital for the establishment of private industrial firms. Unlike his predecessors in the United Kingdom during its industrial revolution, the owner of the small shop or handicraft establishment was not competing with others in a similar position as he gradually expanded his enterprise. Instead, he faced competition from large units set up by merchant-capitalists. His disadvantage was compounded by the tremendous profits of the industrial pioneers. The merchant-capitalists who were the pioneers could rapidly expand their initial industrial holdings by reinvestment of profits. No wonder the industrial structure which emerged was characterized by a high degree of concentration.

Because indigenous commercial banks were almost nonexistent at Independence (existing Hindu-owned banks having shifted to India), and because those that did develop shortly thereafter did not participate in high profit industrial investment, the merchant-capitalist-industrialists dominated the commercial banks that were gradually established. The Pakistan pattern was quite different from the bank-dominated industrial development of some European countries.

Another result of large units and the use of transferred technology was that technical knowledge and formal education were not crucial assets. Both could be, and were, hired as needed. The would-be industrialists with technical experience from handicrafts, workshops, or small-scale industry, but unable to afford hired technical and managerial personnel found it difficult to compete with the talent available to the large-scale enterprise, headed by a decision-maker with no technical experience. However, many industrialists used their high income to obtain formal education and technical training for the next generation of their families. Education and technical competence for industrialists were not prerequisites for, but consequences of, early industrial development.

What Pakistan needed for industrial development was a limited number of entrepreneurs willing to undertake a new activity, to take the risks involved and organize the capital required, and to put together the necessary permits, skilled manpower, and contacts with suppliers and buyers. Most of these entrepreneurs had a background in trade, with some subsidiary experience in manufacturing.

The Pakistan experience suggests that governments who have made the political decision to promote private industrial development need not be discouraged if the country does not possess an experienced industrial class, a well-educated population, or trained technicians and managers. It need not rely on a slow process of expanding the number of indigenous retailers or processors. If it has a small group of profit-seeking merchants (or other price- and profit-oriented groups), a judicious structuring of government policy to force a number of them out of their usual occupation and into industry, and to give them the high profits required for capital accumulation, should achieve the government's aim. However, once an industrialization process in private hands is well started, the country will probably have to cope with a high concentration of control in industry and, if family ties are strong, with the possibility that nepotism and lack of technical competence will perpetuate an inefficient industrial structure. Opening the economy at that point to import competition can largely mitigate these potentially unfortunate consequences. Greater competition will, of course, be resisted by an industrial class accustomed to protection, and comfortable with it, whose economic power is likely to give them considerable political influence. Their political influence will be enhanced if, as in Pakistan, the big industrialists are also active in social, religious, and interest groups.

Appendix

Definitions and Components of Industry Groups

Industry group	Description	Examples of industries included
1. Simple processing	Raw materials domestic Simple technology Capital/worker ≦ Rs. 5000 Traditional in Pakistan	Cotting ginning Jute baling Grain milling Tanning
2. Secondary processing (excludes textiles)	Raw materials largely domestic Technology moderately complex Capital/worker Rs. 5-11,000 Nontraditional in Pakistan except small units	Cigarettes Sugar refining Edible oils Matches Tobacco manufacture Shoes Glass
3. Textiles (cotton and wool only)	Raw materials largely domestic Technology not too complex	Dyeing, printing Knitting Cotton spinning and weaving Wool weaving
4. Jute	Same as 3, but limited to East Pakistan	Jute
5. Import processing—traditional	Raw materials substantially imported Technology not too complex Capital/worker ≦ Rs. 3,500 Small units traditional in area or for Muslims	Printing Utensils, hardware Tools, cutlery, arms Artificial fiber weaving Clothes
6. Import processing—nontraditional	Raw materials substantially imported Technology not too complex Capital/worker ≦ Rs. 4,500 Not traditional in area or for Muslims	Tires, tubes, rubber products Metal and metal products Cosmetics, soaps Plastic products Miscellaneous manufactures

7. Chemicals, cement, paper	Raw materials generally domestic Technology complex High capital/worker Rs. 4,000–47,000 Not previously in existence in area of Pakistan	Paper and products Fertilizer Chemicals, paints Medicines Cement and cement products
8. Machinery	Raw materials almost entirely imported Technology complex (though capital requirement not always great) Small units traditional in many lines, large units nonexistent	Engines and turbines Pumps and compressors Electrical equipment Machinery Communications equipment Ships, vehicles, bicycles Photographic, optical equipment Scientific equipment

Index

Index

Bei Fragen zur Produktsicherheit wenden Sie sich bitte an:
If you have any questions regarding product safety,
please contact:

Walter de Gruyter GmbH
Genthiner Straße 13
10785 Berlin
productsafety@degruyterbrill.com